Reshaping IT for Business Flexibility

Recent Titles in the IBM McGraw-Hill Series

Details of these titles in the series are available from:

The Product Manager, Professional Books
McGraw-Hill Book Company Europe
Shoppenhangers Road, Maidenhead, Berkshire, SL6 2QL
Telephone: 0628 23432 Fax: 0628 770224

Mark Behrsin
Geoff Mason
Trevor Sharpe

Reshaping IT for Business Flexibility

The IT Architecture as a Common Language for
Dealing with Change

McGRAW-HILL BOOK COMPANY

London · New York · St Louis · San Francisco · Auckland
Bogotá · Caracas · Lisbon · Madrid · Mexico · Milan
Montreal · New Delhi · Panama · Paris · San Juan
São Paulo · Singapore · Sydney · Tokyo · Toronto

Published by
McGRAW-HILL Book Company Europe
Shoppenhangers Road, Maidenhead, Berkshire, SL6 2QL, England
Telephone 0628 23432
Fax 0628 770224

British Library Cataloguing in Publication Data

Behrsin, Mark
  Reshaping IT for Business Flexibility: IT
  Architecture as a Common Language for
  Dealing with Change. – (IBM McGraw-Hill
  Series)
  I. Title II. Series
  658.05

  ISBN 0-07-707984-1

Library of Congress Cataloging-in-Publication Data

This data is available from the Library of Congress, Washington, DC, USA.

1234 CUP 97654

Typeset by Paston Press Ltd, Loddon, Norfolk
and printed and bound in Great Britain at the University Press, Cambridge.

Contents

Foreword

The IBM McGraw-Hill Series

IBM UK and McGraw-Hill Europe have worked together to publish this series of books about information technology and its use in business, industry and the public sector.

The series provides an up-to-date authoritative insight into the wide range of products and services available, and offers strategic business advice. Some of the books have a technical bias, others are written from a broader business perspective. What they have in common is that their authors—some from IBM, some independent consultants—are experts in their field.

Apart from assisting where possible with the accuracy of the writing, IBM UK has not sought to inhibit the editorial freedom of the series, and therefore the views expressed in the books are those of the authors, and not necessarily those of IBM.

Where IBM has lent its expertise is in assisting McGraw-Hill to identify potential titles whose publication would help advance knowledge and increase awareness of computing topics. Hopefully these titles will also serve to widen the debate about the important information technology issues of today and of the future—such as open systems, networking, and the use of technology to give companies a competitive edge in their market.

IBM UK is pleased to be associated with McGraw-Hill in this series.

Sir Anthony Cleaver
Chairman
IBM United Kingdom Limited

Acknowledgements

We would like to express our thanks to the many people who have helped in the production of this book.

Firstly we would like to thank the many hundreds of individuals that we have worked with over the past 20 years. We would especially like to thank them for their ideas, for their interest in our ideas and for the many discussions, from which we all learned so much. We obviously cannot mention all these individuals by name, but we hope that when reading this book they can see the contribution that they made.

Secondly we would like to thank our colleagues in IBM for their advice and guidance. In particular we would like to express our thanks to Roger Parr, who carefully and patiently reviewed our work, and to Helena Mercurio for the administrative support that she provided throughout.

Finally, we must thank our families. Without their patience and support we could never have completed this work, so our personal thanks to: Vanessa, Christopher, Joanna and Timothy; Janice, Jill, Nicola and David; Diana and Oliver.

Trademarks

POSIX is a trademark of the Institute of Electrical and Electronics Engineers.

UNIX is a trademark of AT&T Corporation Inc.

Introduction

Here come the years of living dangerously

(*Financial Times*, December 1987)

Purpose of the book

This is a book about technology and business. Both are real, physical matters, and it cannot be a theoretical book. It is practical in tone throughout—based on our experiences with clients all over the world. It is not about complex and detailed logical analysis of business processes, information flows and the like. Nor is it about the planning of business strategy. It is about making technology serve the business, as quickly as possible. It discusses the theory it needs to, but then it goes on to practicality. We offer the reader a real way of bridging a real gap that exists in many organizations—the gap between the business and information technology (IT). Whichever side of the gap the reader sits, we offer a view of the other side—covering the major trends in business and technology at length, and allowing the reader the chance to survey a wide field. We hope that by doing that, we will enable a better dialogue in the reader's organization.

Finally, this is a book about investment. Today's executive wonders about getting the cost of IT *right*. IT managers worry about getting the shape and content of their technology right. The two challenges are related, and we offer our techniques for both. Use them, and business executives and IT people alike will have a common approach and language on which they can build the future.

Motivation for the book

Many organizations are now very dependent on IT—whether it be to compete or just to keep their operations running. It is curious that at the very time when the futures of business and IT seem more and more closely entwined, we should see fewer and fewer close working relationships between the two areas in many companies. This is unfortunate. If technology is one of the forces enabling or driving change in the business world, then the organizations that understand and harness that linkage will surely prosper at the expense of those that do not. There are many barriers to establishing the linkage. Communication is the greatest of them. Business executives and IT professionals these days are both driven by a sense of urgency—one driven by the need for business change, the other by the rate of development of the technology. But often they do not speak the same language. The recondite jargon of the computer world has become ever more impenetrable from the outside. These days it is even becoming a barrier between computer professionals themselves. The urgency of life means that there is little enough time to understand the latest slogans and buzz-words, let alone to explain them to the business person. That explanation is left to the media and to sales people. They paint a rosy picture of technical advance moving us rapidly towards Utopia. Anything is claimed to be possible. If that first impression turns out to have been a false hope, then there is no need to worry. The panacea will be 'in the next release', always just around the corner. The business person sees an ever-larger amount of money being expended in chasing this technological paradise. Yet it never seems to arrive, and there is no effective communication channel to get to the bottom of the issues—to make the situation manageable for the worried business person.

It is our belief that the upheavals and reorganizations currently under way in the whole business world will lead to nothing in those organizations where the distance between business people and IT people remains large. IT is fast becoming a necessity to the business person who wants to survive in this new world. Buying technology as a commodity is not yet possible across the board, so business people are faced with a big challenge—choosing the best technology and products for their needs from the industry that is itself in chaos. This is not an easy task, and it needs the right skills, experience and method to make it happen. In this book, that is exactly what we set out to describe. In doing that, we have to address both audiences—the business people and the IT people—in the hope that each will be better able to talk to the other. In our experience, without that dialogue there is little hope of the successful use of IT in their organizations.

Structure of the book

This is a difficult book. Not for the reader—we have done our best to make it a pleasant experience. But certainly, it was difficult to write. We felt that we needed to talk to two audiences—to the business and IT communities. We also believe that each of the two has a limited understanding of the other's discipline. (Clearly a sweeping statement: nevertheless, our experience in a wide range of organizations makes us believe it to be true. There are, of course, exceptions. Please forgive us if you are one of them!) We needed to address that problem first. So the body of the book is structured into three parts. Parts 1 and 2 survey the business and technical worlds respectively. Of course, the book would fail in its objectives if it stopped at a review of life as we know it. In Part 3 we go on to discuss a practical way of building a language and a map understandable to both the business and the information technology worlds. The account is based on our many years of collective experience with large and small organizations all over the world. It is an architectural approach, concentrating on the key features of information technology needed to support the business before detailed work is attempted.

Part 1
Business trends

Change is not made without inconvenience, even from worse to better.

(Richard Hooker, 1554–1600)

In the first six chapters, we deal with business and organizations. Our intention in these pages is to summarize the key trends and ideas in today's thinking on management and business. The intended reader is the IT manager or professional. Hopefully, the material will also be of interest to many business people—not that these two audiences are mutually exclusive! Indeed, the success of this book depends on them both being interested.

There is a danger in these early chapters, which we should try to avoid from the beginning. This book is definitely, absolutely and without question *not* an attempt at providing some sort of MBA course. If the information technology reader is stimulated by this material to go and discover more, then we have succeeded. Business literate readers may also find the text of interest. They may find it useful as a summary of a very large field. We shall be happy if they emerge from these chapters refreshed and eager to read the rest of the book; happier still if they feel better able to contribute to the development of their own organization.

Our disclaimer gives us a great deal of freedom in what we have chosen to cover, and the manner in which we do so. Our approach will be to survey those directions and fashions—an important word in today's business world—that seem to be most widespread in today's companies and other organizations. In keeping with our promise to avoid an MBA thesis, we shall deal with them in a fairly light way, remembering that our target is to provide an introductory survey, not to deliver the definitive survey of management thinking in the 1990s. There are many topics we could have covered that have not been chosen. There may even be some that the business *cognoscente* would rather see excluded. However, the topics we have chosen are those that we often find under debate in our clients' organizations. They include one idea that is becoming pervasive in management thinking (if not always in association with coherent action plans)—that of federalism. This will be our final destination in these chapters, before we turn to look (in Part 2) at the innovations in technology that are assisting the organizational changes we shall describe.

1
A time for change

New pressures on organizations

There is a tide in the affairs of men, which, taken at the flood, leads on to fortune

(*Julius Caesar*, William Shakespeare)

1.1   Purpose

We cannot look at the many approaches to business and organization without first discussing their origins. That is the intention of this chapter. The new approaches are all responses to change, which is experienced at an ever-increasing intensity in today's world. In this chapter we discuss the forces that are driving the changes, in the context of a simple model that we use to illustrate our arguments in this chapter and the next.

1.2   The anatomy of organization

The organization and conduct of human affairs are probably the most complex and diverse subjects that we could have chosen to discuss. Any attempt at simplifying them is bound to be hopelessly inadequate. Despite that, we need some simple framework to act as a guide to our discussion, and to help us see our way through the many complications and difficulties. So, with pragmatism very much in mind, let us quickly develop a model of any human organization, forgetting its flaws for the moment and concentrating on the benefits of the simplicity it brings to our debate. We shall build up the model pictorially.

We are on fairly safe ground in asserting that any organization is about people surrounded by an environment, which may be both hostile and benign at the same time. Figure 1.1(*a*) illustrates the point. Of course, the environment is not just to do with the weather and nature: is has many other components (see Table 1.1). We shall use the word 'environment' in a more general way than is common today.

Our environment is rarely passive, and is usually unpredictable. Human organizations can be seen as a natural response to the capricious world surrounding us as

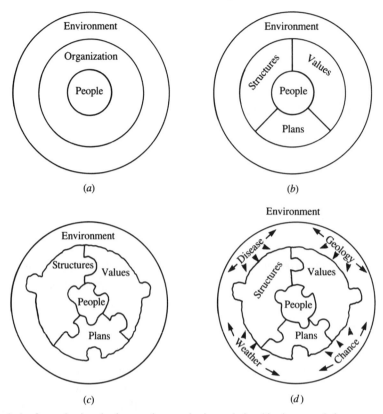

Any analysis of organizations leads us to the complex interrelationships between their component parts. The complexity is made greater still by the inevitability of change in our environment.

Figure 1.1. The structure and environment of human organizations: (*a*) our basic model; (*b*) the anatomy of an organization; (*c*) the inevitability of complexity; (*d*) the ever-changing environment.

individuals. Through working together we hope to insulate ourselves from the dangers around us, and to take advantage of the opportunities that the environment frequently offers us. This has been a hugely successful strategy for us as a species, although as individuals we all know that the specific organizations we belong to have their day and then may well wither, only to be replaced by something newer and more vital. In studying those organizations we move onto more contentious and difficult ground. There will never be one canonical model for the

Table 1.1 The nature of the environment

		Examples
ENVIRONMENT	**Where we live**	Geography, climate, the economy, friends and enemies, social forces, the legacy of history, our collective cultural background . . . .

Table 1.2 The three elements in our model of human organizations

		Examples
VALUES	**Who** we are	Culture, beliefs, customs, ethics, language, dress code
STRUCTURES	**What** we are	Organization, reporting lines, processes, information flows, internal boundaries, external boundaries
PLANS	**Where** we are going	Goals, strategies, objectives, tactical plans

There is no one true model of organization. This one will suit our purpose in the coming chapters.

structure of an organization. Life would be much less fun if there were. There is no ultimate truth to be found here. We shall just choose our own model in the spirit of pragmatism, and make the most sweeping of all possible statements: *all human organizations are made of three elements,* which together with the environment complete our simple model (Table 1.2). Figure 1.1(*b*) shows their interrelationship.

As we have said, life is not that simple. In reality there are many other factors that we could use to characterize human organizations; many ways of describing the same things. The description we have chosen will do for our purposes with just one small change, which is perhaps a last gesture at reflecting the true complexity of the subject we are discussing. It is a subtle change to the diagram—turning it from a regular geometric pattern into a much more irregular jigsaw (Fig. 1.1(*c*)). The change reflects the complex interrelationships of the different elements we have identified. This is the reality. The three elements are indivisibly connected, and make no sense without each other. Without defined structures, our plans lack meaning and cannot be implemented. Without defined plans, we have no way to respond to inevitable changes in the environment. Opportunities will be missed, and eventually negative changes around us will destroy our organization, and maybe us with it. Without values, we have no collective will to sustain us through execution of our plans and in times of adversity.

1.3   No escape from change

There is no stability to be found in this model. The environment is constantly shifting. Even if there were only one coherent global organization, the forces of nature and chance would be there as a cause of major change and upheaval. Witness the recurrent floods in major river deltas (such as the Mississippi). Think of the ravages of drug-resistant tuberculosis, or the spillage of oil from tankers on shores from Alaska to the Atlantic.

Even if the environment stopped changing and went on holiday for a while, the pace of change forced on each organization by its peers and neighbours would still be incessant. The reality is that each organization is part of its neighbours' environments. All organizations are jiggling about together like atoms in a gas. They collide with each other, and through doing that change each other's form and direction (Fig. 1.2).

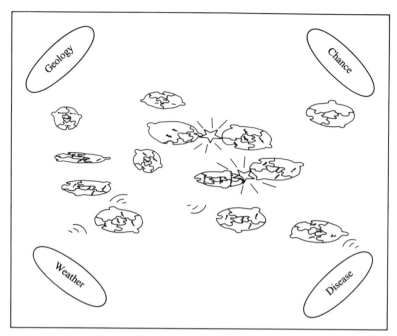

As organizations evolve and interact, so they force responses from their neighbours, who must themselves then adapt. The environment continually forces additional change, and in an unpredictable and random way. As a result change must be regarded as inevitable. The situation is as fluid as the random motion of molecules in the air. The effect on organizations is to alter their shape, to split them apart, and to alter the way in which they behave. All organizations are affected.

Figure 1.2.   Organizations force change on each other.

1.4   The way we were

We have argued that change is an inevitable feature of human organization, driven either by nature or by interaction (not always solicited) with other similar bodies. The change may be radical, unpredictable and irrevocable. There is nothing new in these statements—we have all lived through recessions and social and international turmoil. Yet those of us in the industrialized world saw the shape of many organizations change only very slowly until quite recently. As a result, the fact of change was often pushed to the back of our minds. The *old order* seemed fixed and immutable. Table 1.3 describes the way things were.

Yet the basic elements of business and organizations have remained largely unaltered for many years. Or, at least, they have evolved sufficiently slowly that we hardly noticed the change. At any moment in that period, we would have felt a strong sense of permanence.

Even when the old order seemed at its most successful and stable, the forces that would lead to its change were beginning. The rise of high-growth economies fed by cheap labour in the Far East and the Third World led to increased competition.

Table 1.3 The conventions of organizations before recent times

		The old order
VALUES	**Who** we were	**Freedom within the law** Laws were designed to protect society and its members from harm. If individuals stayed within the law then they could have freedom of action and travel without fear for their safety.
STRUCTURES	**What** we were	**Benign control** A hierarchy of managers all looking after their charges. As a reward they were provided with very great power.
PLANS	**Where** we were going	**Bigger and better** Living standards were set to improve without end. Progress was in the air at all levels of activity, from personal incomes to major civil engineering projects and science.
ENVIRONMENT	**Where** we lived	**History lulled asleep by the cold war** The balance of power between the Western and Eastern Blocs led to stability in many parts of the world, and the view that 'history is dead'.

We have just left a period of remarkable stability in the world order and the organization of commerce. In many ways it was the environment itself which led to that calmness. At least part of it seemed to have fallen asleep—the force of history was far less evident a cause of change than had been the case in other periods of time.

One industry after another was affected. The values of personal freedom, developed more and more during the period of increasing prosperity, made it more difficult to compete by increasing personal productivity, as workers started to value themselves at least as highly as they had previously valued the state or their company. At the same time those same workers expected a continuing improvement in living standards—further impacting the ability of the West to compete. The advance of technology made the problems still greater, as the entry point to industries was lowered and markets became truly open to global competition (see Table 1.4).

Table 1.4 History stirs and starts to provoke change

		Pressures for change
VALUES	**Who** we are	The rise of the individual at the expense of the centre Aspirations of individuals to the 'good life' Erosion of shared values in the West
STRUCTURES	**What** we are	The predominance of consumerism The rise of the Far Eastern economies
PLANS	**Where** we are going	The collapse of the Soviet Bloc The rapid advance in technology
ENVIRONMENT	**Where** we live	Accelerating degree of competition in all industries Globalization of markets

The end of the arms race, and the rise of the 'cult of the individual' in the West has caused upheaval on a global scale. At the same time, the pace of competition has quickened, fed at least in part by the advance in technology. The *old order* will need revision in order to cope in the new environment.

There was an international thirst for the products of advanced technology—
especially those created by the rapidly accelerating progress in electronics. That
was itself a direct spin-off from the arms and space races in the Cold War. It led to
greater and greater pressure on the trade balance in the Western economies. In the
Soviet Bloc, it led to increased pressure for change. The same Bloc was already
sinking under the strain of economic competition. The ending of the Cold War that
resulted seems set to emphasize the call for individual freedom, while at the same
time increasing the degree of competition in all industries. Meanwhile, the pace of
advance of electronic technology, subject to the same competitive pressures, was
accelerating. For many organizations, electronics (embodied as industrial automation and information technology) became one of the few weapons available to compete in an increasingly tough environment.

1.5   Responses to the pressures for change

There are as many different responses to these pressures as there are organizations
dealing with them. We are all different in our history, and in the way we puzzle our
way through difficulties. There is no 'one true path' to some new order that will
replace the old everywhere, and become the new default form of organization and
business. There are, however, some pre-eminent ideas that are gaining widespread
acceptance, which we shall describe in the coming chapters. One of these (federalism) seems to have a particularly wide following at the moment. It will conclude
our discussion of business issues in a few chapters' time. Before that we shall look
at what we observe to be the most frequently recurring approaches and ideas. Inevitably, describing a sequence of such things in a book requires some decision as
to the order of attack. We have chosen an order that we judge to make the most
readable account. The order does not imply any specific ranking of merit or anything else. It may be that all the ideas discussed will eventually 'make it' into some
grand synthesis in the future.

1.6   Summary

After a long period of sleep, history is once again awake and very, very active. We
are living through a period of change more rapid than in any time of peace since the
Industrial Revolution. Those of use lulled into believing it would be any other way
during our lifetimes had forgotten the inevitability of change. Change is the normal
state of human life. Fortunate indeed are those who live in one of those rare times
and places where stability reigns for a long period. We have just left one of those,
and the future is uncertain. This is as true in business as in politics, economics or
our everyday lives.

Behind the changes in business, we see the advance of technology. It is interesting to ask which came first: the acceleration in the use of the microchip, or the
beginnings of change in our organizations and businesses. We are unlikely to find

the answer, and in many ways it does not matter. An interesting question for tomorrow's historians, but for us the key observation is that the two sets of changes are linked. Information technology enables changes in businesses. Those changes stimulate business competition, which in turn gives more impetus to the advance of the technology itself.

There is a cycle here. We leave readers to decide whether it is virtuous or negative in its effect as they read the ensuing chapters. For the next few pages we shall continue to look at one side of the changes—the business and organizational issues, before we turn to the technology. In Part 3 of the book we shall look at a way of linking the two areas together to make sure that the changes we undergo are under our control, and not the other way round.

2
Too slow, bring me another
New structures are needed

There is only one valid definition of business purpose—to create a customer

(Peter Drucker)

2.1   Purpose

We have just discussed the forces for change experienced by many organizations. In the next three chapters we shall describe the ways in which enterprises are reacting to those forces. For the moment, we shall start at the beginning and look at the way most of us have been organized up to now, and the ways in which changes must be made.

2.2   Process bound

. . . and still I seem to tread on classic ground . . .

(Joseph Addison)

Change is everywhere, but that does not mean we should just throw away the past and start again. There are many good things about the way we have organized ourselves up to now, and it is important not to lose sight of them. It is all too easy to see only what is wrong and attempt to remedy that in a single-minded or blinkered way. That approach is evident in many organizations (and countries) today. It is a good way of ensuring that an organization takes on radical change without being hidebound by the past. In the long run, there is a need to soften the approach and retrieve what was good from the past, combining it with the new way of things into a fresh and workable approach. There's nothing new in this. It is very much the lesson of history.

The word 'classic' is worth dwelling on. *The Concise Oxford Dictionary* describes it as meaning 'of the first class, of acknowledged excellence; remarkably typical, outstandingly important'. The way we have organized ourselves up to now has certainly been all of those things at various times and places. What we must do is to find that which is first class, excellent or important and take it across into the future.

Georg Freidrich Wilhelm Hegel was perhaps the most important German philosopher of the nineteenth century. In his *Philosophy of History* he used the term 'dialectic' to describe the inescapable historical force through which the existing order of things is repeatedly broken down and rebuilt. There is a conflict between an existing idea or situation (the 'thesis') and a new idea (the 'antithesis'). The latter comes into being as a reaction against the former. The two are in opposition, and that leads to a process of conflict termed 'synthesis'—which then leads to a new order. The thesis and antithesis are combined in some new way which takes the best of each. Neither emerges in its original form. The new order then plays the role of a new 'thesis', awaiting the arrival of its antithesis. Hegel believed he had discovered a fundamental law of nature, governing all human affairs. He went further and saw the process of the dialectic as a process of continual improvement in which each synthesis was 'better' than the last. This would lead eventually to a perfect state of organization. Marx claimed he had found it. Many of us seemed lulled into suspecting that the corporate organization of the 1960s was the ideal. We have all been proved wrong. We must remember our experiences as we become comfortable and settled in the future. (As an aside, it is worth pointing out that if Hegel had lived as an anglophone today he might have renamed a thesis as a 'paradigm'. It is not obvious what he would have done with 'antithesis', and 'synparadigm' sounds very strange indeed!)

We shall come back to unpicking the good from the bad (or rather, from the 'obsolete') in the next chapters. For now, let us just describe some of the key features of the classic organization, as we have known it. Of all the topics in this chapter, this one will be the most familiar to the reader, particularly the business person. The objective here is really just to make sure we all have the same pictures in our minds for later. If you do not like the pictures, then go back and read what we said in the last chapter about the use of simple models. You may find we agree with you! Hopefully we can also agree to be pragmatic!

The classic model is all about control and planning. It originated in the USA in the years around the turn of the century, as a way of getting the maximum efficiency out of large plants and factories. These were often full of very expensive machinery. There was a perceived need to optimize its use, and also to get the best return out of the growing wages being paid to an increasingly affluent workforce. The same period also saw a very rapid growth in our understanding of science, and in our engineering skills. In an age before quantum mechanics and Einstein's relativity, there was a strong belief in absolutes and in the success of the scientific method. The popular view of science was that all problems could be addressed by a combination of Newton's laws and Maxwell's equations (perhaps with some thermodynamics thrown in for good measure). The whole approach was built on reducing a problem into its component parts, addressing each one in turn, and then rebuilding the entire solution from the results. Given this view of life, it is not surprising to find the same philosophy at the heart of the classic model.

Frederick Winslow Taylor (1856–1915) was probably the first management guru of the twentieth century, and could be said to be the father of today's organizational model. He was originally an engineer working for the Midvale Steel Company. At that time (the 1870s), workers were paid for piecework—for achieving specified output targets. It was up to them how they did that, and at what cost to their employers. The worker had no incentive to over-perform or cut his delivery times. In fact quite the opposite! We all know what happens in most companies to unspent budgets at the end of the accounting period. Over-perform and the targets just get harder next time round. So it was for many workers in the 1870s. In its day the approach had worked well, and had been part of the rapid growth in the industrial economies during the period 1850–1870. But in the following decade, there was a widespread recession in all these countries. There was fierce competition between manufacturers, and radical social change as the population became increasingly urbanized.

Faced with all these pressures, Taylor set out to apply the scientific approach to the operation of his steelworks. In 1881, he was the first to undertake time and motion studies, even more unpopular at that time than they are now. He reduced the workforce and made those that remained more efficient. After 30 years he had perfected his theories into *The Principles of Scientific Management*, published in 1911.

According to Taylor, the key to efficiency is to replace a worker's judgement and freedom in the way things are done, by scientific analysis and coordinated planning. These are seen as difficult tasks beyond the worker's ability. They are to be entrusted to a cadre of professional managers. Only they can understand the whole system of plans and processes. The worker is involved only in execution, working in a way prescribed by the managers. The manager must also become skilled in the (then new) science of psychology, the better to influence and direct the employees. The main responsibility of the line manager is to enforce cooperation, standards, and the adoption of the best environment for the organization's targets to be met.

These ideas became conventional wisdom during the First World War, and until recently were at the heart of many big corporations such as Ford Motor Company, General Motors and General Electric. (The term 'post-

Fordism' is sometimes used to describe the shift in business organization in recent years.) They may have had more than a passing influence on Kafka's *The Trial* (1925) and Chaplin's *Modern Times* (1936).

The result is a complex network of plans and processes, held together by a large organization to staff the production and maintenance of the spider's web, and to supervise execution of its intentions. Let us look at some of the major features of this complexity. We shall do so by following the stages of evolution of a generic organization built along classic lines. We shall assume throughout that the environment is largely unchanging, as was the case during the period of the Cold War (Table 2.1).

In the early stage of our generic organization, God was in His heaven, and life was full of Frederick Winslow Taylor's hopefulness (Table 2.2). This was an

Table 2.1   Summary of the overall environment in the period before the present

The old order

ENVIRONMENT: History lulled asleep

The Cold War. The balance of power between the Soviet and Western power blocs defined the boundaries of the commercial world. It also led to an enormous growth in the defence industries and their suppliers, especially in the West. The race for bigger and better weapons and offensive capability became a very important part of the cold war.

'The end of history'. The stability of the situation created the illusion that the order of things was immutable. The prospect of an eventual global war was perhaps the only major change that people foresaw. For the most part there was a Western preoccupation with progress and consumption.

Industrial pre-eminence of the US power block. The Western industrial base was not centrally planned, unlike that in the East. It was able to be far more responsive to the commercial opportunities presented by the arms race, and to investment opportunities in the underdeveloped world. Its companies flourished, and its workers prospered.

Table 2.2   The original form of an *old order* organization

Stage 1: A bright start

Values: Freedom within the law

We will look after you. Be loyal to the company or the state and it will keep you warm and fed. It will protect you from the misdeeds of others through a set of rules. If everyone keeps to the rules, then all will benefit. Loyalty requires obedience and hard work, in return for the benefits of belonging to the organization.

Structures: Benign control

A hierarchy of managers. The organization is to be analysed and run scientifically. The whole thing must be dissected into small pieces, analysed and then controlled through the understanding gained. This is a great intellectual challenge. Only a very small number of particularly wise and experienced managers will be capable of understanding the whole picture. Less able managers will understand parts of it, depending on their ability. A hierarchy of power based on understanding and ability is needed.

Plans: Bigger and better

Ever onward. The organization is full of confidence that in this, the best of all possible worlds, it can only prosper. Profits, well-being, and market size are all forecast to grow, and are aimed for through the production of detailed plans.

Table 2.3   The successful organization evolves

Stage 2: Just deserts

Values: Freedom within the law

Just do as you are told. Power to make and enforce the rules and to protect the members of the organization is vested in a small number of managers. They are rewarded with status and privilege. They repay the organization through their commitment and the respect of the ordinary workers.

Structures: Benign control

Large centralized staffs to look after and control most aspects of life. The intellectual challenge of the scientific method is indeed very great. Much detailed analysis must be done: not only to plan, but even to measure and hence control. Large numbers of staff workers are needed to undertake these tasks. The complexity is such that they need to be in frequent contact with each other. They are organized into large staff groups to do this, which are often then located in central facilities.

Plans: Bigger and better

Success. The organization has achieved its targets and now sets its sights ever higher. Success follows success and is attributed to the excellent work done in managing the company along scientific lines.

---

enormously positive environment for those who lived in it. It had the feeling of a new and fresh world order, which is exactly what it was when it was first adopted. Hegel would tell us, though, that the thesis it represents must contain the seeds of its own antithesis, and that is exactly what we see arising in the next stage of devel-

Table 2.4   Mounting complexity starts to weaken the organization

---

Stage 3: Growing pains

Values: Freedom within the law

You are just a small cog. The organization is big and complex, and most members know they don't understand it. They are confident that the senior managers must do. As a result, the workers do not worry about the bigger picture, but only about their own jobs and rewards. They have a feeling of detachment from an uncontrollable and large force which ultimately controls their futures. They do not always trust the competence or motives of those wielding that force. That trust has to be earned.

Nothing you do matters. Workers cannot see how their contribution helps the organization. However, they desperately want to help. Frustration results, and morale drops. Some disaffected workers leave or retire.

Structures: Benign control

Many rules. The central staffs work diligently against formidable challenges. Their efforts are made easier by the restriction of the degrees of freedom in the organization. That enables them to concentrate their efforts on the work needed to plan and control the organization's progress. They are puzzled to find their efforts labelled as obstructive and stifling.

Slow, safe decision-making. The pace of life is set by the changes in the environment and the organization's competition. The environment has been largely stable. The competition is organized along similar lines, and no-one needs to break rank by pushing decisions past the point of prudence. There is no need to take avoidable risks, and so the central staff expend considerable effort in analysing decisions and options before they are finally taken. In any case, only the most senior managers have an overall view of the organization. So decisions need to be passed up several levels of management for increasingly erudite approval. Status then dictates that implementation must be cascaded back down the management chain before work can begin. Modification needed in flight, of course, will require the same careful escalation and evaluation process.

Plans: Bigger and better

Bigger. The organization continues to grow and succeed. But increasingly, senior management see the need to plan changes to the internal structure to manage the pain of growth. It is noted that team spirit is not what it used to be, and plans are formulated in response.

---

opment as the generic organization tastes success to justify its previous hopefulness (Table 2.3, opposite). Following its early success, the organization grows, and as it does it starts to become more complex.

Success has now justified the shape of the organization, and gives those at the centre confidence in protecting it, striking a patronizing tone with the organization's members, and at the same time aiming for further increases in prosperity. The nature of the antithesis starts to become apparent. It is that the intellectual effort needed to dissect an organization in Taylor's way, and then to sustain the result as a management tool, is beyond the stamina of humans. Life is too short to peel mushrooms. This becomes more evident in the next phase of evolution, as the organization starts to struggle with the challenges of its own success (Table 2.4, opposite).

Now the strains really begin to tell. But the thesis is still clung to. If Hegel was right, then it would inevitably have to be given up. The fourth stage takes the organization to a stage of maturity evident in many of today's large and well-known corporations and government organizations (Table 2.5). As a rule of

Table 2.5   The organization reaches old age, and turns in on itself

---

Stage 4: End of the road?

Values: Freedom within the law

'I'm all right Jack'. A concentration on their unique and specific situation leads some workers to pay no heed to the plight of those even slightly distanced from them. It is easy to assume that someone else in the organization will deal with all problems, and that each individual need only care for himself or herself. There is little sense of shared responsibility. The value system is weakened as more and more members lose true commitment to it. As a result the organization itself is weakened. One response may be an attempt at greatly increased central control. This has often been fatal (as it was for many farmers in the Soviet Union).

Structures: Benign control

Concentration on perfecting the internal machine rather than dealing with the outside. The world is changing only slowly. Increased profit or well-being will come from internal transformation. Since most organizations take the same approach, there is nothing to be lost by it. Customers and suppliers are not the key focus.

Complexity. The level of resources devoted to analysis and planning leads to an enormous quantity of very detailed paperwork. It describes models for business processes, for the flow of information, financial cases, marketing plans and so on. Often the staff workers producing this material must specialize in specific areas, only increasing the level of detail and the need for specialization. Neighbouring staff groups find it increasingly difficult to communicate, and it becomes hard to summarize the state of progress to senior management. The latter start to feel that not even they understand their own company. Staffs are instructed to simplify, which leads only to yet more analysis and planning. More staff are introduced to coordinate and liaise with the existing staff. The staffs start to grow in size, and the organization sees no way of stopping the trend. It becomes a major item in the profit and loss account, and ever more effort is needed to increase the performance of the rest of the organization to compensate.

Plans: Bigger and better

More freedom. The organization is being stifled by complexity. Individual workers are often disaffected, and have no real sense of corporate purpose. Plans are produced to lower central costs and to delegate more responsibility away from the organization's centre. It is noted that competitors are heading in the same direction, and there are fears of being left behind in an uncompetitive quagmire.

---

thumb, the bigger they are the more likely they are to be close to this state today. They have got to that size in the first place because of the good points in the classic model. Now may be the time to change.

2.3   The reckoning

Many companies that have arrived at stage 4 may see it as the inevitable result of success, which they could see as in itself justifying the whole approach advocated by F. W. Taylor. They might see themselves as being carried along on an unending wave of scientific progress.

   Not only that, but there is a dogged side to some managers which makes them want to carry on with a model through all adversity. Today's conventional wisdom takes the opposite view. It holds that the model has had its day, and should not be held on to. As Hegel might say, this is now the time for synthesis between thesis and antithesis. Figure 2.1 makes the point. It summarizes the evolution we have

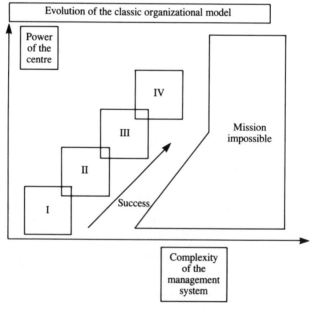

Tables 1.1 to 1.4 took us through the life of the classic organizational structure, as it has been seen in many enterprises. Their evolution has been to do with the migration of power from the centre in the face of mounting complexity. Each stage of the evolution was successful, enabling the country to grow. There is a limit to this growth, which is reached when organizational complexity becomes too great for it to be absorbed any more. The fundamentals of the approach need to be changed.

Figure 2.1.   The four stages of the organization.

been looking at in the last few pages. The management philosophy adopted was to analyse and then control the detailed operations of the company. In its early days that was a success, and led to reapplication of the approach in an ever more comprehensive way. The trouble was that, as things went on from stage to stage, so the degree of analysis required became more and more complex, and the centralized staff functions needed to deal with it became more powerful. The problem here is that sooner or later you run into a brick wall: the 'mission impossible' in Fig. 2.1. That represents a forbidden zone beyond human endurance, in which the complexity of the approach makes it become all-consuming, with no room left for actually doing business! The organization becomes introverted and cumbersome.

Of course, many organizations had already tried pushing into the zone by the mid to late 1980s (or even earlier). They would probably still be trying if the environment around them had remained unaltered. However, the environment, which was based on the same model of organization, collapsed in on itself as described in Table 2.6.

The overall effect of these changes has been to increase competition to a degree unprecedented in modern times. The old organizational order cannot respond; it is caught in a web of complexity. Competitors that are smaller, or are still young enough not to have built large staff bureaucracies, can respond to customers' needs faster and at lower costs. There is no choice but to rethink the organizational model from the beginning.

Table 2.6   The dynamic history is back in evidence

End of the old order

ENVIRONMENT: History wakes up

The cold war stops. The arms race got to the point where it was absorbing huge proportions of the gross national product on either side of the Iron Curtain. The centrally planned and inflexible economies of the Eastern Bloc found it increasingly difficult to take the strain. They had to contend not only with the direct effect of research and manufacture, but also with the indirect effect on their populations' morale and attitudes, which were affected by the affluence seen in the West. Something had to give, and it was the Berlin Wall.

The return of history. With the collapse of the Wall, history woke up (it had actually been stirring for some time before that). The old political boundaries vanished almost overnight, followed closely by national boundaries. New markets and new competitors arrived. At the same time, a new set of military conflicts became first a possibility and then a reality. The certainty of the past had vanished.

Industrial pre-eminence of the developed Asian nations. By the end of the 1980s, Japan had achieved a very strong position in a string of industries from cars to electronics. In other parts of the Pacific Rim, smaller dragons were headed along the path to full industrialization. The largest dragon of all (China) was already starting to indicate a similar future for itself.

Rapid progress of technology. First air travel, and then information technology and telecommunications had revolutionized competition. Global markets had been created, along with global competition. As the progress of information technology continued, new forms of competition became possible.

The pressures described force change onto our organizations. They cannot respond rapidly enough with the complex management systems many of them had evolved during the four stages described earlier.

2.4   Summary

There was much that was good in the way we had structured and run our businesses and organizations up to now. We had optimized our management thinking to the stable environment we lived in. For a long time things went well. Although there were always problems, there seemed little need to make major alterations to what had become a winning combination of management skill and employees' dedication to their small part of the organization. We had all forgotten that history was against us. Nature is not stable for long, and change was inevitable. Of course, there always had been change, even through the period of apparent stability. Some businesses grew; some failed. But the rate of change could be coped with within the conventional model of management and organization. This is a tribute to the intellect of its inventors—F. W. Taylor and others.

As we saw in Chapter 1, the period of stability is now behind us. Aided by the advances in information technology, all types of organization are experiencing changes in their environment on a scale and at a pace not seen since the eighteenth and nineteenth centuries. If Hegel were still alive, he would smile. His *dialectic* is alive and well.

The old way of doing things cannot cope with the new rate of change. Organizations must be more flexible and more rapid in their response to new opportunities and threats. They can no longer rely on the old command and control systems, with their safe but prolonged approach to decision-making. They must find ways of moving faster, more cheaply and with more imagination. Individualism and customers are suddenly back in vogue.

3
Straws in the wind

New management thinking

Take a straw and throw it up into the air. You shall see by that which way the wind is.

(John Selden)

3.1   Purpose

In this chapter we turn from the old way of things and look to new approaches. We shall not try to be encyclopaedic. There are many specialized books that the reader can turn to if that sort of depth is required. We hope that our material will both motivate and equip the reader to do just that.

Our discussion has to proceed in some order. The reader shouldn't assume that the order chosen is some kind of value judgement. It is not. All the ideas discussed are in use or under debate in one form or another in most organizations that we have dealt with. There is one topic that we do believe stands apart from the others in its impact—the federated organization will be given a place of its own in Chapter 4.

3.2   Born to serve

There is one enormous flaw in the classic model that we looked at in the last chapter. It is introspective. When the environment is reasonably stable, that is no problem. The outside world is then a fixed and predictable feature of your planning. But when it starts to move, and move fast, then you need to be able to respond and adapt, or you will become extinct. The trouble is, the classic model develops the opposite tendency in organizations—a cumbersomeness born of complexity and over-analysis. Paralysis by analysis.

Unfortunately (or perhaps fortunately), the world is changing, and those changes are accelerating. Not only that, but the more organizations that manage to adapt, the faster the environment changes for everyone else. It is a snowball, and about as controllable as one rolling down a hill. What we see here is a revolution, a complete change in the order of things.

> *Revolution (noun), complete change, turning upside down, great reversal of conditions, fundamental reconstruction*

> *(Concise Oxford English Dictionary, 7th Ed.)*

The immediate symptom of the changes is increased competition. We could fill many pages looking behind the symptoms for the root causes. If Hegel had his way we would not look any further than the dialectic. Perhaps in 50 years or so historians will be able to write a less philosophical account of the path back from today to the Second World War via the rebirth of the Japanese and (the then) West German economies and the explosion in electronics capability leading from the Cold War. There is little point in trying to guess their conclusions here. We would get it wrong, and in many cases it is not relevant to the purpose of this book.

What is key is the new importance and power of a customer in a very competitive world. The customer has to come centre stage and replace the focus on internal analysis and a tightly orchestrated management system that was at the heart of the old order (Fig. 3.1).

In the modern use of the word, we all have customers. They are the people who pay us, either directly or indirectly. Your employer pays you, but is paid by someone else. Both are your customer. If either becomes dissatisfied with your work,

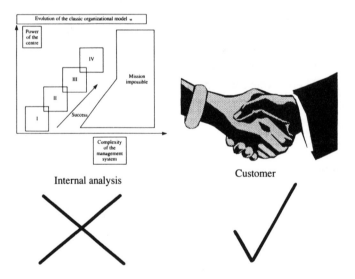

Internal analysis

Customer

The pace of change and degree of competitiveness require new approaches. The former concentration on internal efficiency, and on a tightly orchestrated management system is replaced by a focus on the customer.

Figure 3.1. Turning from perfecting the internal machine of the organization to the customer.

then you are threatened. This apparently trivial insight into human affairs has been responsible for a high proportion of the ideas (all potential 'antitheses' to the classic model) in management thinking in recent years.

We must think even more widely than that, and make sure that we are focused also on our suppliers. We need this because a supplier (i.e. anyone who regards us as a customer) is as much of a competitive issue for us as a customer. The effectiveness of an organization to serve its customers depends to a greater or lesser extent on its relationships with its suppliers. They need to be cultivated in different ways to customers, but just as strongly. Your competitors may be aware of this fact, and are capable of using it to strike at their neighbour's competitiveness.

The situation is made still more complex by the way in which many companies have been forced to diversify into new markets. How, for example, would you categorize the relationship between General Motors and IBM? Perhaps the best analogy here is international affairs, where it is possible for two countries to see themselves as allies even though they compete in some areas.

- General Motors is one of IBM's largest and most valued customers in the world, and has been influential in the direction of many of IBM's products.
- Both General Motors and IBM have strong interests in the rapidly growing area of facilities management, making them competitors.
- General Motors and IBM have collaborated in the definition of various technology standards, making them partners.
- General Motors is one of several suppliers of cars to IBM (UK).

Organizations have made a number of different responses to the new importance of the customer and the supplier. We are going to discuss three here (Table 3.1). All three attempt to adapt the classic model to the new situation, but they do it from different standpoints. As we showed in Fig. 1.1, the various aspects of an organization are interlinked, and cannot be changed in isolation. It follows that even though the three approaches we shall discuss seem at first sight to be separate, in fact they are closely interlinked. In the next chapter we shall look at their synthesis in the idea of federalism (the fourth approach in Table 3.1).

Table 3.1 New approaches to moving beyond the old order

Quality	Give the customer what the customer wants
Value chain analysis	Find out how to make it valuable to him or her
Progress reengineering	Find out how to give it to him or her faster, more cheaply and more attractively than the competition
Federated organizations	Do all of the above, with simplicity as an aim

There are many different ways forward from the former approach to organization. Although it is convenient to treat them as separate ideas, in reality they are closely interrelated. That interrelationship is best seen in the federated organization, to be described here. Only the first three of these topics are discussed in this chapter.

3.3   Quality

Come give us a taste of your quality

(William Shakespeare, *Hamlet*)

It is all to be made of sighs and tears... it is all to be made of faith and service. . . .

(William Shakespeare, *As You Like It*)

There cannot be many people working in a large or medium-size organization who have not come across the 'quality industry'. There cannot be many themes in recent management thinking that have become so widespread and have had such a long history. It has even generated its own international and national standards—for example the International Standards Organization has ISO9001, the UK government promotes a standard known as BS5750, and in the USA, the Federal Government promotes a number of standard approaches, including the Baldrige method with its coveted bronze, silver and gold awards. The subject has its own literature, its own 'trade press', and a galaxy of consultants and gurus—stretching back to the famous Dr Demming, who is the post-war doyen of the subject.

Despite the evidence of maturity, the subject is widely misunderstood. The term 'quality' is used to cover an ever-wider range of management and organizational thinking. Many of the topics covered in these chapters can be found within this broad spectrum. In this sense quality, as a movement, is a major and fundamental aspect of today's working environment. The problem is that the work is in danger of being devalued through its widespread publicity. In many organizations, quality initiatives have failed because senior managers have found it all too easy to buy the banner headlines, but have somehow failed to step up to the challenge of fully realizing the potential of the concepts involved. Often, it fails because of a lack of common understanding across the organization of what 'quality' represents. There is a resultant lack of team focus, and that is fatal. If quality is about anything, it is about people working together as a team, with a common purpose.

Perhaps that last remark needs justification. To do that, we need to look back to the origins of quality. Most discussions of the subject trace it back to Dr Demming's work in the years after the Second World War. Of course, it is really far older than that. It goes right back to Taylor's unpopular time and motions studies in his steel mills in the 1880s, and further. However, Demming's work really led to today's focus on the subject. It is well known that he took his ideas from the USA, where they had gained little acceptance, to Japan in the 1950s. There they found a more sympathetic home, and arguably have been one of the major factors in bringing the Far Eastern economies to their current prominence. It may well be that to the Japanese industrialists of that time, the word 'quality' had a meaning much closer to the everyday use of the term—some sort of subjective feeling of excellence to a product or service. It was certainly true that in those days Japanese manufacturers had an image of low quality, lacking in excellence. This contrasted with the image of the US manufacturing industry, whose products were seen as of the highest quality (design, durability, etc.). The Japanese had a far cheaper labour force, but that was not enough for them to change their image of poor quality. To do that they would need to outdo the USA in product excellence, without raising their product prices so high that no-one would take them. Demming had the answer. By a systematic focus on the quality of each stage in the manufacturing process, not only would the finished goods be of the desired excellence, but they would avoid expensive scrap and rework. So the products could be made to higher quality, at the same or lower production cost. The result was both higher profits and increased market share. The strategy paid off: today Japanese manufactured goods are regarded as some of the most excellent in the world, and Japan's economy has boomed. Of course, at the time of writing, even Japan is entering a recession. Change is always with us.

The early approach can be summed up as 'do it right first time'. It was so successful that by the mid-1960s US and European firms were reimporting Demming's ideas into their countries. Meanwhile, Japanese companies did not stand still, and understanding of the quality concept grew and became more elaborate. In particular, it moved away from statistical control of manufacturing processes towards people—the company's employees. Most of us have been familiar for many years with stories of Japanese companies in which the employees play a very large role in improving their organizations' internal operations. Many Japanese workers will volunteer ideas each year for improvements. Many of these are implemented. This is a long way from stage 4 of the classic model, as described in Chapter 3. It required a radically different corporate culture to the one that was more usual in Europe or North America 15 to 20 years ago. Its success in Japan has led to a widespread take-up of the same approaches worldwide. Of course, indigenous cultures vary from country to country. Not all aspects of Japanese style can be transplanted to Brazil, Denmark or London. But the basic approach can be used—that of creating a company culture devoted to quality as a team affair.

The move towards a people-oriented style to achieve quality marks a transition from the earliest concepts of quality. In the earliest days, quality extended only as far as the manufacturing process, or some other process that was amenable to statistical control. It was measured by the degree to which manufacturing targets and tolerances were met. It did not question too much whether or not these were the *right* targets—it just ensured that they could be met. In the next phase, it was realized that in most organizations, processes and people are so interlinked that the entire organization has to be involved in improvement. There is little point in the plant making tin cans quickly if the marketing function or transport department delays the sale or the shipping—perhaps because the cans are unattractive or are awkward to handle. What is needed here is a team approach in which the 'right' targets are set across the organization, and everyone pulls together to achieve them. Quality now extends across the whole organization. However, its focus is still internal. The difficulty is in determining the *right* targets—the ones that are really best to shoot for.

With only an internal focus it would be quite possible to manufacture a Trabant[1] precisely to specification each time, at optimal cost, and with the full operation of the whole car plant; so that Trabants moved off the production line to customers like clockwork. The trouble is, the strategy relies on the customer agreeing that the Trabant hits the right target: he or she, given a choice, may well opt for someone else's product. Before the fall of the Berlin Wall the customer did not really have much of a choice—the ultimate seller's market. In an increasingly competitive world, quality is forced to shift its focus from the inside to the outside—to the customer. This is the real change, the real quality revolution.

The Trabant story illustrates the final phase in the evolution of quality: the realization that only the customers can decide on the right target, and that only their opinion really matters in the final analysis (Fig. 3.2). Without their approval, the product may as well not have been made. Quality has come a long way in this evolution, from the control of production tolerances and errors through to the involvement of the entire organization in the pursuit of the customers' satisfaction. Of course, that immediately prompts the question of 'which organization?' As we have seen, the old order is slow and cumbersome due to its complexity.

It follows that if we need to keep the customers happy in an increasingly competitive world, we had better be prepared to change our organization to make ourselves more responsive. This is the point at which quality meets the other three topics to be discussed in the rest of this chapter and the next.

In reality, most organizations are now entering the last phase of quality to a greater or lesser degree. The trouble is that as we have moved from phase I to phases II and III, quality has become more and more embracing in its subject matter. At the same time, many organizations just starting down the road find themselves at differing phases. The result is very considerable confusion as to what the subject is now really all about. It has become so large that it really represents an entire philosophy of how modern organizations should be set up and run. The quality umbrella is now wide enough to cover all the subject matter of this book and beyond.

The model above is what we have been looking for to replace the complexity–control diagram we had previously (Fig. 2.1). It represents a shift from introspective to customer-driven purpose.

---

[1] A Trabant was a make of car, and the standard means of private transport in the German Democratic Republic. It enjoyed a virtual monopoly in that country. There was a dramatic drop in sales volumes following the reunification of Germany.

Three phases of quality

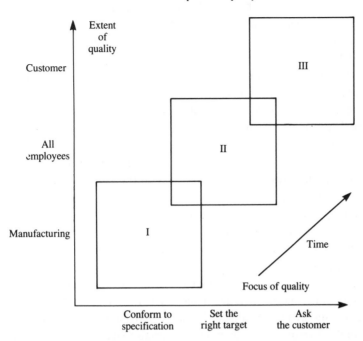

In phase I, quality is to do with conformance to specification, and relies heavily on detailed analysis and statistics. Its roots are in the classical model of organization. In phase II, quality has moved on to involve the whole organization in a search for betterment. The emphasis now is on team building and cultural change, and a common set of targets and objectives. In phase III it is realized that the customer sets the targets and must also be seen as part of the team. Quality is now seen as affecting every aspect of the company's activity. It is difficult to make this philosophy productive within a large and complex organization: getting the necessary customer responsiveness is always likely to be an uphill struggle. So quality points the way to the organizational changes that will be discussed in the next chapter.

Figure 3.2.   The evolution of quality from a production mentality to one dominated by the customer.

3.4   The customer has values

The trouble with customers is, they're always right

(Sales manager of a now defunct company)

As we have seen, in today's thinking on quality the customers are in the driving seat. They are the ultimate arbiter of our success. If they do not value us or our product, then we are in real trouble. Of course, if you had a monopoly in your market you might care a little less about the customers' needs, or their view of you. As a result, the delivered quality of your product would be lower, and the customers would not value it as highly, even though they might have no choice but to use it. For most organizations this is a hypothetical situation. Few have the luxury of being able to ignore competition, and the customers' view of our organization is then extremely important to us. But think about a large organization. Inside it there are divisions, departments, functions, plants, laboratories—all tightly interrelated, all dependent on each other. Many of these groups will have a monopoly on the market for their internal product—the product they deliver to the department on the next floor, or in the next city. The finance department is unlikely to have a rival department serving the same divisions. The plant maintenance group is not going to be in competition with another group from the same company. Each department is a monopoly for at least some of its output. There is a real danger that in the absence of market forces, the quality of those products—the extent to which their internal customer will value them—will be lower than it could have been.

Fine, there may be some internal wrangling within the company, but so long as the external customer sees a high-quality product, there is no problem. Wrong. If I deliver a low-quality product to you, and you do the same to your internal customer, and that goes on all the way to the real customers' door, then they are going to end up unhappy. If we want to avoid that, the whole organization must pull together, and must be customer-oriented. Not just oriented towards the external customer, but also towards the internal customers. Only then can we hope to be an effective competitor in an increasingly tough world.

The concept of the internal customer is key in today's organizations. The ultimate measure of the success of a department's work is the extent to which its customers (internal and external) value it. If each department adds value to the work it processes in the flow of activity from raw materials to delivered goods, then the real customer is far more likely to be happy than otherwise. Michael Porter made this observation in the mid-1980s, and introduced the concept of the value chain to help analyse the situation in real organizations.

Figure 3.3 shows a very simplified value chain for a manufacturing company. This is imagined to be the sort of company that takes in parts as raw materials, processes them and then assembles them into complex goods. We could equally well have chosen a company (say a chemical producer) that takes in a small number of very simple commodity raw materials and makes them into a very diverse range of finished chemicals. Or we could have chosen a financial or service industry. The approach is the same. Divide the chain from supplier to customer into its constituent parts. Then use the analysis to determine where value is added to the raw materials before they reach the customer. In the example in Fig. 3.3 (which omits much of the complexity and many of the functions, such as finance), we can see the way in which the different major functions feed each other. Executive management can use the diagram as a map which will let them point at places where value add is too low, or where surprising linkages indicate the need for change to the structure. Revealing the logical anatomy of the organization allows the management team to diagnose its difficulties, and see new ways to improve it. (It is worth noting that this is an architectural technique—the use of apparently simple diagrams to lay bare the bones of complex situations. We shall make heavy use of this philosophy later in the book.)

Dissecting an organization in this way has one other important result. It allows everyone to focus on the ways in which value is added, and makes each department

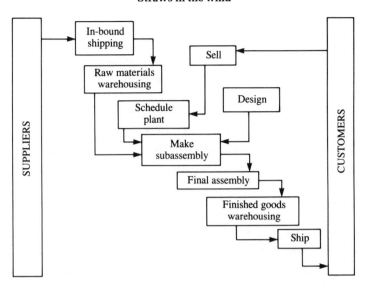

The competitive battle for the customer's attention requires the organization to be seen as different from its adversaries. We talk of the company adding value to its products. The value-chain analysis shows the company's managers where value is added to the product, so that they can see where unproductive (i.e. low-value) activities exist, and where more value could be added than is currently the case.

Figure 3.3.   An example of a value chain.

acutely aware of where their internal customers are, and how those customer–supplier relationships affect the value seen by the real customer. That can lead to a good basis for teamwork, the prerequisite to a successful quality programme.

Making the most of a value-chain diagram (like the one in Fig. 3.3) does, of course, need some good internal knowledge of the company's challenges and opportunities. Without that the pictures may be interesting, but cannot be considered very useful. Without trying to take ourselves through a detailed case study at this point, let us look at a simple example. We shall suppose that we are the board of directors of the company described in Fig. 3.3.

The company has been losing market share. Market research shows us that customers are dissatisfied with a general lack of responsiveness from the company. They have told us they do not like our products, they find us interested only in taking the order, and that we take too long to deliver. Look at Fig. 3.3, and try to see how it can help us to understand these issues!

Take the clients' first point—that our products are unattractive to them. We see from our chart that the customers' main interface to the company is through the sales function. It turns out that for many years the company has been very proud of its sales force's ability to outsell the competition. They had been given higher and higher annual sales targets, which were always achieved with ease. Until last year, when a new competitor from the Far East opened a distribution outlet near our main factory. They undercut us by a fair margin, and previously loyal customers have deserted us in large numbers. We always thought our brand image would be sufficient to keep us going through any threat of this sort, but obviously we were wrong.

Requests for product enhancements were always thought to be fed in through the sales function. Perhaps we have been driving them too hard. Perhaps they are not motivated to listen to the need for future products, but only to sell ever-larger quantities of output. We decide to make two improvements to the value our company provides to the customer.

Firstly, we take a hard look at the way in which the sales force operates, and the value it provides to the customers. Up to now the sales force have really only taken orders. They have not been particularly useful or helpful to our customers. We decide that the sales force must now be made responsible not only for selling the factories' output, but also for customer satisfaction, which they must care about as passionately as they do their selling. We know that this will mean quite a change in culture and attitude in the sales office, so we spend some time planning a strategy to effect that.

Secondly, we note that the only interface between customers and the company up to now has been the sales force. We decide to provide direct interfaces into design and manufacturing, so that the customers now have a strong voice in the way the products are designed and the quality of the manufactured goods. We are now able to draw an improved value-chain diagram, showing the customers' new relationship to the company (Fig. 3.4).

The board also worries about the customers' comments on responsiveness. These days we all expect the gap between aspiration and fulfilment to be as short as possible.[2] The speed with which things are done for us makes them attractive. This has become an important part of the value that customers associate with new their suppliers. Our board realizes this, particularly since we have new competition on our doorstep. We also know that cost is a key ingredient in a customer's evaluation of our services. We look at the value chain and examine where time is lost or cost is added unnecessarily on the route from raw materials to the customer. We find the black spots, and put actions in place to fix them.

This simple example hints at the way in which the analysis of the value chain can lead to improvements in the business. Of course, we can only hope to get a taste of

[2] We live in a society that is increasingly devoted to instant gratification. Whatever you want or need is available with little or no delay. Instant noodles, instant coffee, freezer-to-microwave meals, drive-through restaurants, electronic mail, facsimile, video phones, one-hour film processing, one-hour spectacles, same-day delivery, instant cash, instant credit. Responsiveness is a competitive weapon.

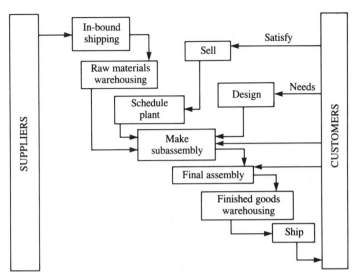

New links have been added between the customers and the selling, design and manufacturing functions. The mission of the sales function is also changed.

Figure 3.4.   The value chain after analysis and improvement.

the way in which the real debate would go. We have no information about the company than the few slender facts given above. In a real situation the senior managers doing the analysis would have a very deep and intuitive understanding of the key issues presented by Fig. 3.3, which would allow them to focus that intuition without getting lost in detail. This is a common feature of high-level architectural diagrams such as Fig. 3.3. They usually mean far more to the people who have to use them than they do to others.

Of course, there is an even more fundamental question—should the processes shown in the value-chain diagrams be there at all? Perhaps there is an altogether different way of doing things, in which some existing processes vanish altogether, and in which things are wired together in a completely new way. This analysis has become known as 'business process reengineering', and is the third and last of the current business approaches we discuss in this chapter. The observant reader will note the close relationship between quality, value chains and reengineering. We drew attention to this earlier in the chapter. In practice, the three approaches beg, borrow and steal from each other—they are all very close cousins.

3.5   Reengineer

> GÉRONTE: *It seems to me you are locating them wrongly: the heart is on the left and the liver is on the right.*
> SGANARELLE: *Yes, in the old days that was so, but we have changed all that, and now we practise medicine by a completely new method.*
>
> (Molière, *Le Medecin Maigré Lui*)

The value-chain analysis lays the organization bare. It allows senior management to question the way the organization is, and to try and redraw it in a new and better way. This rewiring of the organization has become known as 'business process reengineering'. As we have seen, its roots lie back in Demming's ideas on quality. We have traced the gradual evolution of those ideas through their various phases, and this is where they end up. The new ideas have inherited much from the world of quality. They act as a magnet for publicity, and the whole area of reengineering is very much alive and well in many organizations. As with quality, there is much confusion as to the meaning of the concepts, and the ways of dealing with them. There is a rapidly growing library of books on the subject, and the consultancy market-place is full of ideas and approaches to carrying out the tasks required.

Business process reengineering is in some ways a return to the type of 'organization and methods' activities that Frederick Taylor Winslow initiated 100 years ago. But whereas he applied it to maximize the efficiency of large factories, reengineering is today very much focused on the customer, and on the way in which value is created around the organization. Like quality, its banner headlines have caused it some problems. Expectations are high, but are not always fulfilled. In the case of quality, the difficulties are often a lack of focus on driving change forward through a team approach across the organization. Reengineering has an additional challenge, which has led to some of the early failures. It presents an opportunity for an organization to take a radical view of its processes and internal operation, and transform itself by extensive rewiring—effectively redrawing the value chain from scratch. That would allow the cutting out of processes that don't contribute to customer value, as well as optimizing those that do. A prerequisite is almost certain to be some painful organizational or head-count decisions. Some organizations have baulked at the prospect, and have used the techniques to improve the internals of specific processes. The return for their pains is considerably less than might have been the case if they had taken the more radical option.

The most extreme option of all is to entirely dismember the organization into a collection of small businesses, each focused very clearly on its customers and market-place. Many organizations believe this to be the only way of effecting the degree of reengineering that is needed to grasp the competitive opportunity. They would go further, to say that rewiring the organization is not sufficient. To really make these changes work, there has to be a fundamental change in the culture: one that really stands F. W. Taylor's thinking on its head, and gives back to the individual employee the responsibility and freedom of action that Taylor's thinking did so much to remove. Granting these to the employee has become known as empowerment, and is one of the things we shall discuss in the next chapter. For now, let us return to the simple example we were looking at earlier, and draw the reengineered company (see Fig. 3.5). Once again, let us pretend to be the board. This is a very live issue for many organizations today, and is the subject of the next chapter.

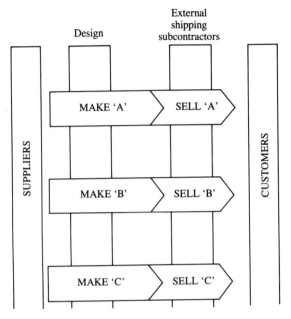

The integrated wiring diagram shown in Fig. 3.4 has been replaced with a completely new structure aimed at serving the customer's needs.

Figure 3.5.   The company has been redesigned.

What we see is very different from the starting point. We now have three businesses, each focused on making and selling a specific product—from subassembly onwards. They deal directly with their own customers and markets, adopting the philosophy that customer satisfaction and value is key, as described earlier. They share a common design function, which maintains the strong links to customers that we gave it earlier. Design and manufacture are seen by our company as the things that it is really good at. In fact they were the things that made our chairman so successful when he first started the business, operating on his own from a garage. His professional skills attracted others to the company, and it has always had a wealth of talent available in both the design shops and the plants. They always feel that they are the soul of the company, and that they really are its best asset—the thing that at the end of the day distinguishes it from the competition. On the other hand, the company has never seen shipping as its main forte. It has always been just something that had to get done, and has over the years built up a small fleet of trucks and delivery vans. We have now realized that the shipping job could be done more effectively and more cheaply by subcontracting it entirely to a company that specializes in that area. We have outsourced shipping and have seen customer satisfaction improve as a result. Not only that, but we no longer need the huge outbound warehousing operation that we used to run. To the delight of the board, most of the shipping staff they had formerly employed have now found work with the subcontractor. They all seem to be far happier than when they worked for us. The shipping company is in an environment where they are valued for their own special skills in their own right, and where they feel they can make a real contribution.

We have avoided the use of the big inbound warehouses. By careful redesign at a detailed level of our manufacturing and scheduling processes, we have struck partnership deals with our suppliers. They deliver stock to us when we need it ('just in time'), and are assured of a steady market. We save on inventory costs, and can make the product far more quickly.

Overall, our situation is much improved. Our customers are happier. Our employees are much more motivated—we have allowed them considerable freedom to implement the business the way they thought best, and they have a clear customer focus as a team. We have reduced costs substantially, and are left with a set of processes and activities that concentrates on our core competencies—not on peripheral activities. That enables us to put all our energies into keeping the customer happy with the right product, at the right time and the right price.

As with everything, there is a price. For us, it is the difficulty of keeping the company together in a coherent way. We believe we are more than just a holding operation for a group of autonomous businesses. We have shared values, and we may need in the future to reengineer the company again on different lines as the market changes. That gives us the headache of balancing a shared infrastructure (from the phones to the pay policy) against the needs of the businesses to be independent.

3.6   Summary

The old order is fast passing away. There are still many uncertainties as to what should replace it. However, for most organizations, the *customer* has now moved to the centre of the stage. In the old world the customer had often seemed to be placed at the rear of the stalls. We see this in businesses, in government departments and even in health care and law enforcement. We see it not only in relation to the real external customer, but also in the way people relate to each other even within the same organization—often regarding *each other* as customers.

The new management-speak used to describe this change varies with viewpoint and guru. Arguably, the common ground is to be found in the concepts and jargon of the quality movement, which has itself moved gently over its 40 or so years of public life from an inward focus on statistical control of production standards towards addressing the customers' real needs. It has led to business process reengineering, via value-chain analysis. We have spent a little time looking at those approaches.

Even from the beginning, the quality movement stressed the involvement of individuals in improving the processes or products of their organization. The pressure for rapid change that we described in the earlier chapters make the individual even more key. He or she is where creativity starts. He or she is the focal point of dealings with the all-important customer. Not surprisingly, the individual plays a key role in today's management thinking.

One of the strengths of the old model was its provision of shared infrastructure that could be relied on to do the job—whether it was drainage, roads, or computer services. In the new world, with its focus on the customer and the individual, there is a danger that these virtuous aspects of the old are thrown out with the bad. They are needed if the individual is to realize his or her full potential.

In the next chapter, we shall look at a new organizational model which offers the chance of liberating the individuals' energies and creativity while at the same time providing him or her with the infrastructure needed for full effectiveness.

4
New foundations
Federal organizations

If I had a hammer, I'd hammer out freedom, all over this land

(Pete Seeger, paraphrased)

4.1   Purpose

New ways of organizing are emerging, as the old order proves itself ill-fitted to a changing world. Much is yet unclear. But the outline of the new order can just be discerned. In this chapter we describe what can be seen, and raise some questions about the parts that are still unclear.

4.2   Collapse

Everywhere you look, organizations are in turmoil. In all industries—from banking to steel, from leisure to electronics—companies are 'deconstructing', 'slimming down', 'flattening', 'empowering', or 'seeking new visions'. In countries all over the world, power is trying to flow from the dams created by central governments towards regional groups or individuals. Sometimes the change has been sudden and dramatic. In the Eastern Bloc, walls tumbled and tyrants toppled. Recession bit, and companies folded. Sometimes the changes have been quieter and less noticeable. Corporations have dismantled their central staffs. Western democracies such as the United Kingdom have spent 10 years and more taking apart centralized socialist infrastructures, pushing even universities, schools and hospitals through a fundamental change in the way they operate and view their purpose.

In this new order, everything is fast and light (Table 4.1). Gone are the huge bureaucracies needed to coordinate all the minute details of life in an industrial or global empire. Level after level of management hierarchy has vanished. In the new 'free' environment power has gone to smaller work groups and to individuals. In many ways it is like growing up. Not only are we given power to determine our own actions, but we are also expected to exercise the power in a responsible way. If we

Table 4.1 The new rules to replace the old

A braver new world

Values: We make the rules round here

Unleashed talent. The individual is freed to make his or her contribution to the organization, and to feel that it makes a difference.

Management is dead. The comfortable faith in an omniscient and benign management system has gone. So have many of the managers who lived in it. The ones who are left are very busy and have no time to look after their people as they used to. Nor do they have the time to operate and maintain a labyrinth of management processes. The staff functions that helped them keep the maze going have also been disbanded. Weeds grow in the gardens.

Make your own decisions. In the absence of the paternal management system, individuals must now display initiatives. They can no longer wait for management to make decisions for them. Some employees welcome this, others find it discomforting.

Stay together or die. The organization cannot be just a collection of individuals. If it has an identity, then that can only come from cooperation between individuals. No cooperation, no organization.

There is nowhere to hide. Now an individual's actions matter to the organization. With that comes responsibility. The individual is now accountable for what he or she does (and does not do).

Structures: Small is beautiful

Big things choke. There is no management time to spare for holding together large and complex organizational structures. The organizational units must be small enough to be easily managed, and to allow freedom to the individual.

Little things run fast and friendly. The way in which individuals are allowed—in fact *required*—to make many of the decisions makes the organization very flexible and responsive to the market-place. The business presents a very human face to the customer.

Stick to the point. Small organizational units cannot cover everything. They need to know who they are, and to concentrate on doing things well.

The sewers do not work. Shared infrastructure across the whole organization requires shared resources to look after it. In this new world, there is far less of those resources, so many of the benefits of the old order are lost.

Plans: Hang loose

What vision? In times of change it is difficult to see far ahead. Many organizations find planning too hard in this situation, drifting with the tide. Yet it may well be that those with the vision and imagination to see opportunities and grasp them in a single-minded way will be tomorrow's winners.

The major change in the new world is the central role played by the individual. Small organizational units are needed to allow the individual freedom, and to free inventiveness and energy in pursuit of the customer. Paternalistic management structures vanish. That leads to a lack of amenity and comfort in what had been a common infrastructure.

do not, then our company, our government department, our nation—whichever it is—will fail to a greater or lesser extent. So this is also about teamwork, about shared values, shared vision and culture. Teamwork, of course, is the point of convergence between these changes and the discussion we had in the last chapter about quality and business reengineering. Clearly, for commercial organizations the changes have been driven by competitive pressures and the fight for the customer's attention. That was where we got to in the last chapter.

However, process reengineering and quality do not explain the endemic nature of these changes, which affect all scales and types of organization from governments to banks, charities and industry. The changes to our model from Chapter 2 are dramatic (see Fig. 4.1).

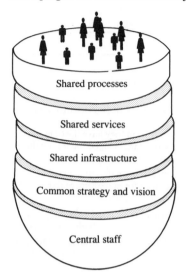

The federation will not exist unless there is sharing. Without sharing, it is no more than the sum of its parts. In a business, many things can be shared. For many of them there may be a need for shared staff to manage the common resources, services of infrastructure. The shared staff does not need to be physically centralized, it could be dispersed among the businesses. A business federation is unlikely to be successful without shared infrastructure. After all, it was partly customer responsiveness that led us to a federal structure. If a lack of shared infrastructure makes us less responsive to customer needs then we have failed.

Figure 4.1.   Shared elements in a federation of businesses.

The changes bring with them an enhanced ability to compete (cost effectiveness, responsiveness, etc.), and a renewed focus on freedom of the individual. They increase the pressures to compete and for freedom—the same forces that created them in the first place. As a result, they spread like a virus, infecting one company or country after another—each forced into a more competitive or more liberal environment by its neighbours. What we are seeing here is a revolution in every sense of the word.

4.3   Baby's bath water

A lot of people wholeheartedly welcome these changes. Many others greet them with at least a hint of regret. Some view them with great unease. As with all revolutions, there is a danger of the good being destroyed with the bad, with no clear idea of what will replace it. The unease can be summed up in two words— 'infrastructure' and 'well-being'. In a centralized world, there is at least the hope that both will be looked after for the common good by 'the system'. If the latter was incompetent or malign, then of course life might have been better without it. But things are rarely that black or white. In this strange new decentralized world it is not immediately obvious who (if anyone) will build a shared infrastructure, or who will look after the well-being of the citizen or employee.

It is sobering to recall that in the latter years of the eighteenth century, a similarly large change in working methods was under way, as the Industrial Revolution took millions from their villages and cottage industries to new work in large factories. In some industries, notably textiles in England, an entire generation of workers lost their livelihoods and never worked again. It may well be that we should expect the force of history to be equally brutal in today's world. The irony here is that the changes in the eighteenth century were the source of the classic organizational model that is now passing away. It was the Industrial Revolution that started building the infrastructure we seem to be in danger of losing.

This is a complex issue, and also a very old one. The debate on this subject goes back to the philosophers Locke and Hobbes, and even further back to Plato. Even so, there is as yet no textbook account of the one true path to well-being in this new world. We can describe the issues, and we can talk about the ways in which organizations are dealing with them today. But we cannot describe the 'truth'. It has still not made its mind up as to its eventual shape and form. We are in the middle of the revolution, and all that we can do is to equip ourselves to understand what is going on and to help shape the outcome in our own organizations and lives.

4.4   Rights to power

If you had been in charge of an old-style regime in a country like Romania in 1989, you might not have had any great decisions to make about the emergence of a new order of things. It might just have happened to you, and then the 'revolution' would have taken its own course afterwards. Most business people (and probably government officials) would rather take the pain of some personal decision-making. Most of the intellectual pain will come from determining the role of the centre—in the new organization itself, as well as in the transition period. In one extreme view, of course, the centre has no role. It *empowers* the factory floor or citizen in the street with all its authority, and then shuts up shop. Market forces and jungle law are then supposed to determine any management structures needed by a process of evolution. The trouble is that in this situation there is no reason why any one of the empowered groups should not just go its own way separately from its former peers, and maybe even set up in competition to them, with their rivals. That is a kind of organizational suicide. The original organization gives up on its identity totally and ceases to exist. The ultimate demerger. This is usually a corporate strategy taken only under extreme threat of external pressure: for example, the demerger of Bell or Standard Oil forced by monopoly legislation, or the demerger of ICI in the face of an exposure to corporate raids.

Most organizations will try to preserve at least their corporate identity in moving to the new order, rather than going for the radical demerger approach. Corporate identity may mean many things, but typically it will include at least a shared purpose and some kind of shared management of the company logo or brand image. It may also go a lot further—for example, management of the asset base or even common ways of performing key business processes. This is where the dilemma lives. On the one hand, there is a need to empower individuals and small work-groups. On the other hand, as we have seen, we want to retain some powers centrally. But which powers?

The philosopher Thomas Hobbes lived through the disorderly period in England leading to the execution of Charles I in 1649. The violence and bloodshed of his day led him to put law and order at the heart of his philosophy. He saw life without government as 'solitary, poor, nasty, brutish and short'. He advocated the protection of individuals from each other's natures by a strong government. Mix this philosophy with the analytic approach of F. W. Taylor and you have the ingredients for some of the more authoritarian organizations that we have seen in the past 100 years or so.

John Locke was of the generation that followed Hobbes, living in slightly less troubled times, and able to take a more sanguine view of human nature. He promoted a much looser form of government than the older philosopher. For Locke, government had only one purpose—to ensure that 'no one should harm another in his life, health, liberty or possessions'. Government was to be a servant of the people, and subject to change by them. In politics, his views led eventually to the flowering of democracy (of course, several later philosophers also had a key role). In business organization, his ideas are only now finding their day. The idea of a federal government, put in place by the federation's members for their mutual benefit and convenience, is very much alive today in the business world.

It is worth remembering that political philosophy did not stop with Locke. In particular, John Stuart Mill noted that Locke's 'government by the majority' could be as much of a tyranny as could Hobbes'. That is certainly one view that can be taken of the turmoil due to the mob in the French Revolution at the end of the eighteenth century. Mill held that the government should be elected by the majority, but should have powers to protect the minority from their will. This represents a flow of power away from Locke's pure democracy to one in which the elected government has powers to control the behaviour of the electorate in some situations. Hobbes' views lie at the extreme end of this path. Most democracies exhibit some sort of balance between the two extremes. It may well be that we shall yet see similar thinking emerge in businesses that have recently formed loose federations. Perhaps we shall see a flow of power back to the centre.

What this comes down to is that the centre must be *right-powered* for the new environment. A good rule of thumb is for it to have the minimum powers necessary for the overall good of the organizations. That immediately prompts the question of where that overall good is to be determined. It also leaves open the question of who will determine the powers held by the centre. Fortunately we can take a short cut, because these questions have been addressed before, by politicians.

4.5   Federated futures

The right-powering dilemma has been faced before, in the USA after the War of Independence, in West Germany in the late 1940s, and today in the ongoing debate on the shape of the European Union or of the CIS in the former Soviet Union. We could also list a range of other situations from Australia and Switzerland to the Trades Union Congress in the United Kingdom. In each case, the solution has been to form a *federation*—a union of separate entities (states, businesses or anything else) joined together to serve common interests while retaining a strong degree of autonomy. Its members stay together because they need each other and, importantly, also because they need to share things. The *centre* in a federation exists as a shared resource or service. It is given power and authority by the federation members. This is quite the reverse of empowerment—in which the centre gives power to the edges. The reversal of view and attitude is the single most important difference between the old and new worlds. In a way we can see 'empowerment' as an interim concept *en route* from the old centralized structures to the new federated organization.

Now we have the answers to our first two questions. In a federated organization it is the federation members that ultimately determine what is best for the organization as a whole, and decide which powers the 'centre' should exercise.

4.6   Granting the right

For any federation, the first major milestone, the act of conception, is the agreement to a constitution. Although federal thinking goes back a long way (to Ancient Greece and before), the word 'constitution' usually conjures up the document drawn up by the newly independent American states in 1787. It is a model document, clearly laying out the responsibilities of the centre, of the state government, and of the individual (whom we shall be coming to shortly). Not only that, but it also describes the processes by which the centre can be changed and constrained. But even more importantly, it lays out the bones of a shared vision and of a shared value system—essential to the coherence of the nation.

Any organization going down this path must form such a constitution. It is the act marking the creation of a federation, and the birth of the new centre. The centre is given its initial powers by this constitution. It should also describe the common vision and collective purpose of the federation, the rules which govern the behaviour of its members in their dealings with each other, and the way in which those rules will be dealt with. It should also lay out the processes by which the

power of the centre will be modified and maintained. It may well be that the constitution will end there. Any additional rules or powers will be determined (rather like
Bills in the USA or Acts in the UK) by the federation through the processes
described in the constitution. That process may also need to define a supporting
organizational structure to deal with three key central activities:

- strategy—the determination of the direction of the entire federation
- execution—carrying out the tasks necessary to follow the strategy
- monitoring—ensuring that the constitution is adhered to as well as any policies
  or rules agreed in addition.

Common sense says that there should be clearly separated functions implementing
each of these. Otherwise strategy will be confused with operational issues, which
will in turn be confused with laws and rules. That is not to say that these 'central'
activities need a large centralized organization to carry them out. Quite the reverse!
They would be better labelled 'shared' rather than centralized. One very effective
way of carrying them out would be to disperse them across the federation—with
different activities carried out by different groups. This would be a good way of
reducing central staff overheads as well as ensuring that the 'centre' does not slowly
acquire more power and authority, encumbering the rest of the organization.

4.7   Shared concerns

We have so far been waylaid from the real question—determination of what
should be given to the centre by the federation's members. (Remember—the centre
may actually be dispersed!) As we have seen above, this should include strategy,
execution, and the monitoring of adherence to the constitution and any additional
agreed rules or 'laws'. However, the 'centre' may also include the following.

1 *Definition and implementation of key business processes* to be run in common
   ways across the organization. Whether there are such things really depends on
   the specific circumstances. Clearly, the federation members would not give
   away their autonomy in this area lightly. But there is a range of processes that
   may be excellent candidates for doing 'right' just once across the organization:
   credit management, meeting environmental legislation, etc. There may also be
   some key manufacturing processes which are common to all members or there
   may be a need to make some processes common to optimize the value chain
   from the federation suppliers to its customers.
2 *Provision of shared services,* used by the members of the federation (Fig. 4.1).
   These may range from 'legal services' through to information technology, or
   publicity and accountancy. Whatever they are, they should be shared between
   the members of the federation and be discarded if they are not used. In a sense
   they can operate as an extreme form of shared process—the process being a
   total subcontract of a particular area to a shared service group. Again, the

federation members must exercise care in setting up these groups. Too many, and a staff organization with a life of its own will develop and be difficult to remove.

3   *Provision of shared infrastructure.* The US Federation's constitution of 1781 was not its first. The Declaration of Independence was followed shortly afterwards by the 'Articles of Confederation' of 1787. These defined a federal structure with a far less centralized power than we see today. Its authors, driven by a fear of centralized authority, had produced a constitution that limited the centre's functions largely to a common defence policy. The reasons for its replacement only six years later include the practical difficulty of building and managing a common infrastructure. Infrastructure is essential to the well-being of any federation. In the case of nations, the key requirements are shared planning, shared funding and shared implementation. In the case of businesses there is one additional requirement—flexibility. Political federations do not need this in the same way. It is unlikely, for example, that Texas and New Mexico will ever amalgamate and redivide themselves into a totally new geographic configuration. Equally, it is unlikely that Switzerland will ever sell one of its cantons to Germany, or that the Australian federal government will ask Queensland to leave the federation. In business, mergers, acquisitions and the redrawing of organizational boundaries are commonplace, and to be expected in an increasingly competitive and fast-moving market. For a stable business, there needs to be a shared infrastructure that can enable the shared strategy, common processes and services. For a changing business, that infrastructure needs to be designed with flexibility in mind. That requires a strong element of design, and is the subject of the next chapter and the rest of this book.

4   *A common strategy and vision.* This is the essence of teamwork. Remember that some time ago our journey passed through the three stages of quality. We said then that teamwork was the fundamental prerequisite to the success of any quality programme in an organization. This is even more true when we get to business process reengineering, and now to federal organizations. We are really on this journey only because of the customers—and our need to have them value us. We saw earlier that a key ingredient of this valuation will be the rapidity of our response. Remember, this is the 'instant' society. It is very unlikely that we will be able to display anything like the responsiveness the customer needs if we allow our organizations to be broken up into a patchwork quilt of disparate and divergent pieces. This is true, of course, of the other areas we just listed. But it is nowhere more certain of being needed than in the possession of a common strategy and vision of where we are all heading.

5   Last (and not quite least), all the items in this list will need some people to tend them on behalf of the federation. In the old world such people rose to positions of great power and influence. In F. W. Taylor's world, they were the management class, of superior vision and intellect to the working professional. In the new world, they are the mere servants of the people. But rather like doctors,

nurses and teachers in today's society (and also, of course, refuse collectors and street cleaners) they are essential to the well-being of the entire community. Therefore they are valued by their peers, by their customers—the ultimate accolade in this new order. Of course, we would not want to see them becoming a repeat performance of the burgeoning and bureaucratic staff functions that we looked at in the classic organization a couple of chapters ago. Many of them do not need to be centralized in any way. Responsibility could be shared out between the members of the federation. But inevitably, there will be a need for some central group of people. The trick is to make sure it is the right size for the job, and not some burdensome bureaucracy.

4.8   The new individual

What we are now seeing in most organizations is the collapse of the old 'centre', and the ascendancy of the individual. Since the latter is the new and active force, we shall discuss it first and then come back to the centre later.

Let us describe an individual in this new order—how he or she feels, how he or she operates, what it means to be an employee or (in newspeak) a corporate citizen. For starters, let us make it clear that this individual is you, or I, or the lady next door, or your father, or your niece when she leaves school next year. He or she may also be the CEO, or the cafeteria assistant; the chief fire officer, or the supervisor in the boiler room, or your secretary. It is all the same. In the new world all our old preconceptions about 'us and them' about status, age, length of service, must be shelved. We start again, with a blank sheet of paper. There will be those of us who cannot do this, who find the old world too familiar or too comfortable. The rest of us must help these people through the transition—because those who cannot make it and find the right-shaped hole in the new world will become homeless. More than that, in general there will be some losers and (mostly) winners in the new world. In fact all of us will gain something and lose something. We have to be prepared for this.

Let us suppose that I work in a new-style organization. I work in a team of fewer than 200 people, most of whom I know by sight, and many of whom I know personally. The familiarity has come about because we tend to work in project-oriented teams which change manning and purpose as customer needs alter. So we work with a wide range of people. It is quite possible for me to lead a team today and have one of its members lead me in a different team tomorrow. There is no status barrier to getting the job done. All this dynamic reshaping is made possible because we share a very strong sense of belonging, of shared purpose and of vision—and, of course, we all care desperately about the satisfaction of our customers. We have few rules that constrain us—really only those that are needed to ensure the smooth running of our business unit, and of the overall business that owns us (there are many more units like ours within the overall business). Our unit is targeted to achieve specific profit levels, and we are paid in relation to the profit we make. We are all actively involved in key decisions on the operation and direction of our business, and I feel I can always voice ideas and comments that would improve our unit's future. We all spend significant amounts of our time in planning and developing our skills—because we know that what is good for us is good for the business. We are a happy, well-motivated and well-paid workforce with no status or hierarchy barriers to get in the way of doing the job.

Readers with a history of working in large corporations may find this account a little naïve. But it is based on the way life feels in a number of big companies that are rapidly heading down this path. It is also the way that many successful small businesses have always been. The trick here is to get the benefits of the small company within the framework of a large one.

4.9   Summary

In many businesses and organizations today, we see the emergence of similar structures replacing the old way of doing them. Power has been taken away from the large corporate centres and given to small business units and to individuals. The corporate staffs are gone. Individuals carry far more responsibility than they did before. They and the small business units characteristic of the new order have far more power than previously. In return, the rest of the organization depends on them far more than it did. Their actions, their ideas, carry far more weight than they could ever have done before.

With the power and responsibility comes danger. The individual may misjudge or blunder. Most organizations think this is a price worth paying. Better to err and move forward in a rapidly changing world than to fool yourself into thinking there is less danger in endless analysis of risks and options, often very far away from the point at which the actions are to be taken. In fact, the person closest to the action may have a better view of the correct approach than 100 people sitting in a staff headquarters building.

With the power also comes the need to carry responsibility in a mature way. Federations need their members to work together for mutual good. That requires giving and taking between the individuals or small organizational units and the larger whole. It needs them to give away some of their power, voluntarily, because they recognize the need for some things to be shared and hence managed on their behalf. So, shared infrastructure, shared strategy, shared support services—all of which need management on behalf of the federation members.

Information technology is an important part of the shared infrastructure in any organization. That remains true in a federated organization. Clearly, in that situation, we must abandon the old-world assumption that all aspects of IT are a shared and therefore centrally planned and controlled resource. That route leads back to large central staff functions. Nevertheless, there may well be some parts of IT that are of common importance to all the federation members, and that need to be planned (and possibly managed) centrally, on behalf of the federation.

We shall turn to this issue for the next two chapters. In Chapter 5 we shall remind ourselves of just how important technology can be as a driving force in times such as ours. Then, in Chapter 6, we shall examine the case for including information technology as part of our shared infrastructure in a federation organization, or indeed any other sort of organization.

5
Order and disorder

The influence of technology

Things fall apart; the centre cannot hold. Mere anarchy is loosed upon the world.

(W. B. Yeats)

5.1   Purpose

In the last four chapters we have surveyed some of the most important themes in today's management thinking. Clearly those ideas represent a significant break with the past. In this chapter we argue that the discontinuity in management think- ing is closely related to the rapid progress of technology in recent years and, furthermore, that this relationship must be harnessed to achieve business success in these difficult times.

5.2   Technology's melting pot

The original causes of the current revolution may well take historians 100 years to analyse and agree. Perhaps it was the new competitiveness introduced after the Second World War by its economic victors, Japan and Germany. Perhaps it was the emergence of industrialized societies with cheap labour forces in the Third World. But one thing is certain, the fires of change are now fanned by the wind of innovation in technology. Cannot compete with cheap labour and production tech- nology? Then automate wherever possible, or give value to commodities by soft additions (new complex functions, services, information linkages between diverse products and companies, etc.). Cannot afford large bureaucracies? Then replace them with dispersed cross-functional teams, and people networks. Cannot com- pete on your own? Then form and reform alliances that can compete effectively as a unit. Cannot keep up with the pace of change? Either expire or adapt into a new organization and infrastructure that can cope.

Information technology is one of a very small number of weapons available to a company to deal with all these challenges. The remarks in the last paragraph need

justification, particularly since it has become fashionable to denigrate the importance of science and technology to our societies. Their practitioners are certainly
less valued and lower paid than they were 30 or 40 years ago. There is an increasing
tendency to typecast them as incoherent and obsessive introverts, and their activity
is in need of wise guidance and careful financial scrutiny. The same prejudice has
been applied to computer professionals, who have done little to discredit it in most
organizations. As a result, the opportunity offered by information technology is
not given much credence by senior managers. Many of them have come to see
information technology as an expensive form of plumbing. One of the key
messages of this book is that their view must change. Why? Because of the power of
technology to change business and national organizations fundamentally, and the
fact that the power is evidently at work in today's organizations—which are indeed
changing rapidly. Let us look at some of the evidence of technology's power in
history.

5.3   The last time around

The period of time that best illustrates the potential of technology as an agent of
change is, of course, the Industrial Revolution. Too much has been written (and is
still being written) about that period to make it worth while for us to go into detail
here. In any case this is not a history or sociology text. But it is worth reminding
ourselves of some of the key facts.

People of vision

The Industrial Revolution was driven by people with vision—moneymaking
vision, the ability to see clear business opportunities from applying steam and
water power to manufacturing. Philanthropic vision too—the prospect of a world
somehow made better for all by leaps forward in transport infrastructure, and
through the creation of wealth. It was also driven by technologists, people who
were fascinated by the challenge of applying the technology to new purposes, or
working out fundamental scientific and engineering principles that could be
applied again and again. Both the visionaries and the technologists were essential.
Today we have plenty of the latter, but few organizations have people with the
vision to make real business use of information technology. There is a void
between the business people and the technology, created by attitudes and a lack of
effective communication between the two. In its own small way, this book is an
attempt at bridging the gap, and for a good reason. The message of history is
clear—organizations that do not have the vision to use advances in technology will
not be able to compete effectively in the new world. They will find that their
markets become obsolete, or their cost base is too high, and they will fossilize.

Time-scales

This was not a revolution in the explosive sense of those in Paris in 1789 or Russia in 1917. It took several generations to complete and (rather like today) it was not apparent that such fundamental changes were under way until well into the process.

Social impact

Within just two generations the whole way of life in Great Britain had been transformed. In 1760 the means of production were decentralized. Work was taken out to villagers in their own homes. By 1810, the expensive and centralized machinery used for production of cotton, coal or steel in bulk had been introduced. There had been a mass migration from the countryside to urban centres surrounding the new means of production. Communities that had existed for centuries were weakened or vanished altogether. Fresh communities sprang up, often dominated by a new hierarchical and autocratic management system associated with the factories.

Infrastructure and communications

The needs of the new factories for raw materials and rapid access to markets led to an explosive growth in the transport infrastructure. In 1750 it took two weeks to travel from London to Edinburgh. By 1820 it took under two days. That kind of improvement enabled the formation of dispersed businesses, and allowed government to disperse some of its powers and to maintain tighter central control over others. Importantly, it also led to a greater degree of common vision and of shared citizenship—contributing to the competitiveness of the nation as a military power.

New winners and losers

The industrial strength of Great Britain and its well-developed infrastructure grew alongside the political foment in France in the early 1790s. Conflict was inevitable, as Britain feared the spread of egalitarian policies over the Channel, and France saw its traditional role as the strong man of Europe under threat as Britain gained industrial power. The result was a series of wars lasting until 1815. They led to the spread of French revolutionary ideas across Europe, culminating in the year of revolution (1848) in one country after another, and the British isolationism that lasted well into this century. After this period, Britain was the uncontested global superpower, financed and provisioned by the labours of its Industrial Revolution.

Clearly, the effects of the new technology were profound. The world we now live in was shaped by it. Every facet of our lives is different as a result.

5.4   The new fire

Analogies are always limited, and it would be wrong to assume that the details of the Industrial Revolution will be played out again 200 years later. We live in a very different age. But the key lesson—that technology can radically transform the world—should be noted. Let us look at the ways in which today's technology is already effecting transformation,

New competition

Information technology is, above all, soft. It can be readily adapted or reprogrammed to serve new purposes. Furthermore, the products of our 'advanced' societies are—rightly or wrongly—increasingly soft in nature, as basic manufacturing of commodities is increasingly exported to the Third World. It follows that the cost of entry into most industries is going to get lower and lower. In the most extreme case it may be the cost of some commodity computer hardware and some programming effort. As entry costs fall, so competition will increase in all industries. International telecommunications will allow that competition to be felt at a distance. No longer will your competitors be the people you went to college with, or can get to in a day's drive. They may be on the other side of the globe. This phenomenon is already with us.

> Ten years ago, if I wanted to have some software written for some particular purpose, I would walk down the corridor and ask my peers in the programming department to do the work. It was full of highly paid professionals, all of them very much valued by the organization. Today, if I had the same requirements I might just as easily use a programmer from the developing world who was prepared to do the work for half the European rate, and to the same quality. The most surprising thing about the arrangement would be that I would never see the programmer. He or she would sit in Lima, or Delhi or Manila, and perform the entire task remotely. All communication to me (including the delivery of the finished software and manuals) would be over a telephone line. The programmer would not need very expensive equipment, but might well use a personal computer for all the work.

New markets

We are moving inexorably towards a global infrastructure of information technology equipment. Anything that can be digitized will be, and will be accessible to anyone on the planet—subject always to payment of fees, security and so on. That means more and more new products are possible based on knowledge: on information and on its processing. It also means that those products—as well as the conventional 'hard' ones—can be sold to anyone, anywhere at any time of the night or day, with perhaps almost instantaneous delivery and payment.

Old markets?

There are those who, probably rightly, decry the vision of Western-style democracies thriving on the basis of only service-oriented 'soft' products. They argue that manufacturing must always be a key component of a sound industrial base. Clearly, if commodity goods can always be produced more cheaply in the Third World, then manufactured goods with a long-term viability in the developed economies must have something that distinguishes them from commodities. The bundling of soft additions to commodities is one possible strategy. Another is to manufacture products which have intrinsic complexity that is difficult to manufacture and which command a sufficiently high market price. Information technology is again likely to be a key component of the manufacturing process here—either as part of the design processes or embedded into the products themselves. Of course, yet another strategy would be to remove the competition on the manufacturing cost of the commodity goods by using heavy automation to move the cost of production onto a new curve. Again, information technology will be key to this strategy.

New employees

If you can talk to anyone, anywhere, any time, what will happen to the idea of the 'work place', and the 'owned' workforce that arrived with the Industrial Revolution? We seem headed for a return to the idea of people working from their homes, and no longer trekking back to the factory or office daily. In that case, does it matter where the employees live? They could be in the next continent as easily as in the next room. It will not even matter if they are 'employed' or 'owned' by you, or if they are subcontractors. In many ways, the latter will be the only sensible arrangement with a widely dispersed workforce—just as it was before the Industrial Revolution.

New industries

When chips are present in everything from the walls of your home to the bath and the kitchen sink, who will supply and control the infrastructure that connects the whole thing together? New companies and entire industries will be born. Think of the scale of the power generation and distribution industries today, and imagine the size of the industry needed to contend with the global infrastructure. Think of the secondary industries that will be needed to feed it—providing not only the hardware, but also information, analysis and software.

New organizations

As we described, large numbers of people may be self-employed—working on knowledge or information from their homes. Others will still work collectively at the sites housing the means of production—manufacturing, repair, or leisure facilities. Yesterday's management structures are unlikely to work or to be afford-able in this new world. Even more importantly, the organization's values and culture may need to be radically different from today's.

5.5   Summary

In this chapter we have argued that the changes now under way in business are fuelled by innovation in technology, and that those who do not ride with this tide face extinction. The Industrial Revolution showed us the power of technology to effect radical changes in business, in society and in international affairs. That led us to survey the wide-ranging impact of today's technology.

In the next chapters we shall continue our discussion of technology's impact—the linkage between business and technology itself. The following chapters will then take us inside the technology, the better to understand what drives its advance, before we get to a discussion of a practical way forward for the business person and the technologist to grasp and use information technology in the organi-zation.

6
Laying the foundations
The need for infrastructure

. . . and he huffed and he puffed, and he puffed and he huffed, but the little house wouldn't blow down.

(Anon., *Three Little Pigs*)

6.1   Purpose

In this chapter we look at the new order described previously and examine the key role likely to be played by information technology. That role will be impossible without vision from the business person and careful planning by the technocrat.

6.2   Highways and sewers

As we saw in the earlier chapters, federal structures really do need some shared infrastructure. Without it, the federation has no cohesion, and may as well not exist. That sounds like a blank cheque, likely to be readily accepted by the old central staff functions. If we are to avoid a financial burden that then becomes a weight around our necks, we had better be very clear about what the infrastructure is going to do for us. Let us start our analysis with a simple analogy, reusing our diagram (Fig. 4.1) from an earlier chapter, and show some familiar objects—some houses set in a community almost anywhere, and supported by the kind of things that we are all used to (although not, perhaps, under the same names) (Fig. 6.1).

Let us simplify the diagram and use the suggestive iconography to add some pipes and connections between the federation members. In Fig. 6.2, these members look like houses. If they were, those pipes might be carrying power, water or gas between each house and a set of shared services. Unless we want the expense of completely separate infrastructure for each connection, we had better have some sharing here, just as we have shown. Other pipes might connect one house to another. These might carry phone conversations, fax messages or even game moves between people in a multi-player computer game (such as 'DogFight' from

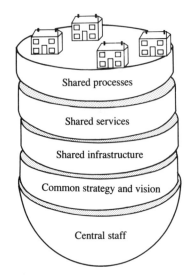

Figure 6.1.   Example of a shared infrastructure. This model was discussed in Chapter 4 and it enables us to explore the role of infrastructure.

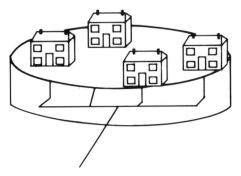

Figure 6.2.   Sharing infrastructure between independent users.

MicroProse in 1993). These are about communication, and require that the two 'ends' have some need to communicate with each other. Again, at least part of the infrastructure had better be common. To show another kind of pipe, let us stretch the analogy a little and make one of the houses larger (turning it into a bank!). Now the pipe is enabling the home owners to query their bank balance and pay bills with a push-button tone phone. This uses common infrastructure to effect a business process that is common to all home owners (or at least the ones who use that same bank). Lastly, let us look inside one of the houses. Now we see an example of parents listening to their child snore with a baby telecom.

There is no need for any shared infrastructure here. The home owner can buy any one of 100 different systems. The choice is with the individual, who values that freedom. Not only that, all the neighbours also cherish that individual's (and their own) rights in 1000 other areas, none of which are to do with shared infrastructure. However, if there is a benefit to be had from restricting that freedom of choice, then maybe the price will be paid. So when our imaginary parents want to attend a dinner party in the house next door, perhaps they would welcome a smaller choice of baby units if they could connect house to house via the phone line. There is a paradox here. A restriction in choice of technology can actually increase the user's degrees of freedom!

So now we can put our iconography back to its original meaning, and see four clear reasons for shared infrastructure:

- to access shared services
- to communicate
- to operate shared business processes
- to gain more freedom by enabling technical opportunity.

6.3 Flexibility

And the earth shall move (again).

(Anon.)

The trouble with organizations is that they change—and never more than in times like our own. So infrastructure had better be future-proofed—capable of flexibility as needs change—and not only the part of the infrastructure that is clearly shared today. For tomorrow fate may arrive and turn your infrastructure upside down, a little like your sister arriving for the summer with her children and expecting her baby intercom transmitter to work with your receiver. So business boundaries are drawn and redrawn as fickle markets and voracious competitors assault you. Now you are organized along product lines, next year along customer lines, and the year after that by function. Your department got moved from one member of the federation to another. Your profession got abolished, or re-missioned and dispersed to different roles in other parts of the company. All this makes infrastructure hard to deal with. It seems difficult to lay down a shared infrastructure that will serve you well through so much unpredictable change.

The simple old-fashioned management answer is to standardize everything. The argument goes that if the entire infrastructure is uniform, then it will be much easier to use no matter what shape the organization is. On the other hand, so the wisdom continues, if standards are not introduced then it will be difficult to maintain any sort of communication and cooperation between different parts of the business. Ultimately, the business will find it has become too fragmented to operate as a whole, and it may as well disperse into its separate business units. There is a great deal of sense in these views. Unfortunately, the idea of centrally controlled standards is counter-culture to most organizations today, as they grapple with the new ideas of federalism. Nevertheless, the area must be dealt with. The trick is to determine the minimum number of standards necessary to maintain the business's coherence and future flexibility.

6.4   A stitch in time

Planning shared infrastructure is hard, but if it is not done the organization will be incapable of running today's business infrastructure, let alone changing to support tomorrow's. You could do it the easy way, but no-one will give you the power to define standards for everything—and in any case life moves too fast. So all that is left is the difficult middle ground—defining a shared infrastructure that meets today's needs and what can be guessed about tomorrow's. That last piece of haziness means that this is an unending task. Shared infrastructure is necessary and must be designed. But it must also be reviewed on a continual basis as the situation changes. And it should never, never get in the way of the business as it evolves.

6.5   Sublime plumbing

The discerning reader will have known this was coming—the inevitable plug for information technology. But do not turn the page yet! Let us just suspend judgement and analyse the case for IT in terms of the concepts we have just been through. Without labouring the point, let us examine the role information technology has to play in each of four areas, recalling that these areas are the essence of the federation as we described it in the previous chapters. As we saw just a few paragraphs ago, a shared infrastructure, and hence a federation, cannot be built without them.

Communication

These days communications are synonymous with IT. This is particularly so in the globalized markets we described in the earlier chapters. As we shall see in the chapter on technology trends, these days communication may mean transmission of almost anything. Technology has already enabled us to put our senses of sight and hearing in direct communication across thousands of miles. Virtual reality will add the sense of touch over the coming years. Who knows just how rich our communication capability will become? Clearly, a shared IT infrastructure will be essential between those who want to communicate, today and into the future.

Shared processes

Shared processes could be paper-based or word-of-mouth. However, the effects of globalization and travel almost certainly mean that these processes will need to have a strong element of electronics at their heart. Again, shared IT infrastructure will be key.

Shared services

Shared services are things that the federation's members all have a common need for, and fund centrally in order to avoid duplication of cost and effort. Legal services, mail rooms and photocopying services are good examples. Information technology has its own scope for shared services, which it offers to its users across a federation. Often access to very expensive equipment such as supercomputers or large databases will be offered as a shared service. So will some sort of central management of printing and other mundane IT chores.

Perhaps the most significant shared service that IT can offer is to provide a vehicle by which the knowledge base of the company can be shared, communicated and stored for future retrieval anywhere in the company. This is particularly important given the dispersion of people and function across the federation. It is a powerful way of enabling the sort of teamwork that we have discussed several times in earlier chapters. It is also possibly the only way of preserving the competence of the dispersed organization in its core areas.

Technological opportunities

As we have said many times in earlier pages, technology is at once one of the prime causes and the main enablers of the move to a new organizational order. The 'instant' society relies on it to enable competition between organizations that seek to outdo each other in the value they provide for their customers. This is true not only from the point of view of responsiveness, but also in cost reduction. If an organization is not able or willing to grasp the new opportunities offered by technology, then it puts itself at a very considerable competitive disadvantage. The trouble is that no organization can afford to create a technological Tower of Babel, in which no part of the organization can be certain of rapid communication with the other parts. Therefore, standards have to be created while at the same time allowing the innovative use of new technology that is so essential to competition.

6.6   Summary

In earlier chapters we argued that the pace of change is newly quickened. We saw that business change is intertwined with the rapid and accelerating changes in technology. The former hierarchical way of structuring organizations is ill-suited to the new situation. It cannot respond to change fast enough, and stifles individuality rather than fostering it as a key corporate asset. New approaches are needed, and we have spent quite some time exploring possible ways forward.

In many organizations, there is a rapid flow of power away from corporate centres towards the sharp end of the business. The same need for responsiveness and flexibility that led to the power shift also forces an emphasis on shared infrastructure. Without the latter, a business will arguably become less responsive and more inflexible if it disperses its power and decision-making. This is especially true of information flows through the organization. Hence we have argued that information technology is a vital part of the shared infrastructure of any organization, especially one in which power and responsibility are dispersed.

This chapter marks the end of Part 1 of the book and our discussion of the business environment. In Part 2 we shall look at information technology itself, since this is both a key driver and a key enabler of the changes that are so common in today's organizations. In Part 3 we shall return to the question of shared IT infrastructure and offer a way of making such a concept a reality, so that the business can make the best possible use of IT in these times of rapid change.

Part 2
Information technology trends

As Tammie glowr'd, amaz'd, and curious,
The mirth and fun grew fast and furious.

(Robert Burns, 1759–1796)

We have seen in Part 1 of this book the nature of some of the changes affecting organizations around the world. Linked to these changes in both direct and indirect ways is the plethora of rapid developments in information technology. Now is the time to change our focus and look explicitly at the technology and the way that the technology is developing.

We can look at technology in a number of ways, and the way that we have chosen is to concentrate on a number of underlying properties. We have not therefore produced lots and lots of charts and tables showing the current leaders in the race for speed or against cost. Such information is not really valid material for any book, because the technology changes far too fast for any meaningful information to be provided in this way.

Up-to-the-minute information on chip densities, operating system functionality, disk packing densities or communications speeds is far better covered in the (more serious) information technology magazines. With the rate of change evident today, a publication frequency of at least one issue per month would seem to be the minimum requirement.

What we have done, therefore, in Part 2 is to look at information technology in a way that we hope will not easily become out-of-date. We have tried to do so in a way that is interesting, informative and relevant to business people and IT professionals alike. In essence, we have gone back to first principles.

7
Off with the blindfold

The perils of prediction

This is my prediction for the future—whatever hasn't happened will happen and no one will be safe from it.

(J. B. S. Haldane, British scientist)

7.1   Purpose

Our dependency on information technology is increasing in almost every aspect of our lives, but especially in the environment within which we work. The cost of making wrong decisions about the way in which information technology is to be deployed is therefore becoming far greater. We are becoming increasingly dependent on our ability to make the *right* decisions.

Because of this, one thing is becoming increasingly clear for more and more organizations, i.e. that an understanding of the future is necessary if organizations are going to build for themselves a sound information technology infrastructure. This understanding has to cover not just the likely developments in information technology, but also developments in the way in which that technology may be packaged and developments in the way in which it may be applied and used.

We are seeing many different trends in information technology at the moment, but the clearest of these trends are those directly caused by the reduction in size and cost of the basic building block of information technology, the ubiquitous microprocessor. This has led to the rapid fall in the size and cost of computers and associated devices. It has also led to a vast increase in the number of components that now typically make up the computing capability of the organization.

So, on the one hand we have a move towards simplicity, with computers becoming smaller, cheaper and far easier to use than even their recent ancestors. On the other hand we have the growth in complexity caused by the sheer increase in numbers of such devices and the relatively primitive ways we have of managing and controlling them. The successful organizations of the future will have to understand the way in which information technology is changing in order to balance these trends continually.

Gaining this understanding is not going to be easy, and we shall have to fall back from time to time on sheer guesswork and crystal-ball gazing. However, the prize that we gain by understanding the way in which information technology is to develop is a worthwhile one, because we have to make decisions today that will shape and constrain our capabilities in the future.

Some of the toughest decisions that we have to make today concern the overall *shape and form* of the technical infrastructure we provide across the organization. As the shape of technology is changed by the trends described above, and as the organization itself is changing shape due to internal and external pressures to succeed in an ever more complex and competitive environment, the danger of getting a mismatch in these two shapes becomes very real indeed.

Decisions about the shape and form of the infrastructure and about the key technologies that will play a major role in that infrastructure are not simple. There is a lot of information around, but there is an equal amount of *misinformation*. Each and every one of us in a position to influence the creation of the IT architecture on which that infrastructure is to be based will have to make a number of assumptions and predictions about the way we believe the future may evolve.

It seems right, therefore, to start by looking at the process of making predictions and especially the reasons why we so often fail to foretell the future effectively, even (or especially) in our own area of information technology.

7.2   Human failing

When we look at the range of technology that is available today and read the computer press discussing the technologies that are being developed for tomorrow, we begin to get a picture of what key trends are in evidence and perhaps, where they may lead. At a very simplistic level, the trends in information technology are associated with the creation of technology that is:

- cheaper
- smaller
- faster
- more reliable.

These are fundamental trends (see Chapter 9) that are easy to understand and demonstrate, yet it is often quite difficult to understand exactly where they may lead.

Why is this so hard? Why are so many people so often surprised by what such basic and simple developments cause? The following list suggests some of the things that make the IT industry so dynamic, and therefore make prediction that much more difficult.

1   The information technology industry is a very competitive one. The relatively large profits and growth achievable in the 1970s and 1980s caused a large increase in the number of organizations offering information processing technologies.

2   The information technology industry is founded on *soft technology*. The cost of entry is relatively low, hence it is an area where innovative people with good ideas and a willingness to work hard can build for themselves success on a truly enormous scale. There is no need for start-up capital of the order of millions or billions. A garage, a few spare hours a day and a bunch of good ideas may be all that it takes to make a global impact.

3   The basic technologies on which the industry is built are not yet stretched by our application of them. We work in an industry that is limited by the speed of light and the size of an electron. We have a long way to go before we see these limitations manifesting themselves as true constraints on our ability to gain further improvements.

4   Commercial and governmental organizations, despite the many and varied failures that have occurred, still (quite rightly) see information technology as a major enabler behind the twin drives of service and productivity. Information technology has a lot to offer, and as time goes on the potential just keeps growing and growing.

5   The IT industry is new, exciting and *fun*. This contrasts somewhat with many other older industries such as agriculture and engineering, which do not have the same fascination or charisma and therefore may sometimes seem a less attractive career opportunity.

6   Between basic research, applied research and product development, there are only a few small steps. Innovations at the university can be seen in high-street stores within a relatively short period of time, and this creates an *immediacy* in terms of the drag-on effect which encourages and fuels such basic research.

All these drivers lead to an industry that is in a continual state of flux. Not only that, but we have been in such a state for several decades now and instead of slowing down, the rate of change is increasing day by day. This creates an environment where change itself is guaranteed but the nature of the change is difficult to predict.

Look again at the quotation that started this chapter. This quotation was chosen very carefully because it suggests two key characteristics of change within the information technology industry. Firstly it suggests that anything is possible, and that certainly seems to be the case; secondly it suggests that no matter who we are, where we live or how we live, we will not be able to hide from change. Perhaps all we can say is that we are going to see a large amount of change, but that does not really help us understand the details of that change. In Chapter 9 we shall present some ideas about what these changes may be, changes based on simple, straightforward developments in a number of key areas.

But it is not just the volume of change or the variety of change that causes us problems. As human beings, we have certain built-in failings that further reduce our ability to predict accurately. Arthur C. Clarke (*Profiles of the Future: An Inquiry into the Limits of the Possible*, 1982) suggests that there are two reasons why, when we attempt to predict the future, we so often fail:

- missing the trick—being unable to predict the future because we are not aware of some key development on which the failure will actually be based
- missing the point—being unable to predict the future because we fail to understand the implications of what is happening.

7.3   Missing the trick

The easiest way to fail is to lack some key piece of information, some simple development on which the future depends. This has to be considered an acceptable excuse. Without some fundamental fact we have to be forgiven for getting things slightly wrong. Consider the following examples:

- electricity
- nuclear fission
- genetic engineering
- lasers
- transistors.

Each of these technologies created a discontinuity (see Fig. 7.1), sometimes large, sometimes small, in what would otherwise have been a fairly natural progression of development. But more importantly, each of them was *unpredictable* until shortly before it was discovered. This is axiomatic: it is obvious that everything is unpredictable until it has been discovered; after all, why is something you lose always

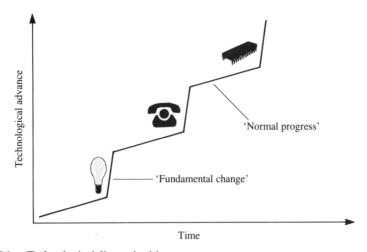

Figure 7.1.   Technological discontinuities.

found in the last place you look? What is meant here, though, is that some fundamental and dramatic change takes place that could never have been predicted in advance, and once such a discontinuity happens, it leads to change. The greater the discontinuity, the greater is the degree of change that will be created.

There are many examples of such discontinuities in almost every area of human development. Before such discontinuities the future seems mapped out and understandable; afterwards everything changes. The three examples shown in Fig. 7.1— electricity, the telephone and the microchip—are all of fundamental importance, all creating change on a global scale.

In addition, the discontinuities lead to changes over a long period of time. We are still finding new ways to use electricity; new applications for lasers such as in optical surgery and compact disc players. Genetic engineering is another area where we are only now starting to exploit discoveries that go back several decades. (The gene was named by Thomas Hunt Morgan of Lexington, Virginia way back in 1910. The term 'genetic engineering' was coined in 1974, and the term 'genetic fingerprinting' in 1985.) Important discoveries continue to be important and continue to be developed over long periods of time.

Once you have accepted the basic principles of electricity, the light bulb, the electric motor, the electromagnet or the electric heater all become fairly obvious. Without the basic principle, each of these devices would seem impossible, perhaps even *magical* and therefore equally impossible to predict.

A single bomb with the ability to vaporize millions of people would have seemed ridiculous in the nineteenth century, but after Albert Einstein had pronounced in 1905 that $E = mc^2$, the destructive force of a nuclear device such as an atomic warhead could be predicted with astounding accuracy.

One of the most interesting examples is that of genetics and genetic engineering. For thousands of years it was believed by most people that all the animals and plants were created by some sentient being. When Charles Darwin published *The Origin of Species by Means of Natural Selection*, the basic beliefs of many people were challenged and ultimately changed. Many years later we have thousands of scientists mapping out the genetic structure of life itself, promising (or threatening) enormous advances in genetic engineering. Could Charles Darwin have predicted this?

Probably not, because without knowledge of the existence of DNA he would have been unable to understand the concepts involved. With this information, it would have been as obvious to him as it is to any of us. The advantage of hindsight is tremendous. Before scientists began to flock to the study of genetics and the popular press started to expose the moral and ethical issues involved, how many people would have predicted serious scientific studies with titles such as *plant transgenosis* or even *animal transgenosis*?

If we are faced with such gaps in our knowledge of information technology, we have the same predictive difficulties. We cannot predict the future if it depends on some invention or some discovery that we are not yet aware of. But is it likely that some key invention or discovery is going to come along in the next few years and change the nature of information technology in dramatic and far-reaching ways? Nobody knows. Predicting the unpredictable is like planning for the unforeseen: we simply cannot do it. All we can do is to try to recognize the problem and proceed.

An interesting question to pose is whether there have been any key inventions, discoveries or developments over the past 20 years that

- have had a significant and lasting impact on information technology capabilities
- were totally unpredictable before they happened.

It is quite difficult now, looking back over the years, to identify discoveries, inventions or developments that have caught us unaware, creating a key change in some fundamental part of the industry, but they do exist. It is worth thinking about what *you* believe these discontinuities to have been. Three suggestions are described below, one in each of the major information technology areas of processors, data and the user interface.

Processors: the transistor

The development of the transistor represented a fundamental change in the basic technology of computing. This small device did far more than enable the ubiquitous (at least it seemed so in the 1960s) transistor radio. The characteristics of the *before* and *after* stages are shown in Fig. 7.2.

The discontinuities here were very significant: almost every characteristic of the most important component of any computer was changed dramatically. The result

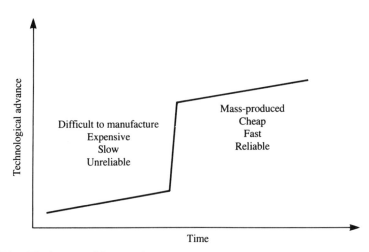

Figure 7.2.   The impact of the transistor.

was, as expected, correspondingly dramatic. The transistor is arguably the single most important technological invention of this century.

Once transistors had been developed and proved, the technological products that were based on them were easier to manufacture, cheaper to buy and faster in their operation, and lasted much longer. Before the transistor we had radio sets that had to be turned on a couple of minutes before the news bulletin so that they had time to warm up. Most houses had a drawer with a few valves in the back of it gathering dust, nobody being really sure whether they were new ones or old ones, good ones or bad ones.

After the transistor we had the ubiquitous transistor radio, cheaper to buy, requiring less power to operate (and therefore portable), which lasted for several years without any significant problems. (One of the first ones appeared in 1955, known as the 'Sony TR-55'. Even in those halcyon days it seems that good names were hard to come by!) After the transistor we developed integrated circuits (see Section 8.11), but this was really a matter of packaging rather than a fundamental new technology.

Data: storage

In the hi-fi world of the audio enthusiasts, great debate takes place periodically about which will be the standard technology for equipment and recordings in the next decade. We have moved from wax drums to black vinyl discs, to 8-track cartridges to cassettes to compact disc and digital tape. (Apologies for the confusion between the spelling of 'disc' and 'disk'. The music industry seems to have standardized on 'disc', the computer industry on 'disk'. Is this a sign of the degree to which the two industries will collaborate when it comes to multimedia applications?) Each technology has offered advantages and disadvantages over the previous one, with incredibly high conversion costs for both the industry and the user.

In the IT world we have had a similar movement, not for musical storage but for data storage in general. However, one transitional step was more fundamentally different from the others, and that was the movement from tape to disc. The reason this change was significant was that it enabled applications to move away from sequential processing of data to processing data in a more specific way.

Before we consider the IT example, consider the more familiar example of the audio tape versus the compact disc. With a compact disc we can select any recording track we want; we can scan quickly through a particular track to exactly the note that we want to hear. We can select the tracks to be played sequentially or randomly, and we can increase the degree of randomness by stacking several compact discs together and letting the player randomly select which disc to play.

Conversely, we play an audio tape forward. If we want to find a particular track then we struggle with the buttons (usually while trying to steer a car at the same

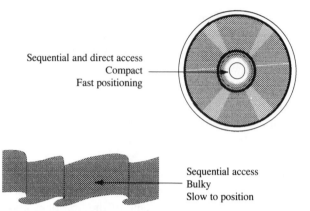

Sequential and direct access
Compact
Fast positioning

Sequential access
Bulky
Slow to position

Figure 7.3.   Changes in data storage.

time), getting more and more frustrated until we realize that the recording we want is on the other side of the tape. The advantages of the compact disc are clear.

The transition from tape to disk technology (Fig. 7.3) has the same impact as the change from audio tape to compact disc technology. The characteristics of the new medium allow a lot more freedom in how the data is used, thereby enabling new applications: random play sequences on a home CD player and on-line applications programs in the commercial data processing environment.

If you wanted to find the details for a particular customer from a file of 10 million customers, the tape drive left little option other than to start at the beginning of the tape and search until the particular customer was found. This could take minutes. Disk technology allowed indexes to be created that pointed straight at the part of the disk where the required information was stored. Thus, the data could be accessed in thousandths of a second.

The speed was important, but far more important was the fact that application programs could now be written that would never have been attempted previously. The development of most on-line programs, such as banking applications, reservation systems, order entry systems and stock checking systems, all resulted in part from the change from a long thin strip of magnetic tape to a small, circular, spinning magnetic disk.

User interface: the mouse

A key development between a single computer and the user was that of what has come to be known as the GUI (pronounced '*gooey*'), or Graphical User Interface. The interface between the user and the computer was tailored in favour of the computer for many years. Console displays, teletype machines or even the so-called *dumb* terminals prevalent in the 1970s and 1980s were never easy or natural interfaces. The computer was always in control; the interface seemingly designed and implemented for the benefit of the machine rather than for the benefit of the person using it. (The term 'user' is a distasteful one. Anyone who uses a computer is termed a 'user', whereas people who use cars are 'drivers', people who use transport are 'passengers' and people who use medical services are 'patients'. We need an alternative, but it does not appear to be forthcoming.)

The development of the graphical user interface required a means of communicating with the computer that was more precise, more immediate and more flexible than the keyboard, which had been the only choice until that time.

The mouse (Fig. 7.4) enabled the development of thousands of *point-and-click* applications. Graphics packages, word processors, spreadsheets, development tools and organizers of every description adopted the mouse as the basis for the communication between themselves and the user. It seemed, almost at a stroke, that the user was *king*, that he or she was in control and no longer being controlled.

This fascinating little device has become a symbol for 'freedom' in computing. The degree to which mice have become acceptable, admired and almost indispensable can be measured by the fact that you can purchase them in different colours and shapes, and you can get covers for them that make them look like real mice. The mouse represented a fundamental change to a whole generation of users.

7.4   Missing the point

Arthur C. Clarke gives us a second reason as to why we may fail in our predictions. This is to do with *vision*, or more accurately, the lack of it. If *lack of information* is our first excuse for failure, then *lack of vision* has to be considered less excusable.

What is meant by this is that we somehow fail to see the natural inevitability of what is happening. Stepping off a cliff edge in thick fog is understandable; stepping off in broad daylight is downright silly, but we all do similar (if less dramatic) things, we all at some time or another fail to understand the inescapable conclusions of what is happening all around us.

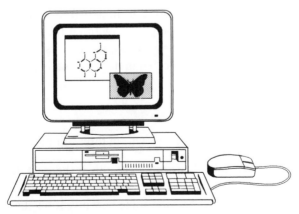

Figure 7.4.   PC with mouse.

If we think back a quarter of a century, back to the early 1970s, what conclusions did we, or could we, draw about the future of information technology? Would we have predicted the emergence and importance of the personal computer, the technical workstation or the local and global networks that we see today? Could we have predicted document image processing, multimedia, client/server or virtual reality?

For most of us the answer is probably negative, even though all the signs were there: the reductions in size, in cost and in power consumption were all taking place, but our ability to visualize the longer term effect of this was limited. Even when armed with all the facts, when we have all the information laid out in front of us we may still fail for the simple reason that we fail to recognize the implications of that information, or we lack the vision and the imagination to be able to really understand what lies before us.

The digital watch is a reasonable example of a product surrounded by vision on the one hand and lack of vision on the other. The Swiss were at one time the dominant supplier of watches across the world. They put considerable funds into research related to time-keeping, and from this research came the idea for the digital watch. The Swiss convinced themselves that no-one would want such a device, discarded it and did not even patent the idea. Along came the Japanese, who realized that a very accurate watch could be constructed at a very reasonable price with a high degree of reliability and considerable novelty value. The rest is history.

Let us also consider the impact of the reduction in cost of processing power in information technology. In the heady days of the vast mainframe computers, the signs were already evident that the cost of computing was falling and would continue to fall for the foreseeable future.

To some, this meant that the cost of the mainframes would come down, but the mainframe itself would continue to be the single and dominant form of computing. In those days the computer and the mainframe were synonymous terms, but as costs came down it actually became feasible to consider computers more as commodity items and less as capital expense items. These commodity items were certainly very different from their mainframe ancestors.

The simple reduction in cost has moved us in part from centralized mainframe computing to distributed personal computing, with all the traumatic effects that this change has had on vendors, organizations, individuals and society. In hindsight the changes seem very predictable, but in the 1960s perhaps they were less so.

7.5 Summary

There are some real dangers in prediction. One of three things is likely to happen.

- We get the prediction right. Unfortunately, this is the least likely of the three options.
- We get the prediction wrong because some new invention changes the ground rules, causing a discontinuity that we did not allow for.

- We get the prediction wrong because we did not see the implications of what was happening, we lacked the vision and the imagination to understand what we were seeing.

If we can accurately predict the future trends and capabilities in information technology, then we can begin to build towards that future earlier than our competitors; we can position ourselves to take the maximum advantage of what comes along.

If we cannot, then we had better do the next best thing: we had better build towards our future in the knowledge that we will have to reposition ourselves continually to whatever is happening, that we will have to accommodate change in a way and to a scale that we have never done in the past.

To build an IT architecture that supports the change, indeed welcomes and absorbs that change in an efficient and controlled fashion, is the most important insurance policy we can invest in now for our future.

8
The long and winding road

A brief retrospective of IT

Hindsight is always 20:20

(Billy Wilder)

8.1   Purpose

In Chapter 7 we looked at some of the reasons why predicting the future is often
not as easy or as straightforward as we would like it to be. In Chapter 9 we shall
put these considerations to one side for a while and try to create some glimpses of
possible futures, some ideas about what *may* happen, based on what we know
today.

In this intervening chapter we take a brief look back down the road of information technology, giving a brief summary of some of the major advances that have
taken place over both the distant and more recent past. The merit in doing this
really comes from the fact that there is no reason to believe that the future is going
to be any different from the past, and reminding ourselves of how far we have come
helps to illustrate just how far we may still have to travel.

At many points in our past our ancestors probably believed that some great technological pinnacle had been reached. Whether it was the discovery of steel or of
printing, of electricity or of nuclear power, it would have seemed that the people
living in this era were seeing something strange and wonderful. Looking back at
their past, they might have felt in some way superior to those who had gone before,
little imagining that in a few short years their descendants would be thinking
exactly the same thing. Why should we be any different?

We have not reached any pinnacle. In terms of technological advancement we
are still crawling through the foothills: there is no reason to suppose that there are
not quite a few mountains just waiting for us. So, a brief look back at where we
have come from should position us quite nicely to take a look at where we might be
going.

8.2 Logical interlude

Before we start looking back at the genesis of information technology, it is beneficial to gain a common understanding of a very fundamental concept, that of the *switch*, or more precisely the *switching speed*.

If we add two numbers using an abacus, the speed with which we can perform the calculation depends on the speed with which we can manipulate the beads on the abacus board. In a similar way, the speed at which a computer can add two numbers together depends on how quickly it can switch its internal electronics from one state to another. To add two numbers together a computer will actually perform many operations, but at their most basic level these operations are simply switching the electronics from one state to another, from on to off. The faster a computer can switch its electronics, the faster it can operate. Modern electronic devices can switch in fractions of a nanosecond (one thousandth of a millionth of a second). Such switching speeds mean that the computer can perform vast numbers of operations in incredibly short periods of time.

Information technology has developed in the way it has because we have had a common set of requirements throughout a fairly lengthy period of time. Initially we wanted to count: whether it was slaves, numbers of cows or camels or numbers of crates loaded onto a dhow, we simply wanted to be able to know how many things there were. Later we wanted to perform more sophisticated calculations to back up the growth in worldwide commerce. We wanted to add lots of numbers together, to work our interest rates and percentages. As our calculations became more complex, they also became more numerous. We needed to increase the speed with which we could perform calculations so that we could perform thousands of calculations in relatively short periods of time. Whether for mathematicians, scientists, engineers or code breakers, the calculations were both complex and repetitive.

Moving into the present day, we need to speed up our calculations still further so that we can perform the vastly more complex calculations involved with manipulating the millions of elements that make up even simple images or voices, with making complex marketing decisions based on the analysis of the purchasing habits of our customers over the past 10 years, with assessing alternative choices in a diagnostic system or providing sophisticated realism to users of electronic games.

Throughout history, the work we have put information technology to has become more complex and more repetitive, both requirements forcing us to increase speed. Let us consider this history in a little more detail.

8.3 Historical developments

Computing is based on the ability to represent the world around us in digital form and then to represent that same digital form in a physical way so that it can be *processed* by a computer. We have been moving inexorably towards being able to represent more and more of our environment in this way and to process that

Table 8.1 Key developments in information technology

Time	Technology
3000 BC	Abacus in widespread use
1617 AD	Logarithms discovered
1642	Mechanical calculator developed by Blaise Pascal
1835	Analytical engine designed by Charles Babbage
1886	Herman Hollerith produced a machine for the 1890 US census study
1937	Alan Turing wrote *On Computable Numbers*
1943	Colossus, the first valve-based computer was used to decode German intelligence data
1943	ENIAC, the first general purpose valve-based computer
1944	John von Neumann developed the concept of storing computer programs electronically inside the computer
1944	Harvard Mark I
1947	Transistor developed at Bell Laboratories
1959	First integrated circuit
1971	First microprocessor

Obviously, a lot of events are missing from this table. The intention is simply to illustrate some of the major ones.

information in faster and more innovative ways for many years, perhaps more years than we sometimes remember.

To help put into perspective the information technology capability that we have reached today, it is instructive to take a brief look at where we have come from and what the major milestones and major discontinuities have been. It is always difficult to look beyond what we have today to try to envisage what we may have available in the future but, as the past shows, some people have had this ability in the past and we owe them a great deal.

Let us start by looking at some key developments (Table 8.1) and then try to break them down into a small number of areas, each to be looked at in a little more detail.

8.4   Sticks and stones

Thousands of years ago, people obviously needed to count. One of the earliest ways of recording numbers was to relate the number to an equal number of stones,[1] or of notches cut on a stick. Obviously this approach had a number of severe limitations. To count the number of bags of flour loaded onto a ship we

---

[1] In the baffling English game of cricket the umpire has to ensure that six balls are bowled each over. At the end of the over the bowling changes direction. To keep count, umpires keep six marbles in their right-hand pocket. As each ball is bowled the umpire takes one of the marbles and transfers it to the left-hand pocket. When all the marbles have been moved the umpire calls 'over'. Simplicity itself.

could perform some physical action every time a bag was loaded, such as picking up a stone and putting it in our pocket or cutting a notch in a stick. This works fine for numbers like two and seven, but what happens when the ship has a capacity for 2000 bags? How big a pocket would we need? How big a branch would we have to start with if we wanted to cut 2000 notches?

8.5 Beads

The abacus[2] was invented 5000 years ago. It usually consists of a number of beads that can slide on a number of rods which are fastened inside a wooden frame. The abacus is still widely used today and the practitioners are extremely accurate and fast. It is fine for addition and subtraction, less so for multiplication or division, but for thousands of Eastern shopkeepers and millions of young schoolchildren it is still a very important device.

If we assume that since the abacus was invented 5000 years ago it has been consistently used by 100 million people, each performing ten calculations per day, then the abacus would have performed somewhere around 2 000 000 000 000 000 calculations.

A workstation today, performing a reasonable 5 million calculations per second, would take around 13 years to do the same number of calculations. At the current rate of performance improvement (doubles every 18 months), by the time the workstation had finished you could replace it with one that could do the same job in about two weeks.

8.6 Slides

Multiplication and division become much simpler if they can be performed by the use of addition and subtraction. John Napier in the seventeenth century developed *Napier's bones*, slivers of bone that were marked in such a way that arithmetic calculations could be performed by moving one piece of bone alongside the other. The basis for this was the concept of the *logarithm*. This gave each number an equivalent logarithm number. To multiply two numbers, all that was necessary was to determine the logarithm of each of the numbers and add them together: the answer was the logarithm number of the result.

A large amount of effort was put into developing logarithm and antilogarithm tables, and the result became the scourge of almost all schoolchildren as they approached examination time. The logarithm tables were important in themselves but, as usual with such discoveries, what was more useful was their application (in the slide rule, a more sophisticated version of Napier's earlier pieces of bone).

---

[2] The word 'abacus' is derived from the Semitic term for dust. In its first form it was a slab of wood covered in fine sand. There is something ironic about the fact that the most modern microchips are predominantly made from the same material (sand, not wood!).

Various designs were produced, but all of them used the principle of sliding two scales (like rulers) against each other, aligning the two numbers to be multiplied and reading the result directly. The slide rule was developed around 350 years ago, and until the 1960s was the ever-present tool of almost every scientist and engineer.

One of the vital things about the logarithm tables was the impetus that they gave to mechanical calculators. Mechanical calculators were needed to help speed up the production of the logarithm tables and to enable the accuracy to be improved.

Try going into a store today and buying a 'logarithm book': they are no longer on the best-seller list. Try finding someone in a store who is old enough to understand what you want when you ask for a slide rule. This is not an 'ageism' complaint, just an indication of how quickly an indispensable item can be made totally obsolete by information technology.

8.7   Cogs

Back again in the seventeenth century, while John Napier was busy working out his logarithm tables, Blaise Pascal[3] was working on something slightly different. He developed a device known as the *Pascaline* which consisted of a number of cogs, each with ten teeth. Numbers to be added were entered into the Pascaline by turning the cogs the required number of times.

Hence, to enter the number 12, the cog on the very right would be turned two positions and the cog next to it would be turned once. To add the number 6 to it, the cog on the very right would again be turned, this time by six positions. The cogs would then indicate the answer, 18. When a cog was turned past zero, the cog on the left would be turned by one position, giving the equivalent of the *carry operation*.[4] The Pascaline was developed hundreds of years ago[5] but, like the slide rule, it was used widely in some shape or form until very recently.

Even today, some accountants still use a mechanical adding machine in which the numbers are entered by pressing on a key pad and then a handle is pulled which, in effect, turns the cogs the required number of positions, much like the Pascaline.

8.8   Engines

Enter Charles Babbage. In the nineteenth century Charles Babbage set down many of the ideas and principles on which all modern computing is based. He was the designer of the first true computer (as opposed to mechanical adding machines).

---

[3] Blaise Pascal was honoured for his role in the development of computing by having a programming language (PASCAL) named after him. In a similar fashion, Lady Ada Lovelace, the daughter of Lord Byron (the poet) and a colleague of Charles Babbage, has a programming language named after her (ADA).

[4] The most common implementation of this today can be seen in almost every car on the road. The odometer, which measures the number of miles or kilometres that have been travelled, is a form of such a device.

[5] Blaise Pascal actually developed the Pascaline as a device that might help his father in his role as a French tax collector.

He designed, but did not build, two *engines*. The first was the *difference engine* which was to be used to calculate logarithm tables automatically; the second was the *analytical engine*. The analytical engine had 50 cog wheels and data were entered using punched cards. It actually had many of the components of what we would recognize as a modern computer:

- a place to store data
- a means of entering data (input device)
- a means of providing data (output device)
- a means of doing arithmetic
- a controller for determining what to do next.

The last point is crucial. In the analytical engine there was a combination of arithmetic operations and the concept of decision-making based on the results of those arithmetic operations. Although Charles Babbage designed these two engines, he could not actually fabricate them. Unfortunately, the ability of engineers to work to the fine tolerances required was limited during the nineteenth century.

It has been argued by some people that one of the major benefits of Babbage's work was the improvement in engineering skills in England during the early nineteenth century, which led in part to an acceleration in the industrial revolution.

8.9   Valves and relays

All the mechanical devices we have considered so far were adapted to the numbering scheme in use at the time.[6] As we move from mechanical to electrical devices, we have to accept a change. Although human beings would continue to work in the Arabic numbering system, the more convenient *binary* system would be used from this point on by the computers. Binary is a good system for electronic devices to work on because it uses only two numbers, zero and one, which can easily be related to some components being *off* and *on*.

During the Second World War, the Germans developed the *Engima* machine which handled the coding of information being sent out by Admiral Dönitz to the hundreds of U-boats in his command. The British had to break these codes, and to do so they developed a machine known as *Colossus*.[7] This was a success: with the help of Colossus, the codes were broken and the U-boat threat to the convoys in the North Atlantic was reduced and eventually eliminated.

---

[6] We are quite lucky with Arabic numbers: they are easy to use. Imagine trying to add two Roman numerals such as XXIV and VIII. Much harder. Even harder would be the Nubian numbering scheme, where numbers up to 9 have one notation, from 10 to 90 another notation and beyond that another notation still. After that, 0 to 9 seems perfection indeed.

[7] One of the designers of Colossus was the British mathematician Alan Turing. Turing left his mark on the IT industry in many ways, perhaps the most famous being the *Turing test*. The test was devised by Turing to explore the debate about artificial intelligence. He argued that if a person were in communication with a computer but did not realize that it was a computer, then it would have to be accepted that the computer was exhibiting intelligence.

A contemporary of Colossus was known as ENIAC (electronic numerical integrator and calculator). This was developed at about the same time in Pennsylvania. ENIAC took three years to build and contained nearly 20 000 valves. It was the first general purpose computer, but was limited by the fact that the programs it executed were stored on punched card or paper tape devices. This contrasts with modern computers which hold the program internally in storage within the computer, based on ideas put forward by John von Neumann. Both Colossus and ENIAC were very slow because they had to operate at the speed with which the lines of program logic could be read from these external devices.

In addition, because the program was stored externally to the computer, it could only be executed sequentially, i.e. from beginning to end. When techniques were developed for storing the program within the computer, it became possible for the program to be executed in a non-sequential manner. This meant that the program could branch from one part of the program to another or could repeat one section of the program a number of times. Both of these operations were of critical importance.

8.10   Transistors

Valves were expensive, fragile, large and slow, and needed a lot of electricity. The transistor overcame these constraints, being cheaper, more robust, smaller and faster and needing far less electricity. It was the ideal device on which to fabricate a computer. There are still computers around today that were constructed using basic transistor technology.

The valve had three components: a cathode, an anode and a grid. The transistor replaced these three components by three thin wires, connected to a small piece of silicon (or germanium). The valve required a heater which was used to heat the grid to create a stream of electrons. The fact that the transistor did not require such a heat source or a stream of electrons (except hidden within the silicon) accounted for the vast benefits.

The transistor was invented by J. Bardeen, W. H. Brattain and W. B. Shockley at the Bell Laboratories. They were jointly awarded a Nobel prize in 1956.

Transistors can detect, amplify, correct and break an electric current. These four verbs illustrate the variety of uses of the device. It can be argued that the transistor is the single most important invention of the twentieth century. The fundamental concept and structure of the transistor are the basic building block of the following two devices, integrated circuits and microprocessors.

8.11   Integrated circuits

As the complexity of the transistor-based computers grew, one problem became apparent. The number of physical connections that was required between the tens of thousands of components was providing to be a real reliability problem.

In the late 1950s, Jack St Clair Kilby assembled on a single structure a number of transistors and other components. This had two immediate benefits for the information technology industry. Firstly, the way that the components were linked reduced the individual soldering used previously: this addressed at least part of the reliability problems. Secondly, the result of placing these components together was a component with increased and fixed function. By combining more and more components in this way, the functionality could be increased. This meant that people could buy an integrated circuit that performed specific tried and tested functions.

8.12   The microprocessor

Finally, up to date with the microprocessor. The microprocessor was the result of assembling all the basic circuitry required for a computer on a single silicon chip. Again, as with the integrated circuit, the microprocessor was (and is) a packaging phenomenon. Consider a tiny selection of the wide applications of such a device:

- in a microwave oven, to control the timing, heating and security features
- in a car, handling the various gauges and displays—in particular, the increasingly popular *trip computer* which calculates such things as average speed
- talking calculators, translating numbers into human speech
- talking watches, extremely useful devices for people with sight problems
- traffic lights, controlling the synchronization of quite complex signalling arrangements
- in the video recorder, controlling signal strengths, the clock, the automatic timer and on-screen displays of information
- in air conditioning units, ensuring the most efficient use of electricity
- in vending machines, taking the money and dispensing various hot and cold drinks according to the selections made
- in door chimes, playing simple tunes in response to someone pressing the button
- in photocopiers, counting the number of copies made, monitoring toner levels, displaying options and diagnostic information
- in games machines, moving Italian plumbers or strangely rounded hedgehogs up and down passages in search of various objects.

There are thousands more applications, and there will be many thousands more in the future. The microprocessor is being seen in almost every area of our lives.

8.13   Just one year

Modern humanity has existed for a little over 40 000 years. If we use the old trick of equating this period to a single year, then our information technology calendar looks something like this.

Date	Time	Event
1 January	0.00	Modern human appears
20 November	0.00	Abacus first formed
29 December	2.00 a.m.	Blaise Pascal invents the Pascaline
31 December	9.20 p.m.	Personal computer announced

This is a sobering way of looking at the developments we have seen so far, the major ones being compressed into such a short period of time. It makes one wonder what the situation will be like when we wake up after the New Year celebrations.

8.14   Summary

We have come a long way over the past 5000 years, the major distance having been covered in only the past 40 years. This is called acceleration. We have tried in this chapter to set the scene, to provide some background points about our industry. The two key points are that

- the rate of improvement in information technology has been accelerating so far
- there have been discontinuities which have enabled radical changes to take place.

In Chapter 7 we looked at two ways of failing to predict the future satisfactorily: lack of vision and lack of information. The past suggests that two things are likely to happen in the future:

- the rate of improvement will continue to increase
- there will be more discontinuities.

If we accept these two statements then our only tractable problem would seem to be in the area of *vision*. The next chapter tries to look at what may happen in the relatively near future: on our one-year calendar, it looks ahead only a few hours.

9
Small, fast and cheap

The technological trends

For I dipt into the future, far as human eye could see
Saw the Vision of the world, and all the wonder that would be

(Alfred, Lord Tennyson, 1809–1892)

9.1   Purpose

As we saw in the previous chapter, information technology has a 5000-year history, but *modern* information technology goes back only to the middle of the twentieth century. In this chapter we are trying to look forward and see where the trends that we have seen in the past and those evident today are likely to lead. What we are trying to do is to train a pair of binoculars on the distant horizon and see if it is possible to gain more understanding, more clarity about the future that information technology may create.

There are many and varied books written on the subject of information technology and the possible role it may play in the future. They approach it from several points of view:

- science fiction, looking at interesting and novel applications of technology as the backdrop to standard stories of adventure and romance
- technology, looking at the underlying technologies, concentrating on the physical, mathematical and chemical processes involved
- information technology, looking at the application of the technology in everyday situations
- sociological, looking at the effect on society of the changes brought about by information technology
- industrial, looking at certain specific business sectors, analysing how information technology can be used to improve standard aspects of that business.

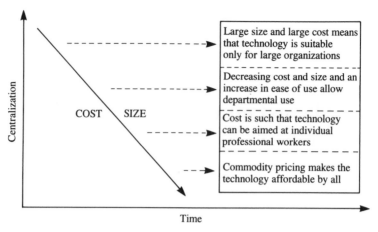

Figure 9.1.   The changing focus of technology.

All these views are necessary: complementarity[1] suggests that to describe some-thing fully it must be described from several different angles, and certainly to understand information technology fully we do need to look at it in several ways.

In this chapter we cannot hope to cover all these angles and we have not tried. Instead, what we have done is to look very briefly at the obvious technological developments—those concerned with size, speed and cost—and then to concen-trate on dipping into the future in a number of ways. By doing this we are trying to show that no matter how dramatic the changes we have already seen, there is a great deal more to come.

9.2   The starting point

Now is a fascinating time to look at information technology and the changes that are taking place within that technology and its application. The focus of informa-tion technology has changed as a natural result of the developments in that technol-ogy (see Fig. 9.1). As the technology became smaller, cheaper and faster, it and its vendors created and developed new applications and therefore new market-places. Large organizations (government and commercial) were the target for the earliest information technology. Only they could afford the massive financial investments that were needed and, to an extent, at that time only they had the mammoth tasks to be performed that justified that investment.

As time went on it became possible for the target market-place to switch to smaller organizations, to divisions within organizations, to departments within those divisions. Technology achieved a level that required far less investment and

[1] In physics, certain phenomena of light can be explained only by assuming that light consists of waves; other phenomena can be explained only by assuming that light consists of particles. Both explanations have to be used to describe fully the properties of light. This is known as 'duality', which is a special case of the more general 'complementarity'.

far less support. Professional workers such as financial officers, managers, scientists, engineers and planners were the next target, made possible by the same changes of size, cost and speed. We are now at the point where the technology is suitable for everyone; ubiquity is just around the corner.

Over the same period, questions have been asked about the impact of that technology; how it could be exploited for best advantage. Those questions now have to be faced by *everyone*, because we are all the willing or unwilling recipients of that technology. In fact the technology is going to become increasingly evident through three routes.

1   As individuals we may *elect* to use some forms of information technology. We may acquire and use personal computers, mobile phones or multimedia games machines. This is all voluntary and we have a great deal of control over the degree to which we immerse ourselves.
2   As members of society we may *have* to become increasingly *technology-literate*. The simple activity of just living is going to require us to use a greater number of information technology devices. Home shopping may become the only option for people living in rural areas; telephone banking may become an economic necessity as banks compete to reduce costs, travelling may require us to purchase tickets from machines instead of people and education may well become far more dehumanized by the application of multimedia than it is at the moment.
3   Finally, as members of organizations we may *have* to spend an increasing amount of our time using information technology devices in one form or another, from the personal computer on our desks to the facsimile machine in the car to the computer-controlled lathe or the computer-controlled warehousing system.

We shall all become much more familiar with information technology than we are at the moment. Whether this is a threat or a promise depends to a large extent on how organizations (again both government and commercial) deploy that technology and on how we as individuals accept that technology.

For the past 50 years we have listened to many debates about information technology. We have been told that we are living in the *information age*, that computers are becoming increasingly intelligent, that robots are going to take over all the mundane tasks and that computer-controlled machinery will push us from a society based on work to a society based on leisure. But now, in the 1990s, an uneasy and strange blend of success and failure seems to be the case. Some of the promises have been fully achieved, some have been achieved in part and some not achieved at all.

What we have seen over the past few decades seems to have been more a trial run, a laudable attempt at creating an information-based society, but no more than that. However, this period is now well and truly over. The capabilities of information technology have reached a series of critical thresholds, and as a result the

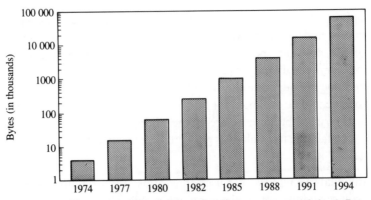

The growth is by about a factor of four every three years (this is an exponential chart). Bytes normally relate to eight 'bits' of memory; each bit is represented by a zero or a one; a byte normally stores a single character. This book contains about 500 000 characters: 16 of these books could be stored on the largest of the chips represented in the chart (64 Mb, i.e. 64 million bits in capacity).

Figure 9.2.   The growth in chip density (amount of memory per chip).

future is almost certainly going to be challenging, frustrating, fascinating, but above all, different!

9.3   The obvious developments

Let us start by considering the obvious changes that have taken place over the past 20 or 30 years. A brief analysis suggests that a number of fundamental changes have taken place and are continuing to take place.

1   Computers, the foundation of information technology, have become

- faster
- cheaper
- smaller
- more portable
- more reliable
- more pervasive.

The heart of the computer, the microchip, is doubling in power (the ability to do useful work) every 18 months.[2] It is available in a broad range of price bands and in both generalized and very specific formats. The chip size is staying almost the same, but the decrease in size of the overall computer comes from better packaging (see Fig. 9.2) and miniaturization of the complete set of components that is required.

---

[2]This is true for some environments. The technology used in mainframe computers no longer achieves this growth rate and is probably nearer the 20 per cent per annum mark. Such a slow-down in the rate of growth may begin to be seen in other areas, but there is no sign of it yet. The growth rate in 'mainframe' computing may well start to climb again as the underlying technology is changed.

2   Software, which enables computers to perform useful functions, has become

- more powerful
- easier to use
- more complex to create
- more difficult to choose from
- far broader in its scope of application.

From the early simple software which ran applications such as order entry or stock control (considered pretty complex at the time) we have now got tens of thousands of packaged solutions covering everything from word processing to language translation, from simulation to visualization, from a complete set of financial products to a full set of encyclopaedias stored on a shiny disc the size of a small plate and accessed by a click of the mouse button.

3   Communication between different computers has become

- faster
- cheaper
- more reliable
- less restrictive.

We have progressed from linking a few terminals at short distances to a large mainframe, to moving those terminals thousands of miles away, to linking a clump of personal computers together in an office, to linking entire city areas. We have moved from copper wires to glass fibres to no physical connection at all.

If these trends continue, what sort of technology will form the basis of our information processing capability in the year 2000? What about 2010, or 2020? The first of these years is within the planning horizon of many organizations today: what assumptions are such organizations making?

9.4   Fantasy land

Let us take a trip into fantasy land: let us assume that some of these trends will continue and that there are no practical limits on the key aspects of the technology. What will we find?

Power

Firstly, the computer will become so powerful in terms of its speed and capacity for work that it will not be a limit to the type of application being run. A desktop computer of today can execute 100 million instructions per second, and this figure is doubling every 18–24 months. Assuming:

1995   100 million instructions per second and a doubling every 18 months, we get

2000   one billion instructions per second (1 000 000 000)
2005   10 billion instructions per second (10 000 000 000)
2010   100 billion instructions per second (100 000 000 000)

How many do we need? Speed is important, not simply because of the time it takes a computer to perform a specific task today, but because of the processes we do not attempt to get a computer to do because we already know it would take far too long. When we look at an internal company telephone directory on a computer, we see names, departments, mail points and telephone extension numbers. It would be useful to see also the face of the individual alongside all of this data, but we normally do not attempt to do this because we know it would slow the overall process down.

If we want computers to add up a bank balance or check the spelling in a memo, then we have probably got all the computing power we need, right now. But the applications which we will need lots more power for are many and varied.[3]

- speech synthesis
- handwriting recognition
- speech recognition
- automatic language translation
- image creation and editing
- image animation
- visualization and simulation
- artificial intelligence
- ultra-intelligent machines (smarter than us)
- holographic television
- virtual reality.

For these applications we are going to need vast amounts of processing power: we are going to need computers capable of performing many billions of simple mathematical instructions per second.

An interesting example of the use to which we can put such vast increases in processing power is in the field of obstetrics. Ultrasound techniques have been used to show pregnant mothers an image of their unborn child. Because these images are produced by complex mathematical calculations (Fourier transforms), the more processing power that can be brought to bear, the better is the quality of the image produced. Many parents in the early days smiled wanly when shown such an image, totally unable to make anything sensible out of the picture that was shown. With the processing power available today, the pictures are far clearer.

---

[3] As these newer and more complex applications grow in function and capability, they grow in the amount of program logic that must be created and maintained. Although it is perfectly possible to double the speed of execution every 18–24 months, we cannot double the speed with which we write program logic, nor can we double the accuracy of the program logic that we write.

Size

Next, the computer will be far smaller than it is today. We have already shrunk computers from the size of a family home to the size of the family album, and we can go further. In the past we drove to work to use the computer, then we managed (just) to drag it out of the office and throw it on the back seat. Then we could fit it in our briefcase, and today we can simply slip it in our pocket. Where will we put it next?

One Japanese company announced its intention to produce wearable personal computers back in 1991, and the Advanced PC Design Centre in Tokyo predicted that by the end of this century people would be wearing their PCs (*Computerworld*, 12 April 1993). It is only a short step from a hand-held personal computer to a contoured one that fits neatly over the shoulder! It is only a short step from this to a personal computer that you have installed, not by some teenager from the support centre down the corridor, but by a doctor or nurse who simply implants the device under the skin behind your ear!

Stupid? Perhaps, but then again, perhaps not. Think of the advantage of always having your personal computer with you, when you're in the bath, at a restaurant, lying on the beach on vacation or even studying the odds in a Las Vegas casino. If you think that this might be beneficial then, so long as there are a few others like you, someone will cater for your needs and provide the technology in such a form. Perhaps we could go even further and genetically engineer future generations so that the 'computer' forms organically during pregnancy, becoming as natural to the owner as his or her hands, and possibly just as useful.

Basic interface

One limitation that has been overlooked in the above is the keyboard. Having a computer so small that it can be implanted or injected with a hypodermic is fine, but it tends to lose some of its appeal if you have to carry a keyboard around with you wherever you go.

But this may turn out not to be too much of a problem. We have seen the size of keyboards decrease significantly as we have moved from desktop computers through luggable, portable, laptop, notebook and currently palmtop computers, but there must be a practical limit: after all, most of our fingers are one or two centimetres across. Some of the palmtop computers or personal information managers now available have taken this size reduction as far as is practical, if not further.

If we cannot shrink the keyboard any further then we have to eradicate it altogether. Manufacturers are pushing pen-based devices as a replacement for the keyboard, and almost certainly they will be at least partly successful. This is a good example of where the vast increases in computer processing power are going to go. It is easy for a computer to detect that you have pressed the letter 'a' on the keyboard,[4] but it takes tens of thousands of instructions to make sense of an 'a' that you have scribbled hastily and clumsily using a stylus.

It is worth considering the degree to which the use of the keyboard has replaced the use of hand-written text. Even though they are anecdotal, a number of straw polls that we have conducted indicate that the replacement of the keyboard by a stylus would not be a welcome move. For people who process certain types of information, for example taking stock checks, giving out parking violations or collecting survey details, the use of a stylus instead of the keyboard may well be acceptable. For the vast number of people who put large amounts of very varied information into a computer, the keyboard takes some beating (sometimes literally).

We know of someone who took a dictating machine home to dictate a report to. He spent the first hour coughing loudly and basically preparing himself for what he obviously believed would be something of a performance. He spent the next hour giggling hysterically as he sat alone in a room trying to speak intelligently to a black plastic box. He spent the third and final hour on the dictating machine trying to edit and change some of the words he had actually managed to get recorded. He spent the rest of the weekend writing the report out by hand.

Better interface

As we are still in fantasy land, let us continue our PC (prosthetic computer?) example and wire it for sound. Ask it what 2 + 2 is and it will whisper the answer; tell it to give you directions to the nearest Holiday Inn and it will do so with ease. And if it takes thousands of computer instructions to decipher a written 'a', just think how many instructions it will take to decipher your voice, especially when you have a cold and everyone else in the same room is chattering away at the same time.

> *Human interface technology will actually be more important than computer performance in 2001*

> (Professor Hajime Iizuka, Seikei University)[5]

Sight is our most important sense, and we have exploited that sense in information technology by the provision of small, flat screens. But they are getting much smaller: already we can (almost) see devices with widths measured in millimetres.

---

[4] The fastest typists can achieve a typing rate of 10 characters per second! Assuming that when a normal word processor is used the computer has to execute 20 000 instructions to transfer the character from the keyboard to the screen (a reasonable assumption), then even when typing as fast as possible, the computer is executing only 200 000 instructions per second, a relatively small percentage of what it is capable of.

[5] We should not mistake the message here. The fact that human interface technology may be more important than computer performance does not mean that computer performance will not be a vital component, but simply that by the year 2001 we shall have achieved very high levels of computer performance: the emphasis will simply switch to the technology that is lagging; the human interface technology.

Placed in front of the eyes, two such devices provide stereoscopic vision (these were seen as futuristic only a few short years ago; now you can buy them mail order). So we can wear our screens of the future as a pair of spectacles or 'head-up display', or perhaps we can implant these also and interface them directly to the optic nerve. Next time you fancy watching a movie, tell the computer which one you want, close your eyes and relax. Why not?

A vast amount of effort is being expended in the area of linking computers with the human senses. Doctors have already performed remote operations: they in one place, the patient (a pig) in another. Such efforts are practical examples of *virtual reality*, of which we are all going to hear a great deal more in the future. Virtual reality is the complete linkage of the computer and our human senses, allowing us to experience a new world, a world stored digitally inside a computer.[6]

The ultimate in exploitation of the five human senses is to link the computer directly to our brains. Let us not consider this just yet; it is not going to happen in the near future. It will happen, there can be little doubt about that, but when it does we shall just throw away the rule book and start from scratch, and the world will be a far stranger place as a result.

Communication

Having an efficient and natural interface directly attached to a very tiny yet very powerful computer is all very well, but all we have got is the ability to process information: we have still got to get hold of the information in the first place. This is where communications come in. Two forms of communication are important. Firstly we want to communicate with people: we want to converse (as on the telephone) and we want to send and receive messages (as in the mail).

Already a number of manufacturers are working hard to tie together the technologies of the telephone, the personal computer and electronic mail systems. (Estimates put the likely number of telephones in use by the end of this century at around two billion. A significant proportion of these will have microprocessors that build on the basic function of the telephone.)

It is interesting to note that if we ever achieve direct sensory attachment of computers and reliable global communication, we shall have achieved a form of telepathy on a global scale. Whether this would be a blessing or a curse is the subject (rightly?) of many science fiction writers.

The other form of communication is communication to data. Want to know the current market value of copper? The dollar–Deutschmark exchange rate? When

---

[6] The current forms of virtual reality rely on 'data gloves', with which the operator interacts with his or her virtual world. You see an image and interact with that image by moving the hand within the data glove. This is primitive, but there are at least nine different senses in our fingertips, each one sensing a different form of movement or pressure. This work is aimed at improving tactile feedback, vital if virtual reality is to be developed much further. The fact that researchers have such a level of understanding in this area is indicative of the importance that is being placed on it.

high tide is in Freemantle next Wednesday? Where your boss is at the moment? How much your partner has spent on your joint account this afternoon? What won the 3.30 race? Just ask. A lot of organizations are going to become very profitable in the near future by providing data such as this, in similar ways to the organizations that today provide stock market information or news information.

Why purchase newspapers containing lots of sports pages if we never look at them? Why not tell the computer what subjects we are interested in and let it do the searching and sifting that is needed? We are going to have access to so much information that we shall have to find smart ways of homing in on only the information we are interested in.

Let us leave our brief analysis there for the moment; we have probably gone far enough. What is important about what we have covered so far is that most of it is based on technology or advances in technology that are quite reasonable. Simply projecting what we have in a reasonable manner leads to an implementation of information technology that makes today's efforts seem primitive in the extreme.

To some, the technological advance is important and interesting in its own right, but this book is concerned more with the alignment of organizations with the technology and the likely trends. For our purposes, we do not need to understand the details of the technology; they will become clear in their own way and in their own time. What is more important is how we are going to employ that technology and what we should be doing now to prepare for it.

9.5   Whimsical questions

If some of the above developments take place, as individuals and as members of organizations, both large and small, we shall have a lot of interesting questions to pose and then answer. A selection are offered below.

1   How shall we assess students in the future if they have access to vast amounts of information whenever they need it? All the chemical formulae, the rules of trigonometry, the dates of all important historical events, the works of every author and the deliberations of all the philosophers, all immediately available.

2   What data will be important in the future and who will provide it? Vast numbers of organizations will try to provide information of value: news information, stock market information, statistical information of every kind.

3   What standards shall we be following? When we move into the *information age* properly, we had better all have similar equipment. If the plugs and sockets in the future are not standard there are going to be some severe discontinuities. It is likely that market forces will dictate the standards, but not immediately.

4   What jobs will disappear? Shall we no longer need estate agents, stock brokers, insurance brokers, travel agents, secretaries, librarians, financial advisers, shop assistants or bank managers? Or will these jobs simply *change*?

5   What new legislation shall we need? Laws of privacy may need to be extended widely and interpreted loosely.

6   What will be the impact on society or the increasing numbers of people who tele-commute and who tele-conference? We need either excellent communications or excellent transport; it is doubtful whether we need both.

7   Will publishers in the future print massive amounts of hardback books and magazines, or will they produce a single master copy and charge us for accessing it?

8   Shall we buy compact discs or their equivalent that contain the two tracks we actually want to hear and 10 others that we find less interesting, or should we build our own personalized disc by copying the data (any musical composition can be stored as a simple, but lengthy, list of numbers) that we want?

9   Will governments disappear when we can all vote from the comfort of our armchair on any of the great and noble issues of the day? Is true democracy achieved when everyone can express his or her opinion on the way in which a country is managed? A situation whereby the information we need is immediately available on our television screens, where all the issues are laid out fairly by both sides and all we have to do is to select the 'yes' option or the 'no' option: is this democracy? Whether it is or not, it is extremely practical.

10 Shall we be allowed to drive our own car in the future when a chip in the instrument panel can record where we want to get to, a chip underneath the dashboard can determine exactly where we are and a chip attached to a cellular communications system can work out an optimal route? Who would risk allowing a human being to take control?

11 Will national boundaries have any significance in the future? If we can communicate with someone thousands of miles away as easily as we can communicate with those in the same town, then we can work with these remote people just as easily; we can form alliances, organizations, interest groups, pressure groups and social groups just as easily.

9.6   Summary

All we have looked at in this chapter is the continuation in the existing trends for reduced size, reduced cost, increased speed and more diverse applications. What is certain is that there is a large and unsatisfied demand for cheap, powerful and convenient computing.

What is less certain is the degree to which this demand will be met. There is a price to pay for such technology, and people are willing to pay only a certain amount for a certain amount of function. The capabilities will be there, of that there is no doubt, but it is far from clear how large a section of the population will feel the price is worth paying.

Some people are 'turned on' by technology itself; many others would rather have a tooth out than interact with information technology in any way. Any discussion of the trends in information technology is almost certain to assume that whatever growth and innovation we can deliver, we will want to deliver. But the qualification must be added and understood that there may well come a point in time when the question is posed of whether or not any further advances in the technology are deemed acceptable. Technology will advance only if there is profit in it for some-one. If society as a whole decides that enough is enough, then the advances will stop.

10
On the catwalk

Different computing models

Rules and models destroy genius and art

(William Hazlitt, 1778–1830)

10.1   Purpose

During the modern (electronic) computing age we have seen a number of models of computing. (There is a great temptation here to refer to these computing models as computing *paradigms*, but we have resisted use of the term, which has suddenly come into fashion and is almost always used incorrectly.) Of these, three models dominate past and current thinking

- centralized mainframe model
- departmental model
- personal model

and a fourth dominates our thoughts about the future of computing

- nomadic model.

These models have collectively represented the contemporary fashion for the development of computer-based systems for the past 30 or 40 years. Just as fashions change, so the computing models have changed, although in our industry we do not appear to have had the opportunity of seeing old fashions become popular for a second time round (at least not yet).

It is easier to think in terms of these models than in terms of the requirements to be met and the solutions to be provided. The models give us a convenient way of discussing something that is complex (this is the primary function of all such models), but at the same time they enable us to gloss over details, to think in terms of stereotypes. Sometimes this can be useful; more often it is not.

In this chapter we consider each of these computing models and look at how they have developed and the types of work that they are used for.

10.2   Major trends

Figure 10.1 shows a simplified summary of the emergence of different computing models since the 1960s. As we described in Chapter 9, we have come from an environment where computers were affordable by only the largest organizations to an environment where microcomputers are glued inside birthday cards so we can listen to a squeaky unmelodious tune every time they are opened. (These appalling devices seem to be still growing in popularity. Those who want to send such birthday cards but do not like the tune can now buy a card with a chip within it where you can record your own greeting: up to 20 seconds of recording that will play repeatedly (until the battery expires). This seems an excellent way of making yourself popular and creating a lasting impression.)

Figure 10.1 is not intended to illustrate distinct boundaries between each phase: the role of the mainframe is not over, and there were personal computers before 1980. Rather, it is intended to illustrate that as the capabilities and characteristics change over time, there comes a point where the changes are sufficiently great to enable a different computing *model* to become established.

As the individual changes have taken place over the past few decades, the IT industry has gone through a series of phases of computing, the sort of phases that make sense only in retrospect. We have worked with hundreds of organizations over this period, and at any one point in time it has been relatively easy to divide them into the following types.

1   Behind the times, still doing things in ways that most other organizations had already moved away from. Making a virtue out of a necessity became some-

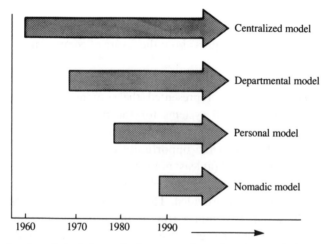

There are no clear boundaries between the four stages shown, but they are distinct and different even though they coalesce and coexist very easily.

Figure 10.1.   Trends in computing.

thing of an art form for organizations that for one reason or another were never able or willing to stay at or near the leading edge of technology.

2   In line with most other organizations, in the general pack of organizations making use of fairly stable technology in fairly predictable ways. This is a safe way of operating and has certain obvious financial benefits, not least the fact that the technology being employed is readily available, is well supported by the vendors and can be supported by skills that are easily acquired.

3   Ahead of other organizations, taking a gamble with the way in which the technology would work out. Taking risks and reaping reward or condemnation in equal measure. Organizations in this category were among the first to start connecting the early personal computers to their centralized systems, the first to implement electronic mail applications and the first to start building client/server systems.

In terms of the four computing models, such positioning has tended to be against the emerging technologies and the newer forms of such models. As each of the models becomes increasingly viable as a form of computing, it enables organizations to

- do things that they could not do previously, or
- do things better than they had been done previously.

So the newer models provided advantages. Far-sighted organizations were quick to grasp these advantages, most organizations adopted them when they realized that the advantages were being gained by others, and some resisted making the move until they were forced to move, for a variety of reasons.

Apart from the speed with which the newer models were adopted, there is another key differentiator between organizations. As new models of computing become available they are seen by some organizations as replacements for the existing models. So the announcement of the personal computer was construed by some as meaning that the previous models would become out of date, would become redundant.

Other organizations recognized that the newer models were incremental or evolutionary, offering advantages in some areas and not in others. They saw that the best way forward was to understand the strengths and weaknesses of both old and new models and to apply each for maximum benefit.

In our experience, the organizations that are reaping the most benefit are those that recognize that every form of computing changes the capabilities of IT, enabling us to improve the way we do some things and to do things that we would not have considered before. They also realize that such changes have to be incremental, exploiting strengths and avoiding weaknesses in all the models.

10.3   The mainframe computing model

At the birth of the electronic computer in the 1940s, the applications ran one at a time. This takes some imagining today. Picture a mainframe computer that weighs in at several tons and generates enough heat to melt a fair-sized iceberg, full of valves and taking a significant time to 'warm up'. Mean time between failures notwithstanding, patient users queued for their 'slot'. The program was read in through a punched card reader and, when the computer was ready, the data followed it. A single computer, a single application program and a single user. The first *personal* computer.

The computer was initially very short on memory, thereby limiting the size and therefore the complexity of the application that could be run; it had little data storage capability and was extremely slow. It was good enough, however, for scientific institutions, government census departments and several brave commercial organizations. It proved its worth and showed significant promise. Life at this stage was exciting, but needed patience, a nocturnal approach to life and a pocket full of spare valves.

The mainframes continued to develop, as did the operating systems that controlled them. With the introduction of on-line data storage, bigger memories and the ability to perform several processes simultaneously (seemingly), the applications became correspondingly more sophisticated. These applications tended to be batch applications. Cards were punched all day by punch-card operators, sorted and fed into the computer where they were queued for overnight processing.

Organizations developed new ways of working, dictated by the 'overnight batch'. Such applications still exist and will probably exist for a very long time. A lot of operations seemingly benefit from being done in this way:

- producing statements of bank balances
- producing picking lists for warehouses
- calculating interest charges and applying them to accounts
- producing renewal notifications for insurance policies
- transferring funds electronically from one account to another
- producing payroll slips
- producing marketing mail shots.

Although it may be efficient and somewhat natural to think of these applications as being inherently batch, they are not; they never were. The computer forced them into a mould that will take a lot of breaking. When we check our bank balance using an ATM (automatic teller machine) today or our television set tomorrow, we do not want to see what the balance was at close of business last night, we want to know what it is now! We always have, but the banks cannot (or will not) tell us. (We should not be too critical of the banks (at least for this) because it is very difficult for a bank to maintain an accurate balance. A cleared balance is always available; it is just a matter of how out-of-date the information is.)

Life at this stage was slightly better, but only when things went well. Having all the eggs in one overnight basket could be (and still is) troublesome, to say the least.

Organizations began to see that there had to be a better way. Why should an insurance clerk spend 30 minutes entering the details of a new policy, only for that data to be formatted as a punched card and put to one side until the batch application is run? Even when the batch application ran there were problems. Because the insurance clerk who typed up the data was fast asleep at the time it was processed, any errors in that data caused that whole piece of work to be put to one side so that the insurance clerk could correct it the following day.

On-line applications were developed to provide simultaneous shared access to the mainframe computer. Results were instantaneous, errors were corrected immediately and everyone was much happier. The demand came for databases, to allow data to be shared, and faster processors to enable more users to process more work, and for more sophisticated networking and operating system facilities. The mainframe came of age, supporting thousands of users in a reliable, predictable manner.

Figure 10.2 shows a mainframe computer connected to collections of non-intelligent terminals in different places. This is by far the most common and the most successful of all the computer models we have seen. The expensive and complex resource was centralized. It was monitored and controlled, tended and nurtured. Procedures and policies were put in place to gain the maximum benefit from it. All the complexity was centralized so that it could be exploited. This is in fact a very simple computer model, and one about which we have learned a great deal over the years.

The large mainframe computing model is currently receiving a bad press, but regardless of what happens to it in the future, it created the environment we have

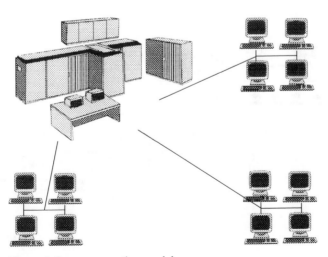

Figure 10.2.   The mainframe computing model.

today. It served, and will continue to serve thousands of end users in both small and large organizations for a very long time.

The organizations used this particular computing model to increase the efficiency of the existing processes. Typical on-line applications were in:

- recording new orders, changes to orders and cancellations of orders
- recording new name and address details for customers
- providing electronic mail facilities to enable people to communicate across the office, the organization or even the world
- the process of developing application programs
- checking the creditworthiness of customers and prospective customers.

With both batch and on-line applications, the organization did not change a great deal: it did what it had always done, but faster and with far fewer people.

10.4   The departmental computing model

The reason the previous model was a centralized one was that it was implemented by a computer (the mainframe computer) that was an extremely expensive and complex resource. Because it was expensive it had to be used in a very efficient manner.

If we can reduce the cost of the computer by some amount, the need to drive the computer as hard as possible, to get the best return on the investment, becomes less of an issue. It is perfectly acceptable to have a computer operating far less efficiently if the cost of that inefficiency is sufficiently low.

This was one of the major drives behind the departmental computing model (see Fig. 10.3). In this model the cost characteristics were such that it became practical

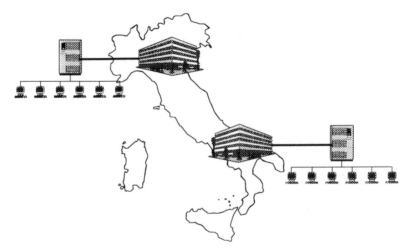

Figure 10.3.   The departmental computing model.

to employ physically smaller computers with sufficient power at sufficiently low cost in situations where the utilization was expected to be low.

In its simplest form, the departmental or minicomputer model of computing looks very similar to the mainframe model. The departmental computer or mini-computer is acting as a mainframe did in the mainframe computing model, although the technology and the metrics associated with cost, power and number of users are different.

Examples of the use of this model are extraordinarily varied, such as:

- in factories, managing warehouse distribution, stock location and stock management
- in financial organizations, serving the need of a single regional or branch office
- at a college or university where it is used during class hours for programming by the students
- in continuous operations such as chemical, oil or steel companies where several of these machines would be located across the complete site, each responsible for a small part of the overall processing requirement.

In these sorts of environment, the characteristics of this model—lower cost, smaller size, better ease of use and better functionality—were all required. When you move from a single tightly managed computing model to one with several computers distributed across different parts of the organization, you cannot afford to support each and every one of these computers with the same number of highly skilled people. They *have* to be easy to use.

Again, as with the mainframe model, these departmental computers were used to automate existing work, existing processes. They enabled organizations to devolve more of their operation away from the centre, and to an extent were responsible for some organizations decentralizing their operations.

It would be wrong to leave this particular model without a brief discussion of a non-technical reason why it gained popularity. With the centralized mainframe model of computing, the onus was very clearly on the IT managers to satisfy the computing requirements of the entire organization. Where the requirements were not met, the removal of support for the central IT function in favour of a local one that was far more responsive to local needs became the objective. The desire for local autonomy was responsible for many organizations developing local IT solutions using the minicomputer model. This movement would be accelerated with the introduction of the next computing model.

10.5   The personal computing model

Reduce the cost of the computer still further, say by a factor of 10, 100 or 1000, reduce the size so that it fits on a desk, make it so easy to use that a child can use it, make it powerful enough to run applications that are obviously useful. Do all this and you end up with the personal computer, just as we did in the 1980s.

In the 1980s, we went back 40 years. Back came the single-user, single-application computer, but this time you could (just) get it through the door. The ubiquitous 'personal' computer had arrived. Technology had created a situation where the cost had been reduced to a level where it was quite acceptable for the machine to be turned off 99 per cent of the time, instead of having to be on 99 per cent of the time to ensure the maximum benefit was being obtained.

In its early variants, the personal computer seems in hindsight to have been a very primitive machine. It had no hard disk to store programs or data. It had a single floppy disk drive and a screen that seemed to display everything in two colours, fluorescent pink and fluorescent green. In addition, it was designed for the elite—those few who could understand what was where on the keyboard. It was short on memory, short on data storage and short on processing speed. If that was not enough, it could not communicate with anything and had a user interface consisting of 'A:\>'.

But for all its faults it had one vital ingredient: it was ours! We could put our arms around this machine. We could retreat into our office or our den and do what *we* wanted to do, not what someone else had decided we should be allowed to do. This was not a computer to be locked away and guarded by strange people talking strange languages, this was a computer solely for our own use. We switched it on, we decided what applications to run and we switched it off. A revolution had arrived.

The applications that could be run on the early PCs were very limited, but two particular types of application made up for the limited choice: the spreadsheet and the word processor. These had two important characteristics. Firstly, they performed a function that the mainframe computers had never addressed, thereby creating a new type of user. Secondly, they were not prescriptive applications: the user was in control, the applications did what the user wanted; not the other way round.

Life at this stage was a little confusing: the technology had escaped from the basement and was running around the building enjoying itself. Whether it would run out of steam or be joined by lots of friends was a question that was asked by everyone but answered by very few.

Although the cost of personal computing has gone down and down over the past decade, the technology has become suitable for more and more workers. Hence, the total amount of money spent on personal computers and associated devices and software is far higher now than it was in the past.

To control this increase in cost, it makes sense to try to share the resources that can be shared. Hence printers, communications lines, data storage devices, modems and software should all be shared between those who work together and perform the same type of work. Local area networks were designed and implemented to enable a group of users to connect their personal computers and share that which could sensibly be shared. Figure 10.4 shows personal computers operating in isolation (stand-alone mode) as well as personal computers linked through a network.

Figure 10.4.   The personal computing model.

A lot has been written about the effect on organizations of the application of personal computing. Most of the people reading this book will be users of personal computers; they will have their own view of how the personal computer has changed the structure of the organization, how it has enabled empowerment, how it has enabled communication in seconds across an entire division or even the entire organization, how it has increased the level of professionalism that individuals can apply to their work, how it has enabled more rapid reaction to market forces.

10.6   The nomadic computing model

The nomadic model in one sense is already with us, and yet we still have so far to go that it is very difficult to see how this model will develop over time. Figure 10.5 shows a simplified view of the key aspect of the nomadic model, the ability to be outside the corporate infrastructure of information technology while at the same time being able to use the vast information, processing power and communications potential that is within it. The nomadic computing model frees users from having to perform their role in specific places, and enables them to move freely while still having access to the necessary data and processing capabilities.

When we say that in one sense this model is here already, we are talking about the millions of people who regularly use portable computing devices outside the controlled geography of the host organization. But these people are only scratching the surface: a significant amount of development of this model still needs to take place.

Consider first a typical worker with a portable computing device of some form or another. It does not really matter what the technology is; the problems (and benefits) are the same. The problems include the following.

Figure 10.5.   The nomadic computing model.

1   The technology, although portable (better than transportable or luggable, both descriptions of a recent bygone age) is still cumbersome. The portable computer fits in the briefcase but usually it gets a bit cramped with the portable printer, external modem, external diskette drive, external power supply, mouse and diskettes. As technology shrinks, these (and more) will all eventually be included within a single device, but for the moment we have a relatively significant inconvenience.

2   The technology usually consists of a computer with a reasonable-sized internal disk drive. On this disk drive are all the software programs (such as word processors and spreadsheets) and all the data that these programs use. In addition there is the operating system, printer drivers, communications software, virus protection software, back-up and recovery software and the myriad of other bits of code that have to exist to make a reasonably functional system.

3   The software becomes out-of-date relatively quickly. That means that there must be some means of getting new versions of software to these machines on a fairly regular basis. This is inconvenient, especially because downloading software over a standard domestic telephone line is still a relatively slow and primitive activity.

4   The data that is stored has value: some has little value; some has a very high value. The portable computer is not a good place to store valuable data. Firstly it can be stolen, and often is; secondly it can be damaged (accidentally or deliberately); thirdly it is not available to anyone who is not using that particular machine.

These problems are caused by the fact that the portable computer is *outside* the controlled infrastructure that we associate with computers that are fixed at certain points within the organization. These can be controlled and managed much more efficiently, and the resources contained on them can be protected and made available much more easily.

So we are not there yet; a lot of developments need to be made and a lot of lessons need to be learned before we really achieve the goal associated with this computing model. This is a suitable point at which to consider what this goal actually is. We hinted at it in previous chapters, especially when looking at the future and the technology that we may see. Let us list a few important objectives of this computing model.

1   The technology must be easily portable. This will require the shrinking of the technology still further and the incorporation within the basic portable computer of all the add-ons that are required.
2   We must be able to power the technology for as long as we need to. Never mind the second briefcase full of spare batteries: we have to avoid the need to be permanently aware of the battery level. We do not need a battery that lasts a month, but we need better than the few hours we have today.
3   We do not want to have to worry about maintaining the software on the portable computer. When the software becomes out-of-date, the process for making it current again should be as near transparent as we can make it.
4   We do not want to have to worry about taking back-up copies of data every night. The data should be secured automatically.

If you look closely at these objectives (and others—there are many), it becomes apparent that the biggest problem with the portable computer is the computer itself. The *real* objective surely has nothing to do with power supplies or data security; the real objective has to be along the lines of:

> *to be able to use whatever application software we are allowed to use and to process whatever data we are allowed to access, whenever we want to, wherever we happen to be.*[1]

That is getting nearer the real objective, and is the baseline for the nomadic computing model. In all the three previous computing models we considered, we were tied to specific processing capability being at specific geographic points. The nomadic computing model goes beyond this, into the area of ubiquitous computing.

This has two implications, firstly for people who are not interested in being mobile (the traditional white-collared or blue-collared workers who do whatever they have to do in more or less the same place each day) and secondly for people who are already mobile.

A percentage of the first group, the static workers, will find in the nomadic computing model an encouragement to consider other forms of working: from home,

---

[1] An Australian has developed the 'wet PC'. This is a personal computer that you can take under water. This may not be as crazy as it sounds: classifying fish, coral reefs or ancient wrecks is all about information; why not capture and use the information on the spot?

or from suburban office suites. They will be encouraged because some of what tied them down in the first place will be relaxed or removed. They will not have to go to their desk to use their computer, their applications and their data. Any computer will do; the applications and the data will simply follow the person around. (For people who use personal computers there is the obvious drawback that any customization of the interface or the applications or the various settings that are used is usually confined to that single physical personal computer. Using a different computer means that even if the applications and data can still be accessed, there will be a different 'look and feel' that has to be understood. It is a bit like getting in the car after the kids have been using it: you have to move the seat, adjust the mirrors and re-tune the radio to something more acceptable. The 'tailored environment' created by each user is as much a part of the computing environment as the data and the applications.)

Already, many organizations are looking at this with some degree of urgency. To be able to increase the mobility of (mainly office) workers has a host of benefits.

A good example to consider is that of a large UK-based financial organization. This organization has several hundred branch offices and one head office. The organization has a two-level IT infrastructure with mainframe computers at the centre and personal computers on local area networks in each branch.

As the organization tries to maintain the minimum staffing level, there obviously comes a time (very often) when the workload in one particular branch is too heavy for the people available. In the past, the organization would bus in several additional workers from neighbouring branches to help out. The ability to keep the workers where they were, but switch them from being Branch-A employees to Branch-B employees would save a vast amount of expense. This is enabled by the ability to switch the applications and access to the data to where the user is, rather than have the user make the move.

Another advantage would exist for the many employees who travelled from branch to branch as part of their normal job: auditors, regional managers, product specialists or product marketing. These people could travel but still find their own information technology environment waiting for them when they arrived; their own files, their own data.

The above example illustrates that there are advantages in the nomadic computing model for people who are not yet nomadic in nature. For those who are, like the omnipresent travelling sales executive, the benefits are obvious, eradicating the control and management issues that we covered earlier.

10.7   Summary

We have looked at four models of computing:

- mainframe
- departmental
- personal
- nomadic.

Which model is best? The answer is obviously that none of them is *best*. Each of the models has advantages and disadvantages; each is suited to some range of activities and not others. In the next chapter we shall look at the design points of these four models and at why, for some time to come, even though the boundaries between the technologies may begin to blur, the different models of computing will all have their part to play.

11
Trains, boats and planes

Different classes of solution

With a name like yours, you might be any shape, almost.

(Lewis Carroll, 1832–1898)

11.1   Purpose

As we saw in Chapter 10, computers come in many shapes and sizes. This is not accidental: the development of the four models of computing has followed a fairly natural progression in terms of technology, its capabilities and its cost. Over a very short period of time, we have created an environment where the power of the mainframe computer can be fitted in a pocket and powered by a battery.

Now that we have such capabilities, does this mean that all our computing requirements will be met by such devices? At the moment we have four reasonably well-defined computing models: do we need them all?

In most of the organizations in which we have been involved in the production of an IT architecture, it has been clear that to meet the current and future requirements of that organization there is a clearly defined role for most, if not all, of the four computing models. There is no *single* model that can satisfy all the complex and ever-changing requirements.

However, this clarity is achieved only when we understand the design characteristics of the various classes of computer. The purpose of this chapter is to look at these characteristics in a non-technical way, using an analogy that allows us to concentrate on the key points without having to understand the underlying technology which provides these characteristics.

There are a limited number of *classes* into which almost every computer ever designed or built will fit, and this chapter uses a transportation[1] analogy to look at each of these classes. This analogy has three characteristics:

---

[1] We are indebted to Allan Oas from IBM Canada for this analogy. Allan developed a presentation for both IBM personnel and IBM's clients that used the transportation analogy to make a number of simple but important points. The ideas in this chapter have been developed from this work.

- it is easy to understand
- it is easy to extend and adapt to our own purposes
- it relates well to information technology; the analogy holds up reasonably well.

The objective is to remove any subjectivity associated with terms such as *mainframe* or *personal computer* and build towards an understanding of the basic characteristics and suitability of such technologies.

11.2 The analogy

A brief word on the analogy that we are using (transportation). There are many forms of transportation available to most of us, a small selection of which are shown in Fig. 11.1. Despite the large number of choices, when faced with a requirement to transport something or someone from point A to point B, we very seldom hesitate. We understand that each mode of transportation has a range of suitability, that it is fit for some tasks and not for others.

For example, if we want to go from the first floor in a building to the 25th floor, we use a lift. If we want to take the kids to school we use a car. If we want to take a class of kids on a school outing we use a bus, and if we want to move 100 000 tons of oil from Kuwait to Rotterdam we use an ocean tanker. Little debate; little room for doubt.

In Fig. 11.1, we show a transportation matrix: the number of people to be transported versus the distance they have to be transported through. We can argue over specific cells in the matrix because we all have our own subjective opinions of which transportation mechanism we prefer and we all live in slightly different environments, but obviously all forms of transportation are better at some jobs than at others. The choice is dependent on more than just distance and number of passengers: we also need to consider cost, comfort, energy conservation, time taken for the journey and ease of access. We do not fly to work and we do not walk to our

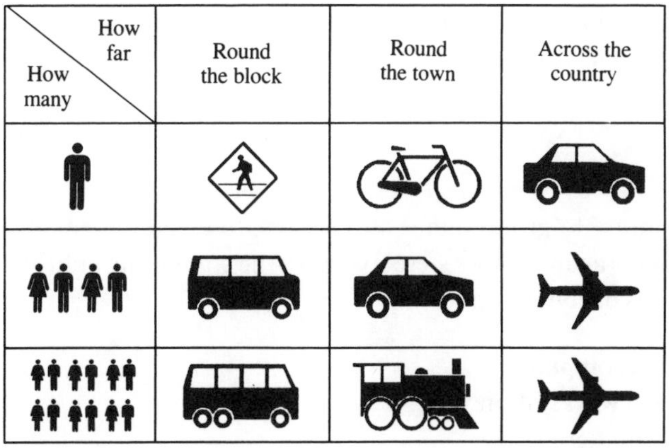

Figure 11.1.   Modes of transportation.

vacation resort (usually). In this chapter we use the transportation analogy to try to show that the same is true in information technology.

We may all have our subjective (personal) opinions of which information technology we prefer, but there surely must be a recognition that all forms of information technology are inherently better at some jobs than at others.

This may seem a trivial message to try to make. It is blindingly obvious that you cannot run the payroll application for the US Navy on a personal computer, or even a few thousand personal computers. It is equally obvious that you do not buy a mainframe computer to write the occasional letter, but time and time again, when we have been involved with organizations large and small, when we have worked with individuals young and old, we have come across the same prejudices and therefore the same subjective assessments. (We know of one organization where some senior managers believed that they should remove the mainframe computer and replace it with a personal computer on everyone's desk. Using our analogy, this is a bit like closing down all the railways and airlines and buying everyone a pair of shoes.)

So, for people who believe that the mainframe is the only real viable computing option, or for those who believe that the personal computer is going to replace every other form of computer, let us ask:

- do you use the same form of transportation all the time?
- do you use the same form of transportation regardless of who is travelling with you?
- do you use the same form of transportation regardless of how far you are going?
- do you use the same form of transportation regardless of how much time you have for the journey?
- do you use the same form of transportation regardless of how much you are prepared to pay?

Let us use the analogy and see if this helps our understanding of the four classes of computer that we have identified.

11.3   The problem

It is human nature to group things into classes, to create stereotypes and then to make judgements against those stereotypes. In the computing industry we have created four classes of computer:

- the personal computer
- the technical workstation
- the minicomputer
- the mainframe computer.

(There are in fact more than just these four classes: we have ignored specialized computers such as those involved in process control or everyday household devices, and the supercomputers traditionally associated with subjects such as meteorology, concentrating on the set of computers that accounts for almost all the computing in existence today.) Asked to illustrate these classes, most of us would come up with a picture similar to that shown in Fig. 11.2. We recognize the classes quite easily, although classification is becoming more difficult due to the growing degree of overlap between them, but the characteristics of each are more difficult to define.

- What is the difference between a mainframe and a minicomputer? What about a small mainframe and a large minicomputer?
- If mainframes continue to take advantage of the technology coming out of the development of the personal computer and technical workstation, will these differences still apply?
- What is the difference between a technical workstation and a personal computer? Both are available in desktop versions; both in single-user and multi-user versions, what is the *real* difference?
- If we take six minicomputers, link them together and manage them as a single unit, is this the same as a mainframe that contains six separate processors within it?
- You can install a card inside a personal computer that simulates a mainframe computer. It enables typical mainframe applications to run on the personal computer. Is the personal computer now a mainframe?

Answering the above questions is relatively easy, but only when we really understand the technology of the computer and the design of the computer. Without this

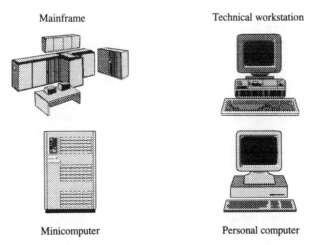

Figure 11.2. The four classes of computer.

understanding we run the risk of making the wrong decisions about the type of computer we use in a given situation, and the way in which we use that computer.

The technology of the large mainframes and minicomputers is moving towards the technology of the personal computer and the technical workstation and the reverse is also true, with these smaller systems becoming just as complex as their larger relatives.

So where does the distinction really lie? Which class of computer is suitable for which type of work? To answer these questions properly, we need to look at the characteristics of each of these classes, and the best way to do that is with some form of analogy which takes us away from any subjective prejudices that we all may still harbour.

11.4   Personal computer

The personal computer is a *personal* computer. We should continually remind ourselves of this fact: it was designed to be a personal computer; it has the characteristics of something that is inherently personal.

For our analogy, the personal computer should be related to personal means of transportation such as:

- bicycle
- motorcycle
- sports car.

Such forms of transport are aimed at a single user, and because of this are exciting. To market products in these areas, the vendors do not stress the load-carrying capacity: they stress the individualistic properties, they stress the colours you can buy it in, the decals and the associated status.

The same is partially true for the personal computer which represents a technology that is available to everyone: you do not have to be a specialist to own and use one; everyone can do it. You buy a personal computer in the same way that you would buy a bicycle—off the shelf. They are commodity items which are immediately available and usable. The personal computer was designed for *personal use* and for *productivity*. Table 11.1 lists the typical strengths and weaknesses of this particular class of computer.

The performance of a personal computer is often compared very favourably with that of the larger mainframe computers. This comparison is extremely confusing. Because the personal computer was designed for personal use, it *has* to have an enormous amount of computing power in reserve, which it can use immediately it is needed by the user. For example, when the mouse is moved across the screen the user wants to see the mouse move smoothly and quickly. The power to do this has to be held in reserve, whereas in a larger, more sophisticated computer, this power is being used by other users.

Now let us use the analogy to explore the basic characteristics of the personal

Table 11.1 Personal computer strengths and weaknesses

Strengths	Weaknesses
Responsiveness	Potentially large hidden costs
Low (and falling) prices	Complexity when multiplied
Ideal for home use	Idle most of the time
Large number of applications	Usually managed by the user
Personal	Data unavailable to other users
Fun	
Easy to use (potentially)	
Colourful, graphical interfaces	

computer. If we have a large department responsible for taking orders over the telephone, we need to be able to maintain consistency over the way in which those people work. Giving everyone a personal computer into which they can record the orders is similar to giving all the children in the school a bicycle and telling them to meet up at ten o'clock at the swimming pool five miles away. We just would not do it.

The personal computer is 'personal'. Trying to use it to provide common services to a wide community is trying to use it for something it was never designed for.

Continuing the analogy, some would perhaps argue that we can attach a collection of personal computers to some central point, another personal computer, and that this central personal computer can then provide common services to the individual users of the attached personal computers. This is the typical arrangement in a local area network, with several computers attached to a single 'server' computer which provides common applications and common data to the 'client' personal computers to which it is attached.

But this form of arrangement means that the 'client' personal computers are not 'personal' computers, they are terminals attached to a shared service in the same way that terminals are attached to a minicomputer or a mainframe. Of course they have better graphics and potentially a better response and a better overall 'feel', but they are no longer 'personal' computers. With this form of connection, the server, be it a personal computer or whatever, is playing the role traditionally played by the minicomputer or the mainframe. In fact the server can actually be a minicomputer or a mainframe and still deliver the same service.

All this proves is that life can be complex, that while we attach convenient labels to things to make it easier to converse with each other, the labels really serve only to mask an inherent complexity. We need to think more about the models of computing that we are trying to build than about simplified views of the technology with which those models may be implemented.

Let us stress again that the personal computer is designed for personal use: it is not the best vehicle for supporting in a consistent manner a large number of people who are working not in a personal capacity but as members of a group.

Remember that a personal computer that is attached to another computer, such as a minicomputer or a mainframe computer, is no longer acting simply as a personal computer. This is equivalent to putting the bicycle on a train. We get everyone to the same point at the same time and still allow an element of freedom when they arrive: perhaps the best of both worlds?

11.5   Technical workstation

A technical workstation is typically one that is based on RISC[2] technology. These workstations were designed for hard work. Following our analogy, the technical workstation relates to forms of transportation such as the

- fork-lift truck
- formula 1 racing car
- jet fighter aircraft
- agricultural tractor.

Like the personal computer, the technical workstation is aimed at a single user, but the latter is aimed at a user who requires very high performance and is willing to pay the price. The strengths and weaknesses of this class of computer are listed in Table 11.2.

Table 11.2   Technical workstation strengths and weaknesses

Strengths	Weaknesses
Very high performance	Many choices to make on lots of features
Good graphical user interface	Requires significant skills
Not proprietary, can choose from a number of vendors	Complex command interface

If the user needs high performance for applications such as imaging, simulation, or visualization, all functions that require incredible numbers of mathematical calculations to be performed, then a technical workstation would seem to be a reasonable place to start looking. It is a specialist environment, as the analogy indicated. Farmers need the strength and flexibility of a tractor for a specific purpose; they do not use it for shopping.

11.6   Minicomputer

The minicomputer provides a *shared* environment. In transportation terms it has similar characteristics to the

- family car
- ferry

---

[2] RISC stands for reduced instruction set computer. The speed of a microprocessor is related to the speed of its clock, which is measured in megahertz (MHz, millions of cycles per second). Speed is one thing; performance is quite another. Performance relates to the amount of work that the microprocessor can perform in a given time. The whole rationale behind RISC technology is to squeeze the maximum amount of work out of the microprocessor for a given clock speed. This means that the components and circuitry have to be of a high specification, and this in turn increases the overall cost.

- bus
- mini-van
- tram

These are all shared means of transportation. They are suitable for a reasonable number of people wanting to get to the same place. They offer a shared solution to a shared problem. Table 11.3 gives some strengths and weaknesses of this class of computer.

Table 11.3   Minicomputer strengths and weaknesses

Strengths	Weaknesses
Range of complete solutions available in package form	Lack the flexibility of the personal computer environment
Can be used in conjunction with personal computers	Less choice, fewer vendors
	If only a small number of users, then the relative price can be high
Highly productive environment for both users and those who have to support them	Software and peripherals can be more expensive than for the personal computer environment
Proven technology	
Built-in capability to support many users	

If we go back to the example of the department of people taking orders over the telephone, the minicomputer is a valid solution. It offers the packaged support in an environment that was designed to be shared by a number of people, all performing similar work.

11.7   Mainframe computer

The mainframe computer was designed to provide *shared service* across an entire organization. In terms of our analogy, the following forms of transportation fit well:

- passenger train
- cruise ship
- jumbo jet.

All these forms of transportation were designed for transporting a large number of people from one point to another. They offer little flexibility to each of the individual passengers. People can embark and disembark at various places *en route*, but once aboard they have little or no control over where they are going (hijackers excepted). Table 11.4 gives some strengths and weaknesses of the mainframe class of computer.

Back to the example of the department of people taking orders. If that department is actually 20 departments spread across 20 different locations, then a single

Table 11.4   Mainframe strengths and weaknesses

Strengths	Weaknesses
Proven technology	No graphical user interface
Proven ability to support thousands of users	Very few personal productivity applications
Very sophisticated operating systems	Needs a large specialized support team
Proven ability to process huge numbers of transactions	

minicomputer placed within each department will not necessarily provide the integrity that is required. It is no use having people taking orders in one location for a product that is now out of stock because of orders taken in a different location.

11.8   Putting the pieces together

Just as no single form of transportation is universally applicable, no single computing model is ever going to satisfy all our needs.

Technology is creating an environment within which more forms of computing model, for example the nomadic computing model, become viable. Transportation has followed a similar technological development. The following list shows different forms of transportation in approximate chronological order:

- swimming[3]
- walking
- running
- canoeing
- horse riding
- sailing
- cycling
- driving
- flying.

As these developments have taken place, they have not negated previous forms of transportation: they have simply provided a greater degree of choice, and we have used that choice to change the way in which we approach transportation problems. We no longer *have* to walk; we have a choice but sometimes we still walk, from choice, because walking is sometimes the most effective means of transportation. We may not want to walk every day, and we may flinch at the prospect of walking 10 miles, but we do not want to lose our ability to choose to walk when we want to or need to.

In a similar fashion, we no longer *have* to use a mainframe computer: we have a choice, but we still use a mainframe for the tasks that a mainframe is best suited to—sometimes the mainframe is the most effective method of computing. We do

---

[3] We were aquatic very early in our development!

not want to use a mainframe to write a letter or calculate our bank balance, but we do not want to lose our ability to choose to use a mainframe when it is the best option available.

What we need to remember is that when faced with a problem, we have a variety of solutions to choose from. Some will be suitable, others less so. We need to think about what we are trying to do and choose the best solution. What happens far too often is that the solution dictates the problem; that the technology is chosen because of the capabilities of that technology and people's perception of the value and strengths of that technology.

In an IT architecture, when we consider the problems faced in total by a large organization, it is extremely unlikely that we can ever solve all these problems with a single solution. For the same reasons that any large city has to provide a large number of transportation solutions to meet the varied transportation problems, most organizations will find that they need to provide several classes of computer put together in several different computer models. Mainframe computing cannot solve all problems; neither can personal computing or client/server computing; but a combination of these solutions put together in a considered way probably can.

Let us illustrate this by looking at a very simple example. Let us take a salesman for a large organization that manufactures and sells beds to the hotel industry, and take that salesman through a typical day, looking at the different forms of computing that he needs to use.

7.00 a.m.

Our salesman, let us call him Dave, begins his working day at home. He is going to make a call on a large customer at 9.00 a.m. and wants to update his electronic diary so that his colleagues and his other customers know exactly where he is. He has a personal computer at home, but his diary is stored on a mainframe computer at head office because this is the only location that everyone in the organization can access with relative ease. If his diary were stored on his personal computer at home it would be of no use to anyone: it has to be shared across the whole organization, and therefore it has to be supported by a computing model that is capable of sharing that data across the whole organization.

Dave signs on to the mainframe computer by using his personal computer and a modem. He updates his diary to reflect what he will be doing all day, leaves a couple of messages for his colleagues and then signs off.

Before he leaves on his call, Dave needs to look at his own records for this particular customer. He wants to refresh himself on what was discussed the last time he called, information that he records very carefully after every visit in his own personal *call report file*. This is information that only Dave uses, therefore it does not have to be stored on the mainframe: he keeps it on his personal computer at home because that is suitable and is extremely convenient. At the end of each day Dave can update this information before settling down to dinner. If dinner is early, Dave can do it later; there is no pressure, Dave has access to his personal computer whenever he wants and he exploits that fact to make his working day as flexible as possible.

9.00 a.m.

Dave arrives at the customer and meets with the buyer. There is an existing agreement between Dave and the customer whereby the customer is to purchase 2000 beds over a two-year period for the refurbishment of 14 hotels. Dave and the customer go over the refurbishment plans and decide that in two weeks' time it will be necessary to ship another 185 beds to a specific hotel.

Dave leaves the meeting to finalize the details and uses his portable computer to prepare a call-off order for the customer to sign. This uses a standard template which is held on the portable computer, a template that is used by all the sales executives but can be stored on each individual portable computer. Although the information stored within the template is shared by all sales executives, they never change the template themselves, so they all stay in line with each other, all using the same template until it is refreshed at some future date from a master copy held on the mainframe computer.

However, Dave has a problem. The price that his customer pays has not been fixed in advance, and Dave knows that the prices for single beds have recently changed. He needs to check, and does so by linking his portable computer to the telephone system at the customer's office and dialling in to the mainframe where the prices are all recorded. Dave checks, finds that the price has been increased by 3.5 per cent, adjusts the call-off order and then prints it out for the customer to sign.

12.00 noon

Dave has the signed customer order in his hand and returns to his car. He has a number of choices now: he can post the order in to his head office, he can call at head office and deliver the order by hand or he can sign on to the mainframe again to record the order into the order capture system himself. He decides to do the last. By connecting his portable computer into the cellular phone in his car, Dave signs on to the mainframe again, calls up the order capture system and transmits the information he has already recorded in the template he completed with the customer. The order is accepted and Dave signs off: a good day's work done and it is only lunch-time.

12.30 p.m.

Just as Dave parks by his favourite restaurant, his cellular phone rings. Another of his customers is calling to complain about a shipment of five beds that has just been received. The beds are not of the design specified. Although the customer has already been in touch with Dave's company to arrange for the beds to be replaced, it is inconvenient and the customer thought Dave should look into the matter and ensure it does not happen again.

Dave decides to call at the warehouse after lunch and look into the problem personally. At the same time he can discuss the arrangements for the shipment of the 185 beds and ensure that the warehouse manager understands the importance of this order.

2.00 p.m.

Dave arrives at the warehouse and finds the warehouse manager, who is aware of the problem with the five beds and is already looking into the reasons that the wrong design was shipped. He has signed onto the warehouse computer and has the details of the faulty shipment displayed on the screen.

All five beds were delivered from the factory into the warehouse on the same pallet. The pallet number is tracked, and eventually they determine that the pallet contained beds that had been ordered for a different client and had been specially built. These beds are not faulty, but they are unsuitable for the customer to whom they had been sent, and the warehouse manager promises to look into the reasons that the wrong products were supplied.

The warehouse computer contains the details of all the products in the warehouse and accesses data held on the mainframe, which records which products are to be shipped to which customers. The data on the warehouse computer is used by the transport department, the quality control department and the accounting department, all located within the warehouse. The warehouse computer is a departmental computer, containing data used only by the warehouse.

5.00 p.m.

Dave is happy that all the problems have been resolved, and calls his irate customer to explain what had happened, apologizing and assuring him that it will not happen again. The customer seems happy and arranges for Dave to call and see him tomorrow about some other matter. Dave then gets in his car and drives home.

6.30 p.m.

Dave gets home. Dinner is not ready, so he uses his personal computer at home to update his call report file for the day's activities and to dial up the mainframe computer at head office to update his diary to show where he will be tomorrow.

On reflection

During the course of the day Dave used all the computing models that we have discussed so far.

1 *The personal computing model* This is the personal computer that Dave uses at home. It doubles as a personal computer and a terminal to access mainframe services.
2 *The mainframe computing model* Dave used the electronic mail system, the electronic diary system, the pricing system and the order capture system (all mainframe systems) because of the need to be accessible in an efficient way across the whole organization.
3 *The departmental computing model* This was the warehouse computer with its limited scope of data: the data and the set of applications needed to support the warehousing operation. This computer was supplemented by data taken from the mainframe computing model.
4 *The nomadic model* The portable computer that Dave uses when out on calls or in his car fits into this class. When it was connected to the telephone system in the customer's office it was no different to the personal computer he used at home, but it was clearly a form of mobile computing when used from his car.

He has also used three of the classes of computer that we have discussed. The only one Dave did not use was the technical workstation, because Dave, as a salesperson, does not need the specialization that such a machine provides.

The example we have used here is without apology a very traditional one. It contains no great technological challenges; it is very much business as usual as far as many organizations are concerned; but it illustrates reasonably well that to get the job done we have to use all the tools in our tool-kit.

11.9   Scope

In any discussion of computing models, the question of 'scope' needs to be considered carefully. In the example we have just considered, the scope of usage of data, of applications and of computing resource are all illustrated quite clearly. Let us consider this in a more explicit fashion.

The data used by any large organization is a valuable resource. We all know that; it is axiomatic. One of the greatest problems facing many organizations today is the seemingly simple question of where that data should be placed across the organization for maximum benefit. Should the data be centralized on something like a mainframe computer, should it be stored at divisional level on a series of minicomputers, or should it be distributed to the four winds, placed on personal computers or on data servers on local area networks across the organization?

The way to approach such questions is very simple: we need to consider carefully the usage of the data, and when we have done that the placement of the data should be fairly obvious. When we have considered the placement of the data we should be in a position to decide on what classes of computer we need at what geographic points to support that data. Hence we should, by understanding the scope of the data, be in a better position to understand the computing models that we need to put in place to support that scope.

Let us go through a simple example to illustrate the various points. A manager of a store may require data that only she needs to see, that only she needs to use. The data could be records of her expenses, spreadsheets that she uses to organize staffing rotas, or letters that she has written to various local companies that supply services to the store. Whether or not we believe that such data should be considered private, if we assume that it is data that only the manager needs access to then the scope of usage of data is 'personal', being used by only that one person, no-one else ever needing access to it.

Now look at the staffing rota for that store. Everyone in the store needs to see the rota; they need to see when they are working and in what position they are working. This data is needed by everyone in the store but by no-one else: no-one outside the store will ever need access to it. The scope of usage of this data, therefore, is 'store'.

The stock levels for the store are also required by everyone in the store, but they also need to be seen by head office personnel and by various functions in distribution, warehousing, marketing and internal audit. Collectively, these functions cover almost the entire organization, therefore the scope of this data is 'organization'.

So, in this simple example, considering only a small fraction of the total set of data that the organization uses, we have established three different levels of scope:

- personal
- store
- organization.

The natural conclusion of having these three different levels is that wherever we place the data, it has to be accessible at the appropriate level of scope. The personal data has to be accessible by the manager, the store data has to be accessible by everyone in the store and the organization level data has to be accessible by everyone in the organization.

This may intuitively seem obvious, but very often data is placed at points in the organization that are inappropriate. The data may simply not be accessible or may be accessible only through some convoluted process.

Jumping straight to technology, we can see that a possible solution for the above data is for the personal data to be stored on the manager's personal computer, the store data to be stored on a data server in the store to which everyone in the store has access, and the organization data to be stored on a mainframe computer to which everyone in the organization has access.

This would work, but it may not be the best solution. Having decided where the data should 'logically' be placed, there are certain other considerations. There may be reasons why the personal data cannot be stored on the manager's personal computer. Perhaps the organization has a policy of not allowing personal data to be held in this fashion, or perhaps the manager is not happy about having to manage the data. The problems of security, of back-up and recovery of the data, may be such that the manager requires the data to be held in a more 'secure' location, such as a store data server. Formal techniques exist for assessing the impact of moving data away from its *scope-of-access* point and finding the appropriate balance.

We are aware that in the above discussion there is an implied 'hierarchy' in terms of this organization. It seems that we are assuming a centralized mainframe, a local area network in each store that is attached to the mainframe and a number of personal computers attached to the local area network. We are assuming a three-level hierarchy with corresponding scopes of 'organization', 'store' and 'personal'.

Many people would argue that there is a move away from rigid hierarchies such as this, and they would be right. However, the question of scope is still a valid one, perhaps even more valid, as we move to information technology that is evenly spread across the whole organization. If in the above example we remove the mainframe, we still need to place 'organization' data at a point where it is accessible by everyone in the organization. We may decide that some of the data be placed in one place and some in another, but it must be accessible.

11.10   Shared or private?

Any given computer is either shared or not shared. Of the four classes of computer that we have discussed in this chapter, two are normally shared and two are normally not shared.

The personal computer and the technical workstation tend to be single-user computers, providing for personal use and personal productivity. They were designed for this. The minicomputer and the mainframe computer tend to be shared. Again, they were designed for this. But the blurring of technology now has to be taken into account.

All four classes of computer can be implemented in a shared fashion:

- the mainframe as a central shared service across an organization
- the minicomputer as a central shared service in part of a large organization or as the only shared service in a smaller organization
- the technical workstation running a multi-user operating system that provides shared services to a relatively small number of people
- the personal computer, like the technical workstation, running a multi-user operating system that provides shared services to a relatively small number of people.

When looked at this way, the only real difference between the classes is (like the transportation analogy) one of scale, the mainframe computer being capable of efficiently supporting a larger number of people than a personal computer can.

When we consider the scope of data, the data that must be shared must be placed on a computer that was designed to be shared. In addition, the computer must have the power and functionality to enable that sharing to take place efficiently. The larger the number of people who want to share, the larger is the computer that must be used to support them.

11.11   A prophecy

The division of computing into two classes, computers that are personal or private and those that are shared, seems to be a fundamental one. The shared computing devices of the future, be they called mainframes, minicomputers, supercomputers or servers, will compete over basic technologies such as microprocessor design, operating system capabilities and the like, but they will be providing a common function, namely the efficient and effective support of shared services, shared data and shared applications.

The personal computers will also compete over similar basic technologies and they will be providing common functions such as personal productivity, graphical user interface, remote computing and communications.

Perhaps we shall still have personal computers that sit at fixed points on people's desks, but we shall also have personal computers that people take with them when they leave to go home or to call on a client. The difference between these computers may be quite trivial, because the function they will be providing should be the same.

The real test for the future is going to be the degree to which we design a computing infrastructure that recognizes these key differences and exploits them, providing shared services which can be assessed efficiently by all the work-force, regardless of where they are. The move towards globalization of large networks is a small step in this direction.

The development of applications that exploit the difference between shared services and personal computing will be paramount. Today, these applications go under the name of client/server applications, the client being the personal computer and the server being the shared resources the client is using. So the future (at least the immediate future) may see organizations doing two things:

- defining a computing infrastructure (IT architecture) based on the separation of shared services (such as company data and critical applications) and personal computing, which allows people within the organization the freedom to use those services in innovative ways
- developing true client/server systems which exploit the advantages of shared services and personal computing in ways that allow the benefits of both to be realized.

Perhaps

$$\text{future} = \text{sound infrastructure} + \text{client/server}$$

is a good motto to move forward with. The need for this sound infrastructure has been covered from a business point of view in the earlier chapters, especially Chapters 5 and 6. To this infrastructure and the exploitation of computing classes through the use of client/server techniques, perhaps we should add the need for innovation. It is absolutely certain that fortunes are going to be won or lost on the basis of how well people or organizations take advantage of what is, and what is becoming, available.

Already we see insurance companies equipping their insurance assessors with a mobile telephone, facsimile machine, video recorder and computer. Making instant on-the-scene assessments saves everyone time and money and, in the end, greatly increases the service being provided to the customer. We should modify our previous assertion:

$$\textit{successful} \text{ future} = \text{sound infrastructure} + \text{client/server} + \textit{innovation}$$

11.12   Summary

We saw in Chapter 10 that there are several different models of computing, and we have seen in this chapter that these models are supported by specific classes of technologies. If, in our example, Dave had been limited to only one computer model or one class of computer, his day would have been very different and much more frustrating. It is a case of *horses for courses*: we have choice, we need that choice and we are always going to need that choice.

We have to select the right tool for the job in hand, and that means under-standing what tools are available to us, what they were designed for and what their advantages and disadvantages are. It means defining and building the right infrastructure, getting the *shape* of IT correctly aligned with the *shape* of the organization and then exploiting that infrastructure for all it is worth.

12
What does the future hold?

The important IT trends

---

*The telephone may be appropriate to our American cousins, but it is of no value here,
since we have an adequate supply of messenger boys.*

(The Times, 1900)

12.1   Purpose

There is always the danger that one will miss the really important trends, since their
effects are often not evident until they are well established. We have discussed
business trends in Part I; here we try to indicate the most significant IT trends of
the middle and late 1990s. In developing a technical infrastructure to support the
business, it will be important to work with them rather than against them.

We cover three types of trend: those in pure technology, which we describe as
hard; those in the way technology is used, which we describe as *soft*; and those in
IT organization, which will have a profound effect on how the other trends can
be exploited. The trends need to be taken into consideration for at least three
reasons:

- to establish a clear IT strategy in support of the priorities of the business, as a
  basis for all IT organizational and technical decisions
- to produce a plan that will implement the strategy
- to ensure that the structure of the IT operation is capable of delivering the
  required service to the business.

12.2   *Hard technologies*

Traditionally, these are the trends the IT community has followed most closely.
They are, of course, important, but there are dangers in trying to keep absolutely
abreast of them. The rate of change is extremely fast, and may still be increasing.
There is little point in trying to describe them in detail except in a weekly magazine.

We list below the ones we consider most significant, but advise you to be prepared for surprises inside and outside the areas we cover.

1 *Processing units* The rate of growth in the capacity of large processors is slowing. This has led manufacturers to produce machines using multiple processing units (normally called multiprocessors). Midrange and workstation processors are still improving in performance/price at a startling rate (most industry pundits believe performance/price is doubling every 18 months). Given the trend for 'downsizing' (see below), and the immense growth in software needing great processing power, these smaller processors are also being organized into configurations of many systems running in parallel. In fact, there is a strong trend towards what are known as 'massively parallel processors' (MPPs). This involves linking tens of hundreds of relatively small processors to provide enormous power for many types of application.

2 *Processor storage* Computers have always needed internal storage to hold their programs and the data they are currently working on. This technology is also advancing very fast. To support the MPPs, gigabytes (thousands of millions of bytes) of internal storage will be needed, and available. By the way, a *byte* is a unit of computer storage capable of holding (roughly) a character or a numeric digit.

3 *External data storage* Over the years, paper tape and cards gave way to magnetic tape and disk storage. The last two are still developing, but new types of storage device are frequently foretold. Some have sunk without trace, such as *bubble memory*; some have proved to have limited use as external devices, such as *solid state storage*. However, *optical storage* seems to have immense potential for archiving, for multimedia use (see below), and increasingly for almost all uses.

4 *Input and output* Capturing data for computers, and printing or displaying it afterwards, has always been relatively slow and error-prone. The next few years will see speech and handwriting become practical input methods, and there will be a flowering of output media—good-quality speech, animation, and high resolution video, for example. This is the world of *multimedia* which may revolutionize home entertainment, the user-friendliness of systems and areas such as education technology. It is leading to the experience of *virtual reality*, where the user can appear to live in a world created by the computer. It is very hard to predict the business effects, but they seem to be mould-breaking.

5 *Communication between systems* As IT systems become more widespread and are used more and more heavily, and as multimedia is more widely used, there will be a need for more and more network capacity to communicate. This is another area of explosive technological growth, full of strange acronyms. A particular technology known as *cell relay* is expected to be able to send up to three million bytes per second down an ordinary twisted-pair wire of the sort used to connect a telephone. This should be adequate for the immediate future.

6   *Software technology* Supporting the new hardware will demand immense improvements in the software provided by manufacturers. MPPS are efficient in many cases only if the controlling operating system is changed very significantly. Multimedia will require input/output control systems to be immensely more sophisticated. Ideas such as COSE (common open software environment) will help providers of software to work to a common standard and coexist, but significant invention will be needed to ensure that the new hardware technologies are used effectively.

7   *Environmental requirements* There is hope in an area that has been a problem to businesses for decades. The new technologies will not need water-cooling; they may not even need much extra air-conditioning. They will be compact and will need less power. It may be that the vast computer room and *data farm* will become things of the past. IT equipment may make no greater demands on the business or the wider environment than today's terminals, telephones, copiers and faxes.

The overall message is that technological change will continue unabated in most areas. Predicting it far in advance is very hard (see Chapter 7). It is essential to keep in general touch with trends and the new possibilities they present. It is wrong, though, to be obsessive about keeping up. The effective use of fairly conservative technology will almost always be better than living on what the industry often call the *bleeding edge*—the front end of the leading edge. In Chapter 16 we suggest who should keep an eye on technology for you, but we do not recommend forming sizeable departments with large budgets to do so.

12.3   New soft technologies

These are not advances in raw technology. Rather, they take advantage of it to improve IT productivity and to provide the business with an improved service.

Application packages

There is nothing new about packaged applications, but many in the IT industry hope that they will become very different over the next few years. Current packages have served many companies well (although James Martin pointed out that the average customer spends four times as much money on amending the typical package as he or she does on buying it). With the rapid growth of more complex multi-manufacturer installations and the trend towards 'open systems', however, there is a need for traditional packages to change. They have for many years been written to run on one, or a few, major manufacturer's technology platforms. They have mainly been intended to do a specific job (payroll, general ledger, stock control, customer service, etc.). Thus they have limitations when operating in an environment where data sharing and the integration of multiple applications are becoming the norm.

The new trend, hoped for by many and promised by some, is towards a different approach. Ideas such as reusability of code, standard interfaces to data, conformance to open system standards and willing customization to specific environments are becoming very popular with prospective customers.

This is excellent news. Packages have always been a problem to fit into an organization's processing environment, since they normally seem to have been designed without much consideration for what that environment might be. Now the more forward-looking package providers plan to correct this problem.

Unfortunately, it is likely to be some years before most major packages are as flexible and independent of their technical environment as would be ideal. Until then, the prospective user needs a detailed and reliable approach to ensuring that an attractive package will run successfully alongside the current application portfolio, and will be able to share in the benefits of data sharing and application integration. This calls for a clear idea of how applications should be structured, how they should communicate and how they should access data. A formalization of the decisions made could become what might be called an 'application architecture' (this concept is described more fully in Chapter 14). In the ideal world every organization would have an application architecture, but the need for it is not always seen fully. It is therefore often expedient in practice to incorporate into the main IT architecture the elements of an application architecture that influence it. Whichever route is chosen, application packages will not yield maximum benefit unless they are selected and installed within the architectural framework.

Distribution of data

Many organizations distribute their IT data widely. This may be because they have distributed their computers to many locations and hold the data on the machine that processes it. It may be because they consciously believe that data should be close to the user or to its owner. It may be for reasons of efficiency (such as a short access time), or security (not having all the eggs in one basket). Some other organizations try to keep all important data in one place, under firm central IT control. Their motivation is normally to ensure its 'integrity'. By this they mean that the same piece of information (say, a customer name and address) should be the same throughout the organization whoever is using it and whoever has just updated it.

The ability to maintain control of the currency and integrity of data plays a vital part in deciding whether it can safely be distributed. Up to the beginning of the 1990s, distributed data was very hard to control and keep in step. The 'centralizers' had a very strong argument that it was dangerous to replicate data across multiple departments, computer systems and locations. In the past few years, however, techniques for maintaining integrity while data is processed by multiple programs in multiple locations have improved greatly (of course, there is a price to pay in hardware, software and program design). At the same time, the pressure from users and technicians to distribute data has become very strong, often overwhelming. Most IT departments have accepted with different degrees of reluctance that this trend is unstoppable. There may still be a case for keeping some corporate data under central control, and argument rages in the IT industry as to where to draw the line. A total agreement across the industry is most unlikely in the foreseeable future.

Given the degree of change and uncertainty in this area, we believe every organization must be ready to deal with distributed data at some level and must be ready to increase the amount of data that is spread across the organization over time. To ensure that this is done in a controlled way, at a pace that suits the business, an architectural platform and an appropriate set of tools and techniques will be essential.

'Downsizing' and 'rightsizing'

As discussed in previous chapters, for three decades the powerful and expensive 'mainframe' computer ruled the IT industry. The 'mini' and the 'micro' slowly gained ground, and a few years ago people began to realize that they provided the potential for lower-cost computing. User departments in the business began to argue that a 'downsizing' of computers made sense. Motivations included:

- a belief that smaller machines provide more 'bang for the buck' (purely in terms of the number of instructions performed per pound or dollar, this appears to be true)
- a desire to have their own data processed in their own department under their own control
- a belief (usually correct) that a better response time during interactive use from a terminal is possible with local processing and data
- a feeling that the typical central IT department is too remote, too expensive and too slow to respond to business needs.

The traditional IT department has counter-arguments to all these points, but in many organizations the reaction is 'Well, they would say that, wouldn't they?'. To retain some of the advantages of centralized mainframe processing and to avoid losing not only much of their budget but also most of their *raison d'être*, IT departments have often argued for 'rightsizing'. This accepts that modern minis and micros are wonderful as workstations and local servers, but argues that mighty corporate databases are best controlled centrally; that massive 'batch' computing runs and specialized 'number-crunching' applications need the power of a *big-mipper* (a very powerful machine); and that system, network and service management gain from a central focal point. They therefore argue for a mixed environment where every type of machine is used appropriately rather than for the relative anarchy of a widely dispersed and uncoordinated population of small machines.

Where the debate will end, if it ever does, is uncertain. What does seem clear to us is that it is necessary to take a view of where your organization wants to be over the next three to five years and, perhaps more importantly, to be able to move smoothly in the direction that provides best value in the long term. This will be one of the major strategic issues in developing an architecture. We give later our reasons for believing that the best solution can only be achieved within the context of an IT architecture.

The client/server approach

In reading about information technology, you will frequently encounter the term *client/server* (or client server). This describes an approach to computing that was first described under this name in the late 1980s. It is considered by most authorities to be the best approach to designing a modern IT system that uses rightsizing, distributed data and other advanced techniques. As the name implies, one element of the system (typically an intelligent workstation) represents the user, and is a *client*, asking for services. Another element of the system, normally a more powerful workstation, a minicomputer or a large host mainframe computer, is a *server* and provides the services. Such services are often thought of as being access to corporate data or to major applications most easily run on a larger machine. They can, however, include printing facilities, archiving capabilities, access to internal and external networks and any other system-wide services provided by the IT organization. When it is operating in the client/server environment, the client machine typically handles only the user interface and requests for services. However, it can also do personal work using programs that require no outside help.

Since nothing in the IT world is ever simple, the idea of client/server has been extended. One common extension is to have a *three-level* system, where a client (perhaps a workstation) receives services from a server (perhaps a minicomputer) which, in turn, passes on some of the requests to a device with more power or a wider scope (perhaps a mainframe with a large database) and becomes the client of this higher-level server. At the other extreme, some programs working in the same computer may be linked as client and server (this allows for the possibility of moving one of the programs to a different computer in future with minimum disruption).

Many will say that the client/server approach is not really new, and it is true that good designers and programmers used the structure (without naming it) in the more complex systems in the early days of computing (the author's experience in this area goes back to 1969). However, the new world of distributed processing and data does call for some such structured approach, and it may be that the term will gradually fall out of use because it is taken for granted as the best way to design complex distributed systems.

New application developmental approaches

While computer technology has improved in terms of price performance by a factor of at least 100 000 in the past 30 years, application development efficiency has improved by a factor of perhaps 4–10. The reasons for this contrast are not entirely clear but probably rest deep in the human psyche, which still wishes to think of application development as a creative activity, subject to free will and individual inspiration. We believe that the other trends we discuss in this book will compel people to take a more rigorous 'systems engineering' approach to the development of business function. 'Traditional' development techniques are not really capable of achieving high efficiency in the production of workstation-centred client/server systems using distributed data to provide rapid and flexible response to new business requirements. To be fair, modern techniques have not yet been sufficiently integrated or managed to achieve general acceptance based on a strong track record. However, they are likely to be successful in the end.

We are referring here to modern approaches based on CASE (computer-aided systems engineering), OOPS (object-oriented programming system), RPCs (remote procedure calls) and other fashionable and promising modern techniques. They have in common a high degree of technical sophistication, an apparent suitability for emerging architectures such as client/server and open systems, and the need for rigorous training and discipline on the part of the developer. They offer the possibility of an order-of-magnitude improvement in the productivity of system development (which will remain some orders of magnitude behind improvements in raw technology), but they can easily lead to chaos if employed in an unstructured way.

There are two major reasons for this.

1 Despite all the publicity starting in the late 1980s, the techniques have been slow to reach maturity. The theoretical basis is well developed and appears broadly sound. However, CASE requires much more education and reorganization than its early pioneers realized. There are few examples of really large development projects using a complete CASE approach to produce the required function on time and within budget.
2 The new techniques still produce systems that are inefficient in actual 'live' operation.

Recently an IT industry magazine carried an article about OOPS. At one point the enthusiast being interviewed said '. . . there is power to spare. You don't have to wring every last cycle out of the machine. You can afford to do things that require a little extra computer power.'

Our reaction to such statements is 'Hold on to your wallet—somebody is after your money'. The history of IT says that most innovative approaches put extra demands on machine performance, and they usually do so before the technology has advanced enough to support them fully. In this case, the stress on improved processing speed does not mean that the system as a whole (including databases, disks, communications lines, etc.) is fast enough to run an OOPS application without performance problems. One of us recently reviewed a pioneering system in this area and had to suggest reversion, in the medium term, to a simpler system to give the user the response time required.

Our solution to such problems is to perform a proper architectural definition which ensures that the technology chosen is mature, stable and capable of developing business systems that are fit for purpose at an acceptable cost. Research and development into new technologies needs to be carried on and properly piloted outside the mainline operational environment.

Open systems and standards

Many in the IT industry would say that developments in this area are the most important trends in the area of 'soft' technology. The idea of industry standardization seems to have started, like so many things in IT, within the United States Department of Defense. The main motives appear to have been desires that are now taken for granted:

- to be able to select hardware, software and applications from a mixture of hardware and software suppliers—the 'best of breed' performers in their specialist areas
- to be able to change suppliers, if better value could be obtained elsewhere, without an impossibly expensive conversion of hardware, operating system and applications
- to be able to set standards for designers and programmers, which could be used for all jobs, so that there was no painful re-education process as each new system was developed
- in the networking area, to be able to communicate with other IT systems within the organization and outside it in a standard and straightforward fashion across a standardized communications network.

Clearly, the fundamental ideas that were to lead to 'open systems' had already been developed.

The idea was taken up by other parts of the US government, by other governments and by US and international standards bodies. New bodies came into being and both old and new bodies became increasingly influential during the 1970s. Such groups as the International Organization for Standardization, the American National Standards Institute and the European Computer Managers Association have remained powerful and influential. Specific interest groups of manufacturers have got together to define UNIX^{TM} International and the Open Systems Foundation. Special bodies such as POSIX have been set up to govern particular types of standard.

Originally, the standards developed and implemented were seen as an enormous aid to the interoperation of different manufacturers' systems in a single organization, or across cooperating organizations such as armed forces, banks and multinationals. With the increasingly wide use of an operating system (which has since expanded to a total operating environment) called UNIX^{TM}, produced by Bell Labs in the 1960s, people became more ambitious. In the scientific and engineering world UNIX^{TM} became pervasive, and most manufacturers provided hardware and software to run applications. Thus, UNIX^{TM} became a *de facto* standard, and it began to be possible to *port* (transfer unchanged) applications and data between the machines and operating systems of major manufacturers. It therefore seemed that every UNIX^{TM} user could enjoy some of the benefits of a truly open system. The anticipated advantage was not simply interoperation of the systems of different manufacturers: once a program had been written it could run on any system, and the customer could buy the cheapest system on offer from day to day. This led to a vast extension of UNIX^{TM} into all areas of IT applications and the birth of truly *open systems*. No longer did the IT users need to be locked in to the technology of a specific manufacturer. They could now shop around for the best bargain.

At least, that was how people saw it in the late 1980s. Since then it has become evident that the hopes enjoyed, and the claims made, in the first flush of enthusiasm for open systems may have been a little premature. A number of problems are delaying the anticipated millennium.

1   Open systems standards have often defined a subset of the possible facilities of an operating system, a programming language, or a database manager. This has been necessary to ensure that all suppliers can meet the requirements (it is rather like a convoy moving at the speed of the slowest ship). Some manufacturers can, and inevitably do, offer extra facilities but if users install them their system is no longer totally standard.

2   There is a vast heritage of existing systems installed across each industry, each country and the world. They must continue to operate and must often interwork with any new open system. This limits the speed at which users can move until they can afford to replace all existing systems.

3   Many manufacturers believe they will make more money by selling their specific 'proprietary' systems, at least for a few more years. So not all new technologies and ideas are first introduced into the 'open' world. This actually increases the number of heritage systems.

4   UNIX^{TM}, the original open system, is not yet the most efficient and economical way to do all IT jobs. Despite rapid development it is not really the system of choice for large banks and airlines with transaction processing systems for millions of customers, wanting service at a rate of hundreds of transactions per second. Nor can it yet provide the level of performance, integrity and recovery for the very large operational databases needed by such users. Perhaps most

critically, it cannot yet provide an integrated set of *system management* facilities needed to operate and control systems with dozens of computers and thousands of user workstations spread geographically and in need of high performance, high reliability and total data integrity.

5   Many people consider it an oversimplification to assume that UNIX™ is the only choice for an open system environment. This is especially true in networking, where its products are often not as efficient or usable as proprietary ones or the specifications of the standards bodies. For this and other reasons, manufacturers are claiming that their own systems can meet standards requirements and provide all the openness a user really needs.

It will be evident that there is room for decades of argument here, but the trend to open systems and the standards that define them is probably irreversible. An IT department that established an IT architecture without considering the place of open systems and standards in its plans would be making a serious mistake.

12.4   IT organization

There are a lot of things happening in the IT industry that the management team needs to consider when developing an architecture. They are concerned with organization of the IT department, of what its function is taken to be, of how other parties can help it, and of what new techniques and approaches exist to improve efficiency and effectiveness. In total they are probably far more important than having the most up-to-date and even the most economical hard and soft technology. Any architecture you develop will be fundamentally influenced by the decisions made in the areas we discuss below, since it must support those decisions.

We can identify the following current trends likely to influence the IT architecture significantly.

Control of projects by users

More and more organizations have realized that IT staff are not always ideally suited to running projects that may make an enormous difference to the efficiency of the department concerned. As a result, it is becoming increasingly common for an insurance policy department, a military logistical unit, a utility's engineering department, etc. to take management responsibility for IT projects. The IT department acts as its subcontractor, providing specialized skills and facilities. It is thus unequivocally the business project or programme manager who approves application design and technology choices on the basis of cost/benefit trade-offs that he or she is best qualified to make. This encourages a very practical emphasis on value for money and relevance to business needs in the IT architecture. Needless to say, the business person should not try to become a technical guru, although increasingly he or she will tend to have a more sophisticated understanding of the application of technology than has been the case traditionally.

For the project or programme manager, such potentially difficult technological choices are much easier when an IT architecture exists: it mandates some decisions and gives strong clear guidance on the rest.

More use of specialized third parties

The major growth areas in the early 1990s have not been confined to the area of hardware or even of operating systems. There has been a rapid increase in the use of software *packages* to provide an increasing proportion of the business function in many industries, and also to provide sophisticated support services in the areas of application development, efficiency of operation, improvement of performance, recovery from errors, distribution of business data and many other facilities. This trend has bred a range of specialized consultants who aim to advise on how to use the packages effectively. Technical consultancy in the areas of database, data distri-bution, cooperative processing (especially client/server) and system management, and of system design as a practical discipline, appears to be booming. Assistance in the management of challenging technical projects, sometimes to the point where a third party takes responsibility for the delivery of a working system, is increasingly popular (see 'Facilities management' below).

The impact of such trends on the nature of an IT architecture may be profound. It must allow not only for the well-understood environment and practices of its own organization, but also for a variety of outside approaches to almost every aspect of IT activity. We shall discuss some of the detailed issues later. The essen-tial point here is that an increasing proportion of the environment in which the architecture is operating is strongly influenced by external expertise which comes from a variety of sources and may be inconsistent or even contradictory. The IT architecture may have to be more general than would be needed in a strictly inter-nal environment, and it must make possible the joint and cooperative operation of a wide range of different products, tools, techniques and practices.

Local freedom for personal computer use

Ever since the personal computer was invented, IT departments have been trying to control its use. As company-wide applications have grown up, with the PC re-placing the old *dumb terminal* in normal operational applications at both local and company level, it has been natural for the IT department to provide code, control mechanisms, services and help desks. However, the increasingly 'business as usual' nature of IT has meant that many users do not simply make use of applications and services provided by the IT department. They have their own spreadsheets, word processing facilities, graphics packages, personal organizers and so on. It seemed in the 1980s that the IT department might regain control over personal computing because most PCs came to be linked to the machines owned by IT. In a way, though, the IT department has been a victim of the growth of its speciality. Computing is now so pervasive and so useful in so many areas of daily business life that many business people have come to take it for granted. Most are prepared to accept a core of standard hardware and software selected and installed by IT, but they want to be in charge of their own private applications and to get good value from the depleted IT operation.

As a result, the IT department normally has to accept that its architecture can be defined and enforced only for departmental or business-wide activities. There will be a lot of software and additional hardware on individuals' workstations that has been bought from local budgets and is used for personal activities. The architecture must both keep out of these areas and put a barrier around them, to make sure they do not interfere with the stability or integrity of shared business activity.

Facilities management (FM)

In the drive to improve value for money, and to contain the apparently inexorable growth of IT departments, a number of firms and government departments are showing an increasing tendency to employ third parties to manage aspects of their IT operation.

Initially, the most popular approach was to hand over responsibility for managing the computer services operation—what used to be called computer operations or some such name. This meant passing over day-to-day management of current systems and of the environment for testing new systems. The idea was that many Computer Services departments had become 'dumb, fat and happy' over the years, and that a third party with a time-limited contract would feel the pressure of market forces more than an internal group.

From this point it appears a short move to giving a third party responsibility for the maintenance of current applications as well as the hardware and software. However, this approach has not yet become widespread—perhaps because third parties are not eager to take over responsibility for the masses of poorly-documented *spaghetti code* that make up so many current systems.

Almost as popular now, although it stretches the plain meaning of the term 'facilities management', is the trend to pass over development projects, and in extreme cases responsibility for all new development, to third parties. This trend is still in its early stages and is clearly a major step to take, since it passes over to 'strangers' the task of providing the business with its essential tools. Nevertheless, there are examples of successful projects carried out by third parties and there is an increasing tendency to believe that the really big, really critical efforts to provide major integrated systems for 'reengineered' businesses are best done by external specialists, often on a fixed-price contract.

A warning is important here. There is normally no specific obvious point at which the transfer of IT functions passes the point where the external control of a vital activity becomes a threat to the business. However, it seems clear to us that the IT architecture should be controlled by the organization itself, partly because it requires a detailed knowledge of the business environment, structure and resources, and partly so that the FM contractor can be changed without major disruption. It is therefore important, when using facilities management at any level, to keep a skilled and powerful architecture function within the business and to ensure that FM contractors abide by its rules.

Smaller IT departments

As a result partly of the trends described above and partly of the drive for staff cost savings that has been a feature of the early 1990s, the number of people employed directly by IT departments has at last started to fall, or at least not to rise in proportion to the additional work done by IT. One effect of this tendency has been to put much stress on more efficient application development techniques, more automation of system operation and a shallower management pyramid.

This makes the IT architecture even more necessary, since there are now no spare people to support the heterogeneous collection of incompatible historic systems that have typically grown up over time. It also means not only that it is harder to find an ideal team to define and implement it, but also that it must concentrate on labour-saving new technologies, tools and techniques if it is to provide good value to the depleted IT operation.

12.5   Summary

An essential point of this chapter has been to show that the trends in 'soft' technologies and in IT organization, although they are not as startling as those in hardware, will be at least as important in creating the need for an architected approach to the future. They really have no chance of success unless supported by a sound architectural structure. It is therefore very common to include a structured approach to application development in the definition of an overall IT architecture. If this is not done, there will be a need for close and continuous liaison between architectural and development groups to make sure that they have a common architectural perspective.

User power, facilities management, new types of packages, the decision to distribute data, downsizing or rightsizing and new approaches to application development all play a part in changing the traditional paradigms and creating new ones. The new environment will be more complex, will change faster and will call for wider and deeper knowledge. There is said to be an ancient Chinese curse that goes 'May your children live in interesting times'. It appears our parents were so cursed, and we have to find ways of establishing a solid base in a moving world. We shall show in Chapter 16 how, at least in the technical sphere, this can be achieved through an architected approach.

13
Heads I win

Linking business and technology

Democracy is only an experiment in government, and it has the obvious disadvantage of merely counting votes instead of weighing them.

William Inge (1860–1954)

13.1   Purpose

So far in this book we have described developments taking place in a number of areas, some organizational and some technical. Making sense of all these changes is not easy; it is something that you can spend your whole working day doing (as a lot of people do), each and every day, and still never really do more than scratch the surface.

The purpose of this chapter is to offer an approach to focusing on the real issues, the technological developments that are important to the organization as a whole and need to be monitored, analysed and managed. Obviously there is no magic wand here; the approach offered is simple and straightforward, but as we have said on a number of occasions throughout this book, even simple approaches can help in complex situations. As one of our clients (Don Ross) continues to remind us:

'what is needed is a blinding flash of the blatantly obvious'.

In the first two chapters of this book we focused on change: the change in the business world and the fact that organizations are having to restructure in ways that are as fundamental as any we have seen in modern times. At the same time, technology is driving those organizations forward, creating opportunities for the innovative and new market-places for everyone.

In this chapter we look at a simple technique for helping an organization focus on the elements of change that are important to that organization—important because to achieve the goals that the organization has set itself, these changes need to be considered.

135

13.2   The technological maelstrom

We use the word '*maelstrom*' because that is the situation that most of us find ourselves in. In our dealings with organizations over the past few years the stated
objective for so many managers within the IT function has been to try to make
some sense of what is going on, to try to limit somehow the vast number of choices,
to find simplicity where only complexity is visible.

We must focus clearly on what is important *from the point of view of the organization*, not simply the things we are told are important by

- magazines covering technologies
- vendors of technologies
- proponents of various technologies within the organization.

We have to look at technology in terms of what it can do for *us*.

Firstly, let us be clear about what we are trying to achieve here. The changes we
are trying to manage are exciting, fun, futuristic and challenging. There is great
temptation to dive into the technology and immerse ourselves in bits and bytes.
While this may (to some) be enjoyable, it is expensive in terms of time and distract-
ing in terms of the real objective, which has a lot more to do with building the right
infrastructure for the organization to exploit and build on during a period of
dramatic change.

In Chapter 18 we recommend that an IT architecture needs to take a well
thought out position in a number of key areas. But what do we mean by *well
thought out*? We certainly do not mean that people should become immersed in
technology: that will come soon enough. What we do mean is that we need (as an
organization) to determine what we are trying to achieve, and therefore what
potential technologies we should be looking at.

Taking a well thought out position on (for example) client/server means understanding what the organization is trying to achieve and whether or not client/server
technologies will help to achieve this, and then going on to consider which particular client/server technologies may be appropriate. The fact that multimedia (or
image processing, or object-oriented databases or any form of technology) is available does not necessarily mean that it is a good solution to anything that a particular organization is trying to achieve.

13.3   Business imperatives

Every organization has a set of objectives. They may be represented as a statement
of the mission of the organization, they may be the introductory phrases used in
the business plan or they may not even be written down in any concise and agreed
fashion. Below the level of the simple and straightforward objectives (such as *grow
ahead of the competition*) will be a number of things that the organization must do
to achieve that objective.

If the objective is to '*grow ahead of the competition*', then one criterion may be to '*develop products faster than the competition*'. As we look for more detail, we can break this statement down into a number of 'business requirements'. For this example, the business requirements may be something like these:

- improve the information available to market research
- enable earlier prototyping of products
- reduce the cost of developing new products
- enable more products to be bought in.

This way of identifying business requirements is 'top-down'. It starts with the overall objective of the organization and breaks it down in more and more detail until eventually a set of business requirements are identified. Doing this work top-down ensures that the business requirements can be traced back to the business objective: they are irrevocably linked and the relationship can be demonstrated clearly.

Another way of gathering business requirements is to start with the line managers within the organization and ask them what they want. This is a form of 'bottom-up' requirements gathering, and the results are usually very different from those gained by the 'top-down' approach. They will certainly be more 'immediate', more related to today's problems. They will certainly be less easily related to the overall objective of the organization, because they are based on the way in which the organization is currently organized, which may or may not be the best form of organization with which to achieve the overall objective.

13.4   Prioritization

However the business requirements are gathered, there is a need to understand their relative priorities. There is no magic wand that we can wave over the requirements, and it is certainly the case that no matter how the requirements have been gathered, they will contradict each other in certain areas. Understanding the relative priorities is therefore vital, so that those that require information technology solutions can be identified and the relative priorities of providing these solutions can then be assessed.

A relatively simple technique for performing this prioritization is not to try to rank them, but to assess each of them in turn against the remainder. This is illustrated in Table 13.1.

Drawing a matrix of all the high-level business requirements against themselves enables us to think carefully about each single requirement in turn. We can look at requirement #1 and requirement #2 and ask ourselves the question: 'is #1 more important than #2?'.

If we assign numbers to the answer, such as:

+2 much more important
+1 more important

Table 13.1   Prioritizing business requirements

#	Description of requirement	Business requirements				
		#1	#2	#3	#4	#5
1	Improve customer service					
2	Reduce operating costs					
3	Develop new marketing channels					
4	Increase market share					
5	Decrease *time-to-market*					

  0   about the same
−1   less important
−2   much less important

then we can very easily prioritize the complete set of business requirements by adding the 'scores' for each row in the matrix, as in Table 13.2.

What comes out of such a process is not perfect, but if the objective is to understand the relative importance of the various requirements, then it at least delivers an answer through a fairly objective process. If the answer appears to come out wrong, then we can go back to that particular row in the table and think again about the numbers that we associated with it.

Using the data given in Table 13.2, we would assign an initial priority to the five business requirements as follows.

Increase market share   + 3
Improve customer service   + 2
Reduce operating costs   + 2
Decrease *time-to-market*   0
Develop new marketing channels − 5

We do not have to get into an argument about the relative priorities of the complete set of requirements; we can argue instead on the relative priorities of only two requirements at a time, a much more feasible prospect. This technique is not

Table 13.2   Assigning scores to business requirements

#	Description of requirement	Business requirements					Total
		#1	#2	#3	#4	#5	
1	Improve customer service		+ 1	0	− 1	+ 2	+ 2
2	Reduce operating costs	− 1		+ 2	0	+ 1	+ 2
3	Develop new marketing channels	0	− 2		− 1	− 2	− 5
4	Increase market share	+ 1	0	+ 1		+ 1	+ 3
5	Decrease *time-to-market*	− 2	− 1	+ 2	− 1		0

unique, it is not perfect; but it does give us a first-pass view of priorities from which we can begin to understand the way in which our limited resources should be employed.

We can adapt the technique by considering groups of business requirements. It may make sense to consider such groups rather than individual requirements, because we instinctively recognize that only the group makes sense. It may well be the case that a group of business requirements would 'have' to be worked on together in order to build an effective solution.

13.5   Levers and dials

One potential problem in getting people to assign numbers in the way described is that many people find it very difficult to quantify something that is inherently *unquantifiable*. This is why we assign numbers to phrases such as '*much more important*' and '*much less important*'. But sometimes this is not enough: we need to go further in terms of helping people make the best decisions that they can. This is where another simple but powerful technique comes in useful, the concept of *levers and dials*.

In summary, this technique explores the relationship between any pair of business requirements in more detail by providing a better framework for understanding the impact of one requirement on the other. Take for example, the business requirement:

   develop new marketing channels.

Imagine a lever associated with this requirement. Pushing the lever forwards is positive; it means that we actually develop new marketing channels. The further forward we push the lever, the more new marketing channels we develop. Pulling the lever backwards is associated with not developing new marketing channels: pulling it backwards actually decreases the number of marketing channels. The lever then can be imagined as having the words 'marketing channels' written on it: pushing it forwards gives us more, pulling it back gives us fewer.

That is the lever; the dial is the result of the movement in the lever. In the example of the marketing channels, when we push the lever forwards, what happens to the other business requirements? A dial usually signifies a measurement of some kind, and in our case it signifies a qualitative measurement of what happens when we move the lever in one direction or the other. Consider the example given in Table 13.3.

Such a simple technique can give a little more insight into the cause and affect of the various alternatives that are being considered. In the example given in Table 13.3, the introduction of more marketing channels is going to be in conflict with the desire to improve customer service. This does not mean that both cannot be done, but it does illustrate that care has to be taken with the way in which these are implemented, and that in turn gives a clearer view of the relative priorities of each. This

Table 13.3   Levers and dials

Marketing channels	Improve customer service	Reduce operating costs	Increase market share	Decrease *time-to-market*
	Will be harder to manage when handled by many different channels	Operating costs will probably increase in line with the number of channels	Market share will potentially be increased	Will probably have very little impact
	Can provide better support via a smaller number of channels	Will help by allowing us to concentrate on efficiency through few channels	Will have to grow organically through the existing channels	Will probably have very little impact

is not a book about management consultancy, an area rich with such techniques, but we have seen used and used this technique with great effect.

13.6   Mapping business and technology

Having got a set of business requirements and having assigned a relative priority to each of them, we can begin to look at the technologies we may need as we look for solutions. Again, this can be a difficult task and it may well be made slightly easier if we continue the use of the simple matrix that we used above. If we list the business requirements in priority order down the left-hand side of the matrix, then we can add columns, each column representing some form of technology.

Again, as with the prioritization process, it makes sense to assign some numeric values to the matrix. This time, the values could be as follows:

+2 this technology is absolutely vital
+1 this technology is important
 0 this technology may or may not be useful.

Having assigned the numbers, again limiting the arguments to a case-by-case argument instead of an industry-wide technological battle, simply adding the numbers in the various columns and rows in Table 13.4 gives us a reasonably clear view of the relative importance of the various technologies. With reference to Table 13.4, we can usefully debate the following topics.

1   The priority based on the total scores per column:
    (a) mobile computing
    (b) open systems
    (c) client/server
    (d) object-oriented

Table 13.4 Mapping business and technology

Prioritized business	Information technologies						
	Object-oriented	Client/server	Open systems	Image processing	Mobile computing	Multimedia	Total
Improve customer service	1	2	0	1	1	2	7
Reduce operating costs	0	0	1	0	2	0	3
Develop new channels	0	1	2	0	2	1	6
Increase market share	0	0	1	0	1	0	2
Decrease *time-to-market*	2	1	1	0	1	0	5
Total	3	4	5	1	7	3	

   (e) multimedia

   (f) image processing.

2 The apparent *density of technology* based on the total scores per row, with the conclusion that any project aimed at improving customer service is going to require a great deal more new technology (and therefore, time, risk, cost, skills, etc.) than, for example, a project aimed at increasing market share.

Using even this simple technique helps to avoid many hours of fruitless, sterile argument. It enables people to concentrate a little more objectively on a larger number of simpler decisions. It may also sometimes produce a number of surprises. Perhaps client/server is seen as far more important than previously; perhaps an electronic mail system is seen as far less important than previously.

13.7   Summary

The two simple mapping techniques described in this chapter provide four clear advantages.

1 They at least provide *a process*. In some organizations that we have seen over the years, the process of prioritization and the process of determining which technologies to focus on have been very subjective. As operating plans are drawn up each year, the battle begins anew. Not only do the more powerful people in the organization have a more significant say in what happens, but also very often the argument is about detailed solutions rather than the impor-tant business requirements for the whole organization. Unfortunately, it is still easier to argue over the solution than it is to argue over the requirements and the process for providing the solution.

2 The process that we have outlined reduces very complex decision-making to a set of smaller and easier decisions. It is easier to argue over the relative priority

of two business requirements than it is to try to solve all the priority questions in one go.

3   Whatever the result, whatever the priority of business requirements identified and whatever the relative importance assigned to specific technologies, the result is demonstrable. It can be clearly shown how these decisions have been arrived at. Those that disagree with the outcome have to find fault with the simple decisions that have been taken or the process that has been followed. Simply disagreeing with the result is no longer acceptable.

4   The result of the decisions that have been taken can (and should) be documented. When it is documented it can be looked at again. We should not have to go back to square one when next year's operating plan is being produced. We have a clear base from which we can start. We can ask ourselves whether the business requirements have changed and, if they have, we can change them in our plan. We can ask ourselves whether any of the existing technologies have changed and if they have, we can change our assessment of their value accordingly.

We can also ask ourselves whether any new technologies have come along that may be useful, or whether any existing technologies are not living up to their expectations, and alter our matrices accordingly. The important things about a process, no matter how simple it appears, is that it can be modified in the light of experience and it can be repeated as often as necessary.

Part 3
The IT architecture

Now here you see, it takes all the running you can do to keep in the same place. If you want to get somewhere else, you must run at least twice as fast as that.

(Lewis Carroll, *Through the Looking Glass*)

We have shown in the first two parts that business, technology and the use of technology are changing fast. Just running faster to keep up is not really going to work. You need to establish a firm base from which you can advance at a sensible pace, governed by the needs of the business rather than the latest technological fashion or the belief that any combination of exciting technical advances will work together for you. This section of the book provides you with some understanding of the basic system concepts you need to form your approach to the future of IT. We then provide advice, based on some years of practical experience, on how you can build an IT architecture, how you can make sure it is used and controlled, and how you can evaluate whether what you have is right for your business.

All the work done feeds into the IT architecture which, in turn, feeds into the individual business applications and services, making sure that they are compatible enough to work together and share important data.

This is the practical part of the book. It recognizes that there is no magic bullet that will shoot down all the challenges in your path, but it tries to provide a set of principles, methods and processes that you can use to pick your way through the unfamiliar country we are all entering.

14
The bones of language
Concepts of architecture

Concentrate first on the scales. We'll get to some music later, if all goes well.

(Mr I. D. Williams, at an early piano lesson for one of the authors)

14.1 Purpose

We have covered a lot of background on both business and technology issues. We have argued that a proper approach to information technology is essential for business success in today's fast-moving and competitive world. The rest of the book lays out such an approach. The approach will lead us to explore a number of differing concepts. In this chapter, we start gently by describing some of those ideas and our approach in a general way.

14.2 Need for architecture

Most organizations are headed towards decentralization of power, creation of smaller business units and so on. At the same time they want to be more responsive to their customers' wishes, and to be able to compete on cost. Anarchy is not the best way of achieving this. We argued in the section on business directions that if the new organizations are to be as responsive, flexible and cost-effective as they need to be, then there must be a coherent IT infrastructure supporting them.

Many information technology specialists will agree with this view. Most business people seem to. That sounds like a good basis for a dialogue. Unfortunately, it usually fails soon afterwards, as the two parties sink into a Babel-like discussion full of fevered acronym poetry on the one hand, and complex business-speak on the other. Each party misses the other in the dark. To make matters worse, the business person detects real passion in the IT person as the latter displays what appears an almost Messianic fervour as to the life-giving properties of the XYZ or ABC system, and notes an equally fervent IT person in the opposite corner of the room who seems to believe that the only route to salvation is the ZYX product. A battle of the Titans is often in evidence, and the business person cannot tell who is right or wrong. Victory often seems to go to the one that can shout the longest, and there seems no simple basis for the outsider to understand the ritual of the prize fight. The business person's hopes of a common and shared IT infrastructure seem endlessly dashed by this process. It is not surprising that so many of them have lost faith in IT altogether—they often think it is an impenetrable and unmanageable area, and they avoid it (and sometimes avoid spending money on it). But, as we have seen, this puts the organization at a competitive disadvantage. There has to be a better way.

In our experience, there is such a way. The secret is to find a common language through which both the business people and the IT people can find a common understanding of what is needed of IT, and what shape it should take. Remember team building. Remember shared vision. They are both essential to the success of quality, or of business process reengineering, or of federal success. That means they are also prerequisites to competitive survival. The common language is based on an architectural approach. We shall make the words more precise in a moment. For the moment, let us remind ourselves of the way in which buildings get built. The last thing you do if you want a new house is to get into a heated debate between two jobbing builders on the relevant merits of five or six inch, yellow or red, facing or internal bricks. You contact an architect who designs the building for you in a way that relates to your requirements, in a way you understand, and which also (amazingly) will be buildable by one of the jobbing builders whom we saw as so passionately involved in the merits of differing materials. Architects will also, of course, display immense cleverness, talking to you in terms of your needs and to the builders in terms of bricks and cement. They will enable the project to carry through, and their work—the architecture—will provide the fundamentals of the structure and all the work that has to be done. In our experience of dealing with many client organizations, all over the world, this approach is also the right one for information technology. The message should be *'let us talk together about what we must build, and not yet about how we shall do it'*. Of course, just as with a building, our architect had better make sure that the plans can be built. At times he or she may advise us that this or that cannot be met without some restrictions or compromises that the technology (the building bricks) force on us. But the discussion remains overwhelmingly architectural until such time as the whole structure is defined and understood. Then the detailed choice of materials and so on can take place. But now it is in the context of an overall plan.

14.3   Definitions

Even architects have their own jargon. It is nothing too elaborate, but it needs to be shared. Architecture, as a design activity, attaches some nuances to particular everyday words. Now is the time to cover this ground, in preparation for the later chapters.

We shall also use architecture in connection with information technology, and because of that the word 'system' will slip in from time to time in the book. So let us start there and work our way round to design and architecture. Here are our four key definitions (the good news is that there are *only* four).

1   *System* A collection of parts (*components*) working together to satisfy a common purpose (*requirement*).
2   *Design* (*noun*) A blueprint for a system from which it could be constructed.
3   *Architecture* A visual sketch of the design for a system demonstrating its key features, omitting all points of detail not needed for that end, and such that the overall design is demonstrably 'fit for purpose'. (It follows that an architecture is intrinsically subjective. We would expect this of a building, but some IT people find it hard to swallow in their sphere. We shall imply the following statement several times in this chapter, so we make it here explicitly for the record: *there is no objective truth in the choice of IT systems.*)
4   *Design* (*verb*) The intellectual activity by which designs are produced for systems. Architecture is at the core of the design activity, which is therefore an intrinsically creative process, because architecture is inherently subjective.

So, the definitions are out of the way. Let us now explore some of their implications.

14.4   The design activity

There are those who would like to see the design of information technology systems as a science. Some people find this view comforting. They are late disciples of F. W. Taylor. If only we could find the one true process for modelling this facet of IT, all would be easy, safe and free of personal responsibility. Unfortunately, that is not the way it goes. Design is *not* a scientific/mechanical process that takes requirements and converts them into a design.

Let us look at the evidence for this view. Think about requirements—those worrying things that IT people spend so much time looking for. The requirements are out there, owned by the IT folks' customers (often known in IT jargon as 'users'). In the past, IT people have been bold enough to approach users and ask them to yield up their requirements. The users are often a little taken aback by the request. They will usually come up with something, and if the IT people are skilled at their job, after a lot of questions a requirements statement will be written. The trouble is that each user is different. So when the IT people go around 15 of them, they get 15 different answers: rather like giving your children free choice at a soda bar. So, the IT people do the best they can, they make a judgement as to the best fit to all their users' needs, and use that to build the system. Even then, as they get into the real mire of technical detail, they will find (large numbers of) little things about which the requirements statement is silent. They will make their own subjective judgements about how to best deal with them, and then pass on. Since many of the qualities of an IT systems are not quantifiable, the prospect for comparing even the fit-to-purpose requirements of two designs in some scientific way is slim. There is no Holy Grail of product design. It is all ultimately a matter of taste and personal judgement. Even if a particular way of making a product becomes standardized in its design, sooner or later someone will come along and attempt to gain a competitive lead by altering the design. The process is inherently fluid and unpredictable.

If the design process is subjective, then we must accept that at some point its progress will depend on some mental approach other than logic. The human mind is capable of great creative insights not accessible via logic. The mathematician Gödel showed that in any system of logic there are truths that cannot be proved by a finite sequence of logical steps. The implications for the architect or the IT person are clear—he or she cannot shed responsibility for insight and decisions. Experienced designers know this only too well. The moment at which their insight and judgement becomes evident, often at the early architectural stage, is sometimes known as the *moment of magic*. The ability to practise such magic is a learnable skill, but it takes time and experience. We hope this book will help.

14.5   Illustration

In later chapters we shall describe the way in which an architecture is produced, and in doing that we will need to show examples. To prepare the way for that work, and to make our definitions a little clearer, we offer a very high-level version of an IT architecture for some imaginary company.

Figure 14.1 shows the basic shape of the company's information technology. It is very simple, and would be full of meaning to those who had produced it, i.e. it is subjective. It would be backed by much textual explanation. We shall develop this example further in later chapters.

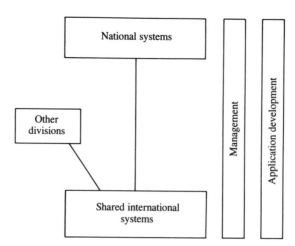

Figure 14.1.   A very high-level technical architecture for an imaginary company.

14.6   The importance of architecture

If the designer's task is subjective, then the last thing he or she wants is to be over-whelmed by a sea of complexity. In the IT world, unfortunately, this threat is always present. The requirements themselves, however well presented they may be, are often very detailed and voluminous. At the other end of the job, real IT systems often require a bewildering array of decisions across many areas in parallel. At both ends, the designer is assaulted by those who delight in this detail and confu-sion (see Fig. 14.2):

- the IT professional who insists on the value of long descriptions of business pro-cesses or information flows
- the user who has a very detailed account to give of the way in which informa-tion must be presented on his or her terminal
- the IT guru who uses 15 acronyms to the second, and rarely has any reliable simplification to offer
- the business person who insists on expressing everything in imprecise or highly political terms, and sees a detailed statement as some sort of failure.

Some people react to the challenge by dealing only with one end or the other: either with the requirements alone, taking the view that the 'componentry' is 'only detail—IT is a commodity and should be able to cope'; or with the components, with the view that 'the users never did know what they want'. Both approaches are understandable, since for the designer faced with this situation for the first time, it is difficult to see how the two seething masses of detail can ever be reconciled into a working system.

The only way of serving the real need here—to provide an IT infrastructure that will serve the organization while at the same time enabling it to take future

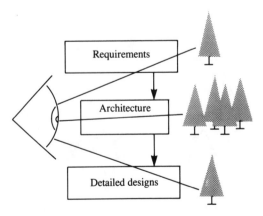

Seeing the forest rather than the trees.

Figure 14.2.   The importance of architecture.

technology opportunities—is to build a bridge between the two. This is what IT architectures represent. They provide the designer with the ability to deal with a far lower amount of information, clearly related both to requirements and to the potential that technology will offer. An architectural approach is the way to climb above the individual trees and start looking at the shape of the forest they grow in.

14.7   The importance of viewpoint

In physics the principle of complementarity states that multiple and mutually exclusive views of a system are needed to understand it fully. As it is with electrons, so it is with IT architectures. (Just for the record, one of the authors is both a physicist and an IT architect. He hopes that any readers with a similar background will forgive his paraphrase of Niels Bohr's principle.)

There is only one system, one company or organization that the IT architecture will address, but the way in which you see it depends on where you stand. To get a complete view (complementarity) you need to put together several different viewpoints (Fig. 14.3). So, for IT infrastructures we need views from the data, applications, process, organization, business and technology viewpoints. Each of these is a map of the organization—the system—we are dealing with. Of course, which particular set of viewpoints are of most importance to an architect will depend on what the objective is. We shall discuss these different architectures again in the following chapters.

If we return for the moment to our definition of architecture, we can see that we were careful to point out its subjectivity. That was partly because of the possibility of different viewpoints (Table 14.1). In fact, each of the viewpoints leads to a

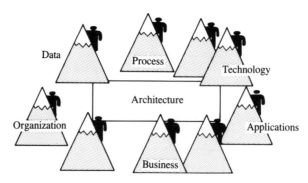

Different perspectives give differing insights into the system that is being designed. A full view of the system can only be obtained from amalgamating several of these viewpoints.

Figure 14.3.   The importance of viewpoint.

Table 14.1   Differing architectural viewpoints

Data architecture	A description of the data that the business uses in its operation. The architecture will identify all the key groups of data, and how they are interrelated. A good data architecture will normally move beyond descriptions of data in purely abstract terms to defined policies on such practical matters as the ownership of data, responsibilities for its maintenance, and the rules that govern its placement in the differing types of computer systems in the organization.
Applications architecture	A description of the applications of information technology in the business, and the way in which they are related to one another. A good applications architecture would normally also cover such issues as the standard interfaces between applications, the rules governing placement of application programmes onto differing types of computers at differing locations, and methods by which the applications will be produced.
Information technology architecture	A single definition of the technology platforms that will be used to implement the business's IT applications. A good information technology architecture will also go much further, and cover the management of computer systems, migration plans, and some aspects of the data and applications architectures.

These are some of the most important architectures we shall be dealing with in this book. Our prime focus throughout will be the information technology architecture.

different architecture, which conforms quite nicely to our definition (a visual sketch demonstrating key features and demonstrably fit for purpose).

14.8   Architectures and IT or IS strategies

In this book, our main concern will be the information technology architecture, although we will sometimes need to mention the others. In fact, most of the approach we will describe can be applied to determining the other architectures as well.

A common source of confusion is the relationship between the architectures and what are sometimes known as IS or IT strategies. It is worth trying to clarify our terms in this area (Table 14.2).

Of course, these elements are tightly interrelated. As we have argued earlier, IT is key to business success in today's world. It follows that all the elements may well help to form, as well as be formed by, the business plan, In fact, we can envisage a series of feedback loops in which all the different elements influence each other (see Fig. 14.4). The following chapters describe a practical way forward in establishing the architectural elements in this loop. If a good job is done in building them, the business person sees more and more value from IT and so wants to give it more of his or her time. That will usually enhance the quality of the architecture, and a virtuous cycle can be established.

14.9   The role of science in architectural design

It would be wasteful not to use the full power of our minds when engaged in design. Our creative faculties cannot be avoided. There are also pieces of work that benefit from the use of logical analysis. For example, it would be foolish if the skilled architect did not check that the performance requirements of a group of users were

Table 14.2   The elements of planning in a business and IT

Business plan	The company's strategy and tactical plans by which it intends to meet its objectives. It will usually be expressed in terms that the main board directors will understand.
IS strategy	The company's strategy for using the processing, storage, retrieval and communication of information in support of the business plan. It will usually be expressed in terms that the main board directors can understand, for example:

- enable the salesman to send in his call reports from his hotel room
- enable us to access all the hotel chain's booking information at the booking clerk's desk
- stop errors in the production process by better communication of information between the design office and the plant.

IT strategy	The company's plans for implementing information technology in support of the IS strategy. They will be expressed in terms understandable to the IT director and his or her senior managers (apart from some key components—the architectures—which must also be understandable by the business people). So, for each of the examples shown under IS strategy in turn:

- provide the sales person with a colour laptop computer, and provide a mainframe application for him or her to feed with call reports
- implement EDI and ViewData links between our local area networks and the hotel chain's midrange computers
- implement compatible electronic mail systems in both the design office and the plant, and also allow direct access from the plant to the database of engineering drawings.

Architectures	The set of architectures (as discussed earlier) that are required to support the IT strategy. These are important pieces of work, defining the corporate infrastructure that must underlie the whole of the IT and IS strategies. It is therefore important that they can be expressed in a way that is meaningful to the business person, as well as having content for the IT professional.

Table 14.2 describes the key planning elements in business and IT. These are all interrelated. There is clearly a top-down sense in which the business plans will shape the other elements. However, if the IT and IS strategies are well produced, they contribute to shaping the business strategy. Architecture is a key vehicle for enabling the dialogue through which that contribution can be made.

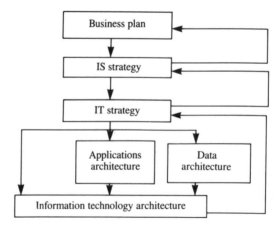

Figure 14.4.   The interrelationships of architectures and business plans.

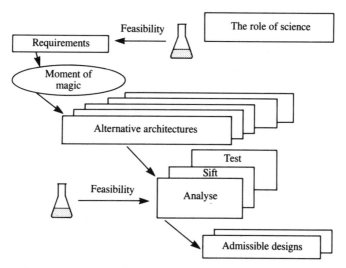

Figure 14.5. The points in the design process where logical analysis or science is useful.

achievable. Equally, it would be wise to use some systematic approach and criteria in analysing or testing alternative designs. The art here is to know when to be creative and subjective and when to be logical and scientific. The designer's job is a difficult one, and needs a wise and experienced head (Fig. 14.5).

14.10 The need for method

A methodical approach (which must incorporate both creative and logical processes at the appropriate times) is needed at these points (see Fig. 14.6):

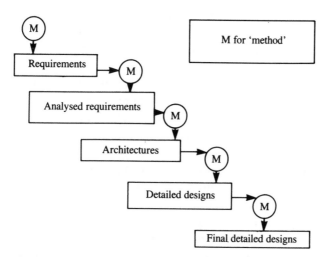

Figure 14.6. The use of method in architectural work.

- in gathering requirements
- in analysing requirements
- in designing the architecture(s)
- in detailing the architecture
- in producing the final detailed design
- in transferring the detailed design into an implementation project or activity.

In Chapter 17 we will describe how the generic steps outlined here can be turned into a process for producing architectures. For now, we shall leave it at that.

14.11   Who needs architecture anyway?

There is a view that the advance of technology will make IT infrastructure planning unnecessary. The argument goes that the rapid emergence of open systems standards will mean the whole IT infrastructure is easy to construct and reconstruct, rather like a set of children's building blocks. Although this may one day be true, that day is still some way off.

We discussed the issues in Part 2. For now, let us just amuse ourselves with a parable, constructed to illustrate the point.

Once upon a time, there were three little orphaned pigs. They were on their way to make their mark on the world. Uppermost in their thoughts was a nice place to live, a trough of swill and a land free of wolves. As they went down the road, they came upon a group of piglets standing around a huge pile of varied building materials. The first of our travelling pigs said 'Just look at this stuff. You could build anything from it. I'm staying right here.' So off he trotted, and was soon joined with the crowd in pulling out one brick or joist after another—debating its colour, strength or shape with his neighbours. Our other two travellers watched the somewhat anarchic scene for a few minutes, and then passed on. After a while, they came to another crowd of piglets, who were standing by a neatly ordered collection of building bricks, all sorted into piles by type and shape. The piglets were walking around the piles measuring the bricks with a template marked 'standard', and would occasionally frown and throw one aside. Our second traveller said 'Oh, this is much more civilized. I'm going to stay and build a house right here!' Off she trotted, and after some instruction was measuring the bricks with the rest of them. Our last pig went on his way, and after a while came to a most peculiar sight. There, sitting on the ground were a group of very wise piglets wearing glasses and suits. In front of them were some huge piles of paper covered in drawings. Now and then one of the wise ones would write out what looked like a shopping list, and rush off with it down the road. Our last remaining wanderer despaired of any prospect of shelter here, until he noticed a wise pig returning with piles of bricks from the last two stopping places. She emptied them on the floor, referred to her papers, and started to build straight and true. Our traveller smiled, and sharpened a pencil.

Enter a mean and hungry wolf. Up he trots to the place where we last saw our first traveller. There he finds an oddly shaped, half-built wall. Beneath the wall he finds our little friend still in deep and heated debate about his preference for seven-inch rather than six-inch bricks. The wolf eats well. After some time spent tripping over scattered bricks, he finds the road once more and soon arrives at the second site. There he finds a collection of identical houses. Unfortunately, they do not yet have a roof, or window glass. He rapidly eats all assembled piglets—who objected because he was not of the approved species. Now bloated, he arrives finally at the third building site. Once again, a collection of buildings greets him. They are all different, and some are of a very odd shape. Recognizing some of the brickwork as being of the same materials as at the last site, he runs at it, sure that he will again find no roof to impede his plans.

Unfortunately, he trips over a boulder labelled 'wolf destruction process, phase 1', and falls straight into a pit full of pointed sticks. He eats no more.

Moral: Real systems don't yet come in neatly standardized packs.

14.12   Summary

In Part 1 we argued that any organization, including the new federated structures, needs a shared infrastructure if it is to be responsive and flexible in dealing with rapid change. Information technology is an important part of that shared infrastructure—particularly as companies become more and more dependent on their information flows and their knowledge base.

In Part 2 we saw that the speed of change and the diversity associated with information technology itself makes any form of IT planning a formidable challenge. Yet we need to build a shared IT infrastructure! In this chapter we have argued the case for a particular approach to this difficult and important task. It is based on the concepts of *architecture* and *design*. We spent some time examining the meaning of these words, and the nature of the work they involve. We saw that architectures are a way of understanding a problem and its solution without getting trapped in a morass of business or technical detail. It follows that they are an important means of communication, a kind of language bridging the gap between business and IT.

Architectures try to capture and deal with the essence of a situation, avoiding minutiae. However, since the devil is usually to be found in the detail, a good architecture is one from which something can be built. That thought is an important part of the approach we shall describe in the remainder of the book. In other words, we shall describe a practical approach.

15
A means to an end

Secondary benefits

The noblest motive is the public good

(Sir Richard Steele, 1672–1729)

15.1   Purpose

There are many reasons why an IT architecture is useful. Chapter 14 discussed some of these reasons, and in this chapter we want to capture some of the less obvious uses that we have come across. It is often the case that the desire to build an IT architecture comes not from the desire to help understand the way in which the business and IT should be integrated, but from far less visible motives.

It is worth focusing on these, because although we perhaps see them as of secondary importance, they will certainly be seen by others to be of real and fundamental importance. In such situations we can use such views to add to the list of the perceived benefits of producing the IT architecture.

15.2   The current focus

Throughout the history of IT, covering as it does a period of around 30 to 40 years, there has never been a time when we have seen more fundamental change than we do now. A time where almost every aspect of IT is being challenged, where nothing that existed in the past seems to be of any importance or relevance, where the IT of the future is positioned to change not just the way we work, but the way we live.

Nearly all the IT organizations that we work with now have a single agenda, a single focus. It is expressed in many ways, but under the surface it is the same—understanding the basic IT infrastructure that they should be using in order to position themselves to take advantage of the advances in technology and those in management style and corporate structure. What they are looking for is what we believe an IT architecture is, or at least what an IT architecture should be.

The reasons for placing this at the top of the agenda are many and varied. Often it is the recognition that the currently used infrastructure is the one which, according to the computer press, is out of favour. Often it is the belief that the costs of IT outweigh the benefits. Increasingly, it is simply the fact that the current infrastructure is seen to be inflexible, preventing the organization from doing the things that it believes it needs to do in order to survive.

Whatever the reason, however it is expressed, there is a growing desire to re-architect IT, to go back to first principles and define:

- what technologies should be employed
- how they should be employed
- how they should be managed
- exactly how IT itself should be organized.

During most of the past 20 years we held an almost immutable belief in certain forms of IT solution, all of which have been thrown in the air over the past few years. It should come as no surprise, therefore, that the key issue we are now facing is the re-establishment of the basic architecture for IT in our own organizations.

During the 1970s and early 1980s, the vast bulk of data processing was being performed in an environment that consisted of one or more mainframe processors driving hundreds or thousands of terminals. This technology changed, but only on the surface and in a predictable manner. Mainframe processors became faster, the operating systems became smarter and the data storage became more efficient; but nothing *really* changed for many years. The basic *shape* of IT within an organization stayed the same and looked like staying the same for the foreseeable future.

IT planning during this period concentrated on prioritizing the development of new applications and keeping the metrics associated with the overall IT system in control; metrics such as costs, manpower, processing power, data storage, and communications bandwidth.

But the shape of IT has now changed, and IT planning must be changed accordingly. Just as technology has become more pervasive and more complex, the IT planning process must be prepared to move outside the glasshouse and tackle the complexity head on. In our experience, the following list reflects the sorts of questions being asked by many organizations as they try to do this.

- What is the overall shape of IT? How much of IT should be centralized? How much of IT should be distributed?
- If we distribute IT in terms of hardware, applications or data, should we centrally control it, and if so, how?
- How do we minimize the technology platforms that we use?
- What rules do we need to put in place to ensure all parts of the organization are doing the right things with IT?
- What technology do we need to build ourselves?

- What are our competitors doing?
- What skills should we be building or hiring?
- Should we be going '*open*'?
- We want ubiquity in terms of applications, so what strategy should we adopt?

The above are simply examples, but they illustrate the variety of the questions that have to be faced and answered by almost every organization. Although an IT architecture is difficult to define, it is very easy to identify one common theme that runs across the IT architecture for any organization, and that common theme is *change*. The IT architecture is:

- a catalyst for change
- a vehicle for making changes
- a means of identifying what changes are needed
- a way of managing change.

These are important aspects and often, in isolation, they represent the hidden (but noble) agenda behind the decision to create the IT architecture.

15.3   Catalyst for change

The creation of an IT architecture is a way of catalysing change, of making change happen. Many organizations, especially those in retail markets where competition is especially fierce and profit levels are low, have maintained a very close financial control over IT. Staff become accustomed to this force and respond in part by closing their minds to opportunities to increase revenue, outsmart the competition or capture new customers by providing new services. Instead, the focus is totally on cost reduction, IT being seen as a cost item, no more or less important than the cost of transportation or the cost of real estate.

As times goes on, the staff rise through the management line and become the managers themselves, still with an outlook that can most kindly be described as 'parsimonious'.

Now, in the 1990s, there is a recognition that the IT mainstay of such organizations, the mainframe computer, may no longer be the lowest cost solution, that smaller processors such as workstations, departmental minicomputers or personal computers may well provide an environment that, overall, is cheaper for some functions. The real problem for organizations such as these is that the investment in such technology has been held back in the past: there is now a giant chasm that has to be bridged between the centralized and the decentralized worlds. For some, this chasm may well be seen too late or be judged to be too wide to cross, requiring an investment that is simply too great.

A new manager brought into such an environment needs a catalyst for change; he or she needs to find a relatively quick way of creating an awareness of the opportunities that IT can provide. The creation of an IT architecture is an ideal way of doing this, allowing the manager to charge his or her staff with the responsibility for looking at IT with fresh eyes, by challenging them to look for ways in which technology can be better employed. By doing this, an awareness of not the cost, but the *value* of IT can be created, perhaps loosening the purse strings the required amount.

One organization that we worked with a couple of years ago went through this process reasonably well. A new IT director was appointed from a retail organization that had always understood the value of IT and had exploited it to their advantage for many years.

She initiated the building of an IT architecture, using two key members of staff, one from the 'data centre' and one from 'development'. The result was that these two people very quickly established an IT architecture that was a very fair balance between accepting the benefit of newer technologies and accepting the pragmatic fact that the starting point was not ideal.

The IT architecture built on the strengths of their current investment (centralized operational data, very efficient warehousing systems) and extended it in the areas of personal computers, networking, relational databases, standard workstation software and electronic mail. These were not in themselves revolutionary, but the result was a reasonable amalgamation of the old and the new and was a good base from which further innovation could then take place.

Cost constraint is not a characteristic unique to the retail industry: the above example could have equally well been seen in many other organizations. What is important is that once the process of building an IT architecture has started, once people see that change is not only possible but practical and desirable, then ideas start to flood out, releasing good ideas and new approaches to solving existing and potential business problems.

15.4   Vehicle for change

A lot of senior IT managers suffer from 'vision'. This is a strange malady because the sufferer cannot understand why everyone else has not got it, and no-one else can understand what the sufferer has got!

In effect, this means that the IT architecture exists as a vision: a loosely assembled, probably subjective but almost certainly brilliant view of the future. The holder of the vision cannot implement it in isolation. Producing an IT architecture that enables the vision to be created, to be 'fleshed out', while at the same time forcing others to share it, to be seen as contributing towards it, is often the only way forward.

A large life insurance company had an IT director who had such a vision, and it certainly represented a radical step forward. However, four years later the same IT director still had the same vision, it no longer looked as radical as it had initially and it was absolutely no nearer to being realized.

In this instance, the IT architecture that was created did little to help. Over a three-month period the IT architecture was created, but it leaned very heavily (too heavily) on pragmatism. The participants never really understood the vision, although they understood fully the problems that the vision was trying to overcome.

The resultant IT architecture was a realistic view of what could be done *now*. It reflected currently available products and techniques, through which the vision could never have been properly implemented. Their work was rejected by the IT director and the communication path to get any further simply did not exist. Vision and pragmatism make very unsuitable partners.

There were two failures here. Firstly, the IT director failed in not understanding that the only way of achieving the vision was to take a small number of steps in the right direction. Pragmatic steps, which would get them on the right road and enable them to see the next part of the journey with a little more clarity.

The second failure was on the part of the process for producing the IT architecture. The vision was correct and was vital, and as such should have been thought through in a lot more detail, looking for the fundamentals, the principles on which it would have to be based, if not now, then some time in the future.

Now, four years on, the products on which the vision can be realized are beginning to become available, but they are now available for all life insurance companies. Failing to build the vision into the IT architecture has removed the advantage of having the vision in the first place, the advantage of being one step ahead.

15.5 Means of identifying change

Often an organization knows it has to undergo some significant change in IT. For example, it may be an insurance organization looking at workflow management or image processing, or a retail organization looking at point-of-sale equipment, or a manufacturing organization looking at robotics or computer-aided manufacturing technologies. Difficult decisions have to be made and there is a perceived need to find some objective way of assessing the various options.

To increase the objectivity with which the decisions are made, the organization often looks for a process that will help. The process of constructing an IT architecture fits well, mainly because if it is done properly, it makes rational decisions about IT, based on a rational assessment of the organization and what it is trying to achieve.

An interesting example of this was the approach taken by a relatively large governmental organization. The basic problems here were the differences in approach being taken by different parts of the organization and the historical difficulty in linking investment in information technology to real tangible benefits.

The process of building the IT architecture brought the different parts of the organization together, including the part that held the purse strings, and forced them through a relatively rigorous process. The objective here was not so much the IT architecture itself, more the consensus on which it was based.

15.6   Means of managing change

For many organizations, the IT architecture may exist in part or in full on bits of paper, in several reports, in a few heads, within a few committees or on a few acetate foils. Within this chaos may exist the makings of an excellent IT architecture, but it needs bringing together, planning, managing and implementing.

An IT architecture delivers most benefit when it reflects the needs and directions of an entire organization. To have different parts of the organization assuming different things, forming different opinions and going off in different directions is obviously not a sensible way forward.

Large organizations, however, have a difficult job coordinating efforts in this way. The IT architecture for a large multinational bank may be immensely complex. At the detailed level it may well be *too* complex to manage as a simple entity. At a higher level, though, the IT architecture might well not be too complex; it may be manageable and if so it will provide the framework from which more detailed architectures for specific parts of the organization can be built and coordinated.

Fear of complexity is not a valid reason for starting to build an IT architecture; it is a valid reason for understanding the limits of our organizational ability and ensuring that we do not try to coordinate at a level of detail that provides little or no benefit or, quite simply, cannot be done.

15.7   To balance control and chaos

As an organization develops, it has to achieve a very delicate balance between chaos and restriction: chaos caused by too little control over events and restriction caused by too much. A democratic society itself has the same challenge, trying as it does to allow people the freedom to say and do as they please while at the same time placing restrictions on the extreme behaviour that may prove detrimental to the society as a whole.

Now, as we face some of the most fascinating technological developments, trying to make sense of them in terms of their potential for exploitation, we have to think very carefully about how the essential balance between chaos and restriction can be achieved.

What makes this debate even more vital is the fact that the bulk of the technological change is aimed fairly and squarely at the individual: personal workstations, personal communicators, graphical user interfaces and nomadic computing, all requiring us to consider how our own organization, our own microsociety, will legislate for their use, maximizing the benefit both to the individual and to the organization as a whole.

It is possible for an organization to attempt to legislate very tightly, to control the spread and use of the technology. But this, by definition almost, requires centralized control over what is certainly a distributed technology. This approach did not work very well during the late 1980s with the humble personal computer, and there is absolutely no evidence that it will work in the future.

On the other hand, the organization can delegate the responsibility for the technology that is used, who uses it and for what purpose, to the individuals concerned. Supporters of this approach point out that it is simply a flavour of the concept of empowerment, a natural progression aimed at putting the decision-making further and further from the centre, thereby making organizations *leaner* and *fitter*.

But the truth is that in most situations neither of the above approaches allows for the right technology to be applied in the right circumstances. Where an organization tries to centrally dictate the wrong policy, users will rebel. The policy makers will lose in the end, in the same way that they lost in the battle between the centralized mainframe and the distributed personal computer. In the 1990s and beyond, the users of the technology have the power and are increasingly keen to use it. A centralized policy in the short term will constrain the adoption of new technologies, and in the longer term will be eradicated in favour of a more 'user-centric' decision-making process.

With organizations that decide against a centralized policy, the natural result may be as it was with the personal computer: chaos. Different technologies implemented in different ways. This also leads to a technological impasse, as in a short time the organization has to try to re-establish control.

Think back to the transportation analogy that we used earlier. Do we force users to travel by train even when they do not live anywhere near a railway or just do not like travelling on trains? Or do we allow them all to own and ride their own motorcycles? The train at least gives a degree of control, allowing those in charge to ensure conformity and standards. The motorcycles may give rise to a few exciting moments with a few notable successes and failures, but the control is non-existent.

So perhaps both extreme approaches, centralized policy making and user-centric decision-making, both lead to the same situation, an inability or difficulty in moving forward with technology because the reins were either held too tightly or not held at all.

The IT architecture has to provide a common view of a way forward, balancing both forces to the benefit of individuals and the organization as a whole.

15.8   Summary

In Chapter 14 we saw that architectures for information technology are vital to the success of organizations in today's changing world. They enable the building of the necessary shared infrastructure, the *glue* between the units of organization. They also allow business people and IT professionals to talk together to mutual benefit, allowing the organization to take advantage of technology advances. They have other benefits and uses, and in this chapter we have discussed some of those we find most often among our clients. These represent ways of challenging or benefiting the individual units themselves, as well as the organization as a whole. The examples covered in this chapter are the tip of an iceberg. There are possibly as many objectives for IT architectures as there are organizations trying to build them. Although an IT architecture is not a universal panacea, it is useful and, as the examples showed, useful in ways that are not always immediately obvious.

We have now spent a little while looking at the philosophy and purpose of architectures. We move on to their production and implementation.

16
Designing the future

Producing an architecture

An excellent plumber is infinitely more admirable than an incompetent philosopher.
The society that scorns excellence in plumbing because plumbing is a humble activity,
and tolerates shoddiness in philosophy because philosophy is an exalted activity will
have neither good plumbing nor good philosophy. Neither its pipes not its theories will
hold water.

(John W. Gardner)

16.1   Purpose

A worthwhile IT architecture needs both good philosophy and good plumbing.
This chapter covers preparing the ground for an architecture, taking account of the
IT trends discussed earlier, selecting a team to produce the architecture and, finally
and in more detail, defining the architecture and planning its implementation.

16.2   Preparing the ground

It will be necessary to put together a skilled multidisciplinary team to create the IT
architecture. This is not a job that can be done by one person, even (perhaps
especially!) if he or she believes that this is possible. Before a formal definition
project starts, however, there is work to be done to establish its scope and context.
Some members of the eventual architecture team may play a part, but the issues
here are not the technical topics in which they will be most expert.

Some fundamental questions need to be answered, such as these.

- What does the organization need?
- What are the objectives of the organization?
- How do we use IT trends to our advantage?

What does the organization need?

Since the whole purpose of an IT architecture is to support the present and future needs of the organization, it is sensible to start from the business plan. We shall for the present assume that this exists, although one major clearing bank in the UK has one only because the IT director persuaded the rest of the board that he could not give them an IT architecture unless they produced a business plan. The plan may be in many forms, from ideas in the head of the chief executive to an impressive set of documents supported by wall-sized data and process models. Whatever its form, it needs to contain the following types of information.

- What will the organization be doing differently in the next five to ten years in terms of business areas, product and services? Will it be taking over other companies? Will it be growing organically? Will it be shrinking?
- What will be the shape of the organization within the planning horizon? Will it be more centralized, strongly decentralized, or much as it is today?
- Will large parts of the business be 'reengineered', and how might this affect the way people use the system?
- Where will it be operating geographically, and in what size of unit?
- Who will be the users of the present and planned business processes? What sort of thing will they be doing? How skilled are they expected to be in the mysteries of IT?
- What data will people need to do their jobs? Where will it come from and who will own it? How will they obtain access to it?

These are by no means all the questions to be answered, but they illustrate the sort of information needed in developing an IT architecture.

What are the objectives of the organization?

The broad objectives will be fairly clear from the chapters of this book, but every organization will have different priorities both in terms of what is most important and in terms of what must be done first.

Support of the business is essential. In different organizations and at different times the emphasis may move towards saving purchasing, maintenance and support costs; ensuring that the IT function can react rapidly and effectively to business change by developing new ways of working, perhaps on new tasks, rapidly and reliably; helping to gain competitive advantage by making available new technology that genuinely offers a competitive business edge; or assisting (at the very least not inhibiting!) major organizational, geographical or functional restructuring.

The nature of the architecture will be affected by the primary motivation for its development or extension at a given time. One of us worked recently on an architecture study whose objective, in the first major stage, was to establish what currently exists, whether it can really be dignified with the name of an architecture, and whether it can support the current strategic projects, let alone the future. Other architectures look five years and more into the future with the objective of establishing well in advance a technical platform for initiatives not yet imagined.

Some words of warning may be in order here. Although an architecture with a limited perspective may not yield all the possible benefits, it is a far safer first step than an attempt to traverse the whole IT universe at a single bound. The project to provide for all the needs of a major manufacturing company, bank or government department may be too big to handle sensibly in one stage. Moreover, an architecture that tries to allow for the possibility of an indeterminately large amount of change without disruption will probably cost an indeterminate amount of money. You should set objectives to achieve specific, defined, improvements and benefits through a carefully defined and manageable project.

How do we use IT trends to our advantage?

Every IT architecture study needs a view on where IT is going over the next few years. In this area technical skills will be an advantage, although many of the trends are not strictly technical. Obviously you must consider elements such as processor, storage, network and software technology. Equally, though, there is a need to take into account changes in the less concrete areas described in Chapter 12. Examples are:

- trends in IT organization
- the growth of 'facilities management'
- a hoped-for change in the way 'packaged' applications are structured
- new approaches to application design
- advances in data distribution and access.

16.3   Selecting the team

When the preparatory work has been done, it will be clear that the team that produces an IT architecture needs a variety of skills. However, it should not be large. This is not a committee-style activity where the criterion for including members may be whom they represent rather than what they can contribute. The usual rule is that it is difficult to get anything actually done with a team of more than six to eight people (if in doubt, consider the British Cabinet and the UN Security Council). Within this limit, the smallest team that brings all the required skills to the table is best. One of the most successful architectural projects we know had a team of four, one of whom was part time.

This raises the familiar problem. To do so vital a job, the best people are needed. The best people are usually the busiest and most critical to day-to-day success.

What is the best way to acquire the best people? We have seen two approaches work well.

1   Bite the bullet, and pull out a small number of the best people to do a high-pressure, high-speed, high-quality job. This requires determined management, not because the good people will be reluctant—most of them will be enthusiastic supporters of the initiative—but because they will tend to be 'irreplaceable' in their main job.
2   Plan the project as a series of 'workshops' a week or so apart. The longest should be two to three days in duration; one day should be normal. The workshops are used to discuss important issues in a structured way, to generate ideas, and to make decisions. Frequently, there will be a need to obtain more information or to record and structure facts, views and decisions between meetings. Such work can be done by less critical staff, guided by team members. In this way the critical team members maintain much better control over their work plan and can use others to do the more mechanical and time-consuming work.

As you would expect from a group of consultants, we can suggest an approach that will prove useful using either method. This is to employ a third party skilled in both process and the content of producing an IT architecture. There are formal offerings on the market that are intended to simplify, speed up and formalize the process of producing an architecture. There are also consultants skilled in 'facilitating' the process—defining the scope, keeping people on track and on time, producing a useful set of deliverables. We would, unsurprisingly, recommend the use of such methods and people but would stress that they cannot do the job for you. Your best people know what you need and what will work in your environment. Their close involvement is essential, as is their commitment to the results. This activity cannot sensibly be fully 'outsourced'.

Within the small group, and any third parties they use (still within the overall limit of six to eight regular members of the team!) the following skills seem to us essential.

1   *Knowledge of the business* We are not looking here for a Harvard graduate, but for someone who can represent the needs and plans of your business over the architectural time frame. You may well be able to plan to use such a resource only in the early and late stages of the project—the middle part can get very technical—but significant input, and concurrence with the architecture, will be critical.
2   *Analytical skills* You will need one or more people with the ability to take a clear, structured, unbiased view of current systems and future needs and to understand what is needed to convert the real present into the desired future.
3   *Architectural skills* One or more system designers with the rare ability to think architecturally, in terms of structure, interfaces and complex relationships, will

be essential. Such people are hard to find in most organizations. You may be tempted to buy in this skill, but you should remember that you will need at least one such person to carry the architecture forward after it has been built and installed.

4   *IT knowledge* Of course this is necessary. It is not simply a matter of which PC chip runs, or will run, fastest or even whether one operating system will oust another. Judgement across a wide range of technical topics is crucial. Knowledge in individual technical areas can be borrowed or bought but, since the architecture must operate as a whole, it must be designed by people with broad technical understanding and depth of knowledge in critical areas.

5   *Process skills* You will need one or more people who know how to run a project of this type, where the subject matter is broad, the skills are highly technical, the scope for diversion into interesting side-alleys is great and the deliverables must be clear and of practical value. We mention elsewhere the need for a method. It is equally important to ensure that the process of using the method runs smoothly. This may be an area where an outside facilitator is valuable.

16.4   Producing a definition of the IT architecture

With an understanding of our needs, what we are trying to achieve, a view on the trends in IT, and a skilled team, we are now ready to produce a description of our desired architecture. This is clearly a crucial stage, but in some ways it is the easy bit. Developing requirements and clarifying the mind about exactly what we hoped to achieve was hard. It will become clear that making the change to the new architectural base is also very hard. Both are typically difficult because we are dealing with real people with different ambitions and abilities, with different views of the past and present (*'Your* Datacentre runs like clockwork'; *'His* Datacentre never delivers what we want when we need it') and different visions of the future. All the architecture team has to do is define what the architecture is and make good and consistent technical decisions. These decisions will often be complex and there will be few absolute rights and wrongs, but the problem is bounded. Thus, a good team with a good process will do a good job in this area.

A word of warning about processes may be timely. The reader who agrees with the primary thesis of this book may be keen to go and do something about it. We would thoroughly support this decision. However, great care is needed. We have observed empirically that most people who come to us for help with an IT architecture have tried it on their own first and have failed. This is not, so far as we can see, a problem of lack of technical depth: when we have subsequently worked with them, they have not primarily needed technical support. Some of the others who come to us have not failed, because they have looked at the challenge and have decided they need help. Some have got a certain distance (in one case after spending more than £1 million) and have then been unsure how to complete the job. Why should this be so? There seems to be a number of reasons. For example:

- a failure to cover a wide enough scope, e.g. omitting operational considerations, or not appreciating the importance of a data architecture
- not appreciating that a collection of individual 'best of breed' products may work together like a set of quarrelsome mongrels
- not starting from a clear and agreed set of requirements, with an emphasis on business need
- producing a technologist's dream which may have been deeply satisfying intellectually but was of no measurable value to the business
- a combination of the above.

We assume that a number of organizations do define successful architectures without significant outside help, but we believe they are the ones that use a sound method. It will be evident that earlier sections of this chapter have been based on the approach we favour. We use a six-phase method to ensure that the right things are done in a sensible sequence, and that an integrated result is achieved. The phases are given in Table 16.1.

We would be the first to agree that there is nothing remarkable about such a skeleton for a method. In fact, though, some hard lessons are incorporated. For example, we carefully separate the gathering and analysis of data because we have found that in-flight analysis is inevitably based on a partial view of the data, and may even colour one's views of later data. The reverse can also be true: and subsequent discoveries or decisions can call for the modification of earlier work, so we allow for iteration as needed during phases 1–4. We also produce a management action plan before we publish our definition to ensure that at least we believe that the architecture can be implemented, maintained and improved. In fact each phase is broken down into multiple steps, and guidance is provided to the team on what can be decided when, what can go wrong, and how problems can be avoided. Such a level of detail is too low for this book, but on the basis of extensive experience we stress that you should not use a method that does not include it.

Table 16.1 Six phases of architecture definition

Phase	Phase description
1	Gather current status and requirements
2	Analyse requirements
3	Build an architectural model
4	Evaluate and select components
5	Produce a management action plan
6	Report and gain agreement

16.5   The critical elements

Without going into the details of the necessary process, once the business requirements and the objectives of the IT architecture have been established there seem to
be three critical questions.

1   What technical capabilities must the IT architecture have?
2   How do I choose the right hardware and software?
3   How do I ensure that people use the architecture?

To illustrate the right way to develop an IT architecture, let us go through the
major phases, showing how they help us to answer the three questions.

Gather current status and requirements

Current IT status

It is necessary to start from where the organization is today in IT terms. The following questions need to be asked.

- Where are we today in terms of hardware, software techniques and tools?
- How do we ensure that we meet the requirements of the business?
- What do we do that is good, and what do we do that is not so good?
- What are we investing in?
- What skills do we have, and what skills are we short of?
- How are we organized within the IT Department?

All these questions help to build up a picture of the current *de facto* IT architecture.

Business requirements

The architecture design team needs a very clear understanding of what the organization requires. This cannot be achieved intuitively; it requires dialogue at many
levels within the organization, including the highest.

It is at this stage that *vision* comes back into play. One organization we worked
with had a single overriding objective, stated as *ubiquity*. What this meant was that
all the information technology (including all applications and data) had to be available to every user, no matter who the user was and no matter where the user was.
This is a very simple objective, but one that gave us a high degree of understanding
and clarity that is not always achieved.

If you ask users what they want from IT, you get answers that vary from 'a
bigger notebook with a better screen' to 'ubiquity'. The former is of little use in
building the early stages of an IT architecture: it does not provide the basis on
which the architecture team can work. What is required is a high-level statement of

what the organization is trying to achieve and how it sees IT helping in the process of developing it.

In some organizations this clarity is not easy to obtain, but this is understandable the first time round, and we have to find ways of helping to elicit the sort of information we need. In many organizations the sort of questions that have to be asked will not have been asked before. In far too many cases the business plan is an operational one, covering a short period of time and looking at the enhancement of existing products and services in a predictable manner to achieve the level of growth or profitability that is deemed acceptable or desirable. There may be no clear role for IT within this plan other than to continue to provide the same sort of services but at a reduced cost. In trying to understand the key requirements that the IT architecture must address, the architecture team must get beyond this barrier: by questioning deeply, by suggesting options for IT, or by highlighting the direction in which the IT industry is moving and how competitors are reacting.

One common response from senior management within an organization is to state a general requirement for 'flexibility'. They rightly argue that the future is unclear and that they must be able to react to market pressures faster than the competition. This requires flexibility from IT. What they may be saying is that IT has in the past been an inhibitor of business change and this cannot continue into the future. This is true, but is not a complete answer. In some areas flexibility will certainly be needed, but a stable base is still necessary. An understanding of the degrees of freedom required by the organization is valuable input to the definition of the architecture, but becomes useless if it is seen as a panacea.

Analyse requirements

Although we have been judgemental in describing the process of gathering requirements, it was critical (because of the dangers of going off at half-cock) that we limited ourselves during the first phase to listening and asking for clarification, or for the resolution of apparent contradictions. Now comes the hard work of interpreting what we have heard in such a way as to make it a sound base for developing an architecture. This requires the application of judgement to what we have heard—not in second-guessing the business people about what they want, but in assessing what is needed to achieve it technically.

Almost certainly, the first of a number of iterations will occur here. It will be immediately obvious that some requirements are mutually contradictory and that priorities need to be established. A good example might be the requirement for 'ubiquity' mentioned earlier. This is an extraordinarily hard thing to achieve technically, especially when starting from a typical current status. It may not be too extreme to say that, in this area of total access to all data and applications, the requirements for total flexibility in the medium term can lead to costs that are unpredictable in detail but are certainly likely to outweigh any imaginable benefits. This is one of the areas where current systems can rarely be improved to the degree needed without being totally reengineered. In such a case, it may be wise for IT to return to the business people and discuss the need for prioritization before undertaking a very costly design and development exercise. The goal can be achieved with patience, but we may be talking of several years to achieve total ubiquity. Fortunately, there may be stages on the way that will provide 80 per cent of the benefit for 20 per cent of the cost and effort.

When requirements have been analysed critically and carefully, it will become clear that the new architecture must provide a range of technical capabilities that will support the strategic business direction of the organization. The capabilities your organization needs will be unique, but are likely to include the list we give below.

Technical capabilities

This is a set of capabilities that most modern IT systems must have. We use the word 'modern' because some of the original systems described earlier in the book did not really need everything that is now taken for granted. The essentials can be listed thus.

1 *The ability to run a wide range of jobs* This entails both those clearly business-oriented and those that support them. Depending on the type of user, the type of external customer being served, the area of the business and the urgency of the output, one might need on-line teleprocessing, overnight batch work, management information systems, computer-intensive 'number-crunching' applications or application development and testing capabilities.

2 *Access to and care of data* We are talking about information technology, so making available and looking after data is critical. This can vary from vast, up-to-the-second customer databases, through departmental invoicing files, down to Dave's records of what he has sold today. Data can be in many forms (records, files, databases, text, image, vector, etc.) held on a variety of media (disk storage, optical storage, tape, etc.). It can be anything from critical (requiring duplication, logging, archiving and data protection) to temporary (useful today, discarded tomorrow). It may be so sensitive that it must be encrypted or so public that anyone can access it.

3 *Communication between systems* Computers must be able to 'talk' to each other, locally on a local area network, or at a distance on a wide area network. Distant computers may be within our organization or may belong to a customer, a supplier, an information provider, a bank or a government department.

4 *A variety of systems* Our own computers, let alone others that we talk to, may be of very different types. We may have big, powerful, multi-application 'mainframes'; we may have 'minicomputers' or 'local servers' scattered across the country; we may have hundreds or thousands of programmable workstations

on desks, in homes or in briefcases; we may have special-purpose process-control or scientific machines.

5   *System and service management* The management of the total service given by this wide range of machinery, data and applications has become critical to successful operation. We need a sub-architecture to handle reliability, perform-ance levels, recovery from failure, the introduction of changes, the detection and resolution of problems, the control of assets and the management of security.

Our IT architecture has to be able to support and manage this wide range of capabilities and ensure that an efficient service is provided. It must do this as cheaply as possible and must be flexible enough to change with the business require-ments, which may demand new capabilities in any area. An important part of defin-ing an architecture, therefore, is to record what is needed in an organized and comprehensible way and to show how the architecture satisfies these technical needs.

Organizational capabilities

Before doing this, however, it is necessary to establish what the current organiza-tion and resources are capable of achieving, starting from the current environment. It is necessary to understand:

- what processes the organization needs to perform
- what data the organization will need to perform these processes
- who will be performing these processes
- where these people will perform the processes.

The answers to these points are critical to the overall design of the architecture. Your work so far should have provided answers: if not, then further iteration will be needed.

Build an architectural model

This step requires a combination of clear thinking and imagination (in Robert Ornstein's original model of the brain, both left and right lobes need to be involved). For someone new to it, the process is difficult, although experience rapidly adds to confidence. The essential task is to build a high-level view of the *shape and form* of the IT architecture. Figure 16.1 shows an example of this: the example shown is a more detailed version of that shown in Fig. 14.1. Figure 16.2 shows a slightly different example.

To do this successfully requires the ability to be able to see through the vast mass of information that has been collected, to understand the priorities associated with the requirements, and to develop one or more outline solutions. There is no magic algorithm that the architecture team can use at this stage and, so far, few relevant techniques have been developed. Nevertheless, the output of this phase is of pivotal

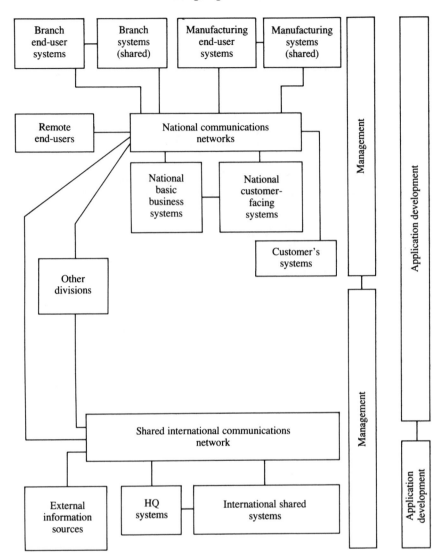

Figure 16.1. Sample architectural building blocks 1.

importance to the success of the architecture, so it is important to avoid major mistakes and omissions.

This is an area where experienced outside help can be especially useful. A word of comfort is possible here. Because a sound method permits iteration, getting things wrong at this point does not guarantee a disaster. There is the opportunity to return to this step if later work shows that it has been too prescriptive, too incomplete, or simply wrong.

The approach that we recommend is to record a set of architectural building blocks that illustrate high-level elements such as those mentioned above (the list is

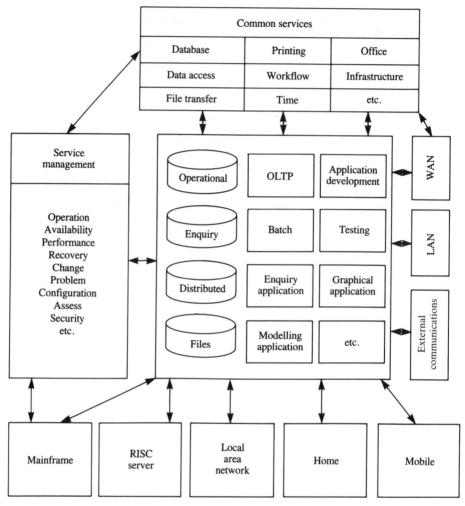

Figure 16.2.   Sample architectural building blocks 2.

not comprehensive). The simplest representation of these buildings blocks, and therefore of the architecture they represent, is a one-page diagram. This can prove a good way of presenting the architecture to senior and non-technical staff and it is a good basis for a table of contents for an architectural definition document. The diagram needs to be backed up by explanatory text, but we believe that the purely visual representation is primary. Written language is not very suitable for explaining and structuring the complexities of an IT architecture. There are too many components, related in too many ways, and there are too many technical 'dimensions' (functionality, implementation, performance, reliability, development, system management, etc.) for words to be clear and comprehensible on their own. Indeed, two-dimensional paper or screens are not ideal, and much ingenuity goes into devising representations that stimulate more dimensions. Figure 16.1 is a simple example of an overview at the building-block level. Remember that it is still at a high level: the building blocks and the connections between them are still capable of much more detailed definition.

With a lot of work, therefore, it is possible to represent in a structured way the technical capabilities required from the architecture. If this is done well, orderly decomposition can generate a valid hardware and software combination to achieve the objectives of the IT architecture.

Evaluate and select components

Designing in detail

Once the shape and form of the overall environment have been established, the details of the various components can be defined through a process of 'functional decomposition' (breaking down the high-level building blocks into the full set of functions they must perform). At this point we are defining at the functional level a specification of each component. We may have identified a major component such as a 'software distribution system'. We identify the functions it must perform, for example:

- distributing software
- keeping a directory of all destinations for software of a particular type
- recording the 'release level' of all software at each site
- providing licensing information.

This enables us to define the detailed characteristics required of the component, such as the following.

- It must allow distribution via all the communications protocols we use.
- It must be capable of distributing a complete set of replacement software or an incremental update.
- Because end users at many locations have few IT skills and want to go home sometimes, it must be able to distribute PC operating software without the need for anyone in attendance at the user site.
- It must be able to distribute software to all sites overnight (so performance and line capacity may be important).

It will be evident that this activity is an essential link between the overall model and the actual selection of the products that will make the architecture work.

The right hardware and software

It is often difficult not to delve into the area of product selection sooner. Discussing the relative merits of one product versus another is far easier and (to the typical IT professional) more fun than trying to identify what capabilities are needed. There is always likely to be one member of the team who has 'a technology looking for a requirement'. However, until this stage we are not ready for detailed product discussions. Only when we have identified the capabilities that are required for each of the component parts of the solution can the selection of specific products be performed, by achieving a reasonable fit between the desired functionality and the capabilities of the product.

Let us be honest from the start. The use of the word 'right' in this context can be misleading. All one can really hope for is a valid combination. There is no known way of demonstrating that it is uniquely 'right': the optimum solution. Even assuming a clever mathematician or logician found a proof, it would no longer be valid within a few days or weeks. Organizations change, business imperatives change, the capabilities of technology change. Our apparently modest aim must be to provide a system that works well today and can be developed fairly easily to work well tomorrow. For all sorts of reasons even this is hard, and the phase in defining an IT architecture where we select products is long and demanding.

Even with our modest aim there is a very wide range of possible choices. Elements include:

- at least half a dozen manufacturers of large computers, twice as many manufacturers of 'server' systems, twice as many again of workstations—and each manufacturer may have multiple versions of each category
- at least a dozen 'mainline' programming languages
- a wide variety of storage media—magnetic tape, magnetic disks, optical disks, solid-state storage, massive main memory, etc.—attachable to a variety of (but never, it seems, all) computer systems
- an extraordinary variety of communications controllers, line splitters, 'front ends', multiplexers, routers, etc. in the networking and communications field
- application 'packages' to perform (after a fashion) most of what most business people have ever wanted to do
- document readers, cheque readers, image capture devices, printers of many types, wall-sized display screens, heart monitors, missile detectors and a host of other input/output devices
- a list of communications protocols as long as your arm
- databases of varying levels of functionality and performance.

We could go on, but why inflict further punishment? The essential point is that decisions must be made between this array of products and that the result must work. Do not lightly assume that it will.

A very large bank performed an IT architecture definition by dividing into 10 teams according to technical topic, and publishing the results of the teams' deliberations. It then decided to use the 'architecture' on a bank-wide application.

Each team had chosen 'best of breed' products for its own area—how could they accept second-best? The new application demanded that centralized mainframe systems talk to departmental server systems and that both should talk to branch systems. When the branches tried to talk to the departmental systems they could not. The different teams had chosen incompatible hardware/software combinations. The cost of this error was weeks of delay in a vital project and significant money to change hardware, software and programs. Such experiences have led us to prefer a chorus of competent products that work together harmoniously to prima donnas that sing superbly but tread on other people's feet.

In order to avoid such pitfalls it is essential to develop a broad-ranging set of product selection criteria that measure not only the functional capability of a product but also qualities such as its ability to interoperate with others, its reliability, its conformance to our architectural principles, its ability to fit into our security policy and a number of other factors that make it fit into our planned environment. Naturally, cost is a critical criterion, but we recommend looking at cost of ownership rather than crude initial price.

The product selection phase of an IT architecture definition is usually lively. Lovers of spreadsheets produce amazingly sophisticated tools to evaluate, measure and compare. Unreconstructed technical gurus fight for their favourite products. Brilliant programmers and engineers want to build their own perfect solution. Potential suppliers of products bend every ear and fill every stomach they can reach. Ultimately a valid architecture can be defined only by close adherence to a sound process, a lot of hard work, and agreement to abide by the results of a carefully constructed set of criteria.

Produce a management action plan

The subject of making the architecture happen, and ensuring it is used successfully in practice, is covered in Chapter 17. The foundations for making the architecture work must be laid by the architecture team. They need to outline a positive set of actions in the areas of implementation and reorganization of the IT Department. The output of the architecture definition project should include recommendations for:

- transition to the new architectural base
- migrating applications to the new base
- methods of achieving conformance to the new architecture
- an appropriate management structure to maintain and enhance the architecture

- a set of processes that can be used by the new management structure to decide when the architecture needs to be modified, and for agreeing and implementing the necessary changes
- training all those who need to understand the architecture—project managers, system designers, development analysts and programmers, data administrators, application maintenance staff, computer operators and technical support staff.

All these recommendations will be much more useful if they include cost, time and resource estimates for each element. Of course the architecture team's recommendations and estimates will be preliminary and at a high level, but they should be a suitable basis for the detailed planning that will come later.

The definition of an IT architecture cannot be considered complete until these issues, most of which are not wholly technical, have been addressed in a practical and realistic way.

Report and gain agreement

We do not believe in giving everyone a vast quantity of detailed information on topics where they have little understanding and less interest. The architecture team's main report should therefore be brief (not more than 30 pages) and at a level that serious non-technical readers will understand. Inevitably, there will be a vast amount of detailed back-up documentation, all of it valuable and much of it essential. This needs to be structured and organized according to who needs it, whether it is temporary or permanent, whether it records permanent features, current facts or long-term trends, etc. It can then be preserved until it is needed.

Meanwhile, suitable presentation materials need to be prepared for all the audiences to whom the architecture team needs to carry its message. Unless all these people accept the message and are prepared to contribute time and resources as needed, the project has not been a success. The 'gain agreement' process must continue until all valid objections and reservations have been met and satisfied or until it is decided that the organization is not yet ready for an IT architecture. In the latter case the least to be looked for is a plan to bring the organization to the point of readiness.

16.6   Summary

We have attempted to outline the process that is needed to produce a practical definition of an IT architecture.

Great emphasis has been placed on ensuring that the architecture is built to satisfy a set of clear and agreed business objectives. We have suggested the sort of people who should be on the architecture team during the definition phase, and have stressed the need for a range of skills and knowledge. A generic process for producing such an architecture has been outlined, indicating that there is a best sequence for tackling the job but warning that provision for controlled iteration is essential. We have also given warnings on the pitfalls that await the unwary or the inexperienced. We have gone through the architecture definition process at a high level to give a feel for the sequence in which things should be done and to indicate some of the considerations critical to producing a usable result.

We have stressed that the business must organize itself to implement, control and enhance the IT architecture and to use it effectively. We have emphasized also that gaining agreement to the existence and the content of the IT architecture from all interested parties is essential. These points are developed in the next chapter, which suggests how we should use the definition we have produced to improve IT's contribution to the business.

17
Making it work

Moving to the architecture

The cloud-capped towers, the gorgeous palaces,
The solemn temples, the great globe itself,
Yea, all which it inherit, shall dissolve
And, like this insubstantial fabric faded,
Leave not a wrack behind.

(William Shakespeare, *The Tempest*)

17.1   Purpose

The most glorious architectural visions can fade in the harsh light of reality, as Prospero pointed out. We have recommended that the IT architecture should be developed by a team and that it should be published initially in the form of a document. This is clearly not enough.

Recently, one of us was in a remote photocopying room in an IT department and noticed that it contained two large anonymous grey filing cabinets. When inspected they proved to contain operating manuals for dead software systems, programmers' guides for past operating systems, manuals for products no longer in use and programming standards for the last hardware/software environment but one. This was 'shelfware' that nobody used and few remember.

Such a fate can befall an IT architecture unless very positive steps are taken to see that it is fully understood, kept up to date and, above all, used. This could happen to your IT architecture. In this chapter we address the elements required to ensure you produce a valid, usable and properly-managed architecture.

To achieve the objectives for which it was developed, it needs at least:

- a senior executive sponsor whose success in his or her job depends on the efficiency and effectiveness of the IT operation
- a clear plan to install and enable the new hardware, software tools and techniques that make up the architecture

- a clear strategy to ensure that all future applications are installed on the new architectural base, and a policy about the pace of moving current applications onto it
- a management structure to ensure that the architecture is properly documented and understood, that it is used, that its rules are followed, that it is reviewed regularly and that it changes when business pressures or technological opportunities justify change
- a guardian group with the technical, administrative and leadership skills to support the major objectives of the management structure—as is explained later, this group should have a strong service orientation
- a system for handling exceptions where a deviation from the IT architecture is, on balance, justified.

Only when all the above are in place will it be possible to answer the sceptic who says 'That's all very well, but how are you going to make sure people use it?'.

17.2   Implementing the architecture

The architecture definition will describe principles, structure and technical platform. As mentioned earlier, the team that developed the definition must have considered transition to the new world. Specifically, it must have thought and advised about:

- how to install the new technical environment
- how to convert the full application portfolio, over time, to the new platform
- who will do the work and how.

Much confusion can be caused if the first two items on the list are not clearly distinguished. Words like 'migration' and 'conversion' sound clear but can conceal the difference between a purely technical problem (installing new hardware and software to provide a technical base) and a business decision (what to put on the new base, how fast, and at what cost and benefit). The two activities are performed by different people, with different motivations, at different times. We shall therefore treat them separately.

Transition to the new architectural base

Some members of the architecture definition team would be the worst possible people to manage or perform this task. They will have been selected mainly for their analytical, judgemental and conceptual skills. It is therefore wise to have at least one member of the team who is of a severely practical disposition, and can see the issues surrounding all aspects of implementation from a practical viewpoint. He or she may be particularly useful at this next stage. However, you should pass formal responsibility for the implementation of the new technical platform to the department best qualified to make it happen and best qualified to support and enhance it. In the majority of organizations nowadays, this will be the group going under the title of 'IT operations' or 'computer services' or something similar. These days it normally controls the technical support function, which keeps hardware and software up to date and helps when technical problems arise. This will be the group that can say 'Development only has to make a system work once: we have to make it work every day.' Such groups normally have enough specialized project management expertise to run a complex hardware/software installation project. However, it may be that application development or system development is deeply involved and strongly motivated, in which case a joint development effort may be appropriate. A strategy or architecture group may also be involved, but is unlikely to have the project management skills to lead such an effort.

You may recall that we recommended in Chapter 16 that the architecture definition document should include an outline 'implementation plan'. One part of this will cover the transition to the new platform. It will include considerations such as how soon the new platform is needed; what seems to be a sensible sequence in which to build it; approximate resource, hardware and software costs; testing and acceptance methods and criteria; and checkpoints along the way to completion. It should, of course, be viewed as a base for the actual implementation plan rather than a tight constraint on it. Problems will arise only if it is wildly optimistic or, less likely, pessimistic. In the former case, the implementation team may have to go back to the sponsor for confirmation that the benefits of the architecture still justify going ahead on the new scale envisaged.

When the project does go ahead, it is likely to be a major one. Activities will normally include:

- confirming and configuring in detail all selected components
- planning the phases in which components will be installed to fit in with operational imperatives and maintenance changes
- writing any special software for your specific environment (this is often called 'middleware', because it lies somewhere between software and application code)
- testing new components, in each phase, against each other and the unchanged part of the system (normally the greater part) without disrupting normal operation
- installing one or more 'pilot' applications to check that the architecture operates as envisaged (this may be done initially by providing a 'test bed' environment on machinery not normally used daily for critical applications)
- ensuring that, in an environment where 'change is the only constant', the architectural platform displays the characteristics of operational stability, good performance and ease of change that the architecture definition team built into the design

- maintaining a team to ensure that, as applications are migrated across to the new technical platforms, all goes smoothly.

Migrating the applications

For new and, we hope, modern applications, the architecture should be the ideal base. Thus there should be no difficulty, if they are structured properly, in installing them directly onto the new platform. This may be your only requirement and you may be content to leave existing 'heritage' applications on the old platforms. However, this would give you only half an architecture. One of the great truisms of IT is that 'Old soldiers never die; they simply fade away'. If you take no positive action, the 'old soldiers' will be around for some years (even decades), becoming more out of date, harder to maintain and enhance, and less well understood. So a positive approach may be needed. There are three popular strategies.

1 As just described, you could put new applications on the new platform and leave others to fade away over time. The advantage of this approach is that there is no need for the new architectural base to allow for the idiosyncrasies of old programs and databases or files. This can make the new system more robust, more predictable, and easier to operate. The first advantage is that you will not have produced the single coherent, maintainable, reliable, cooperating, enhanceable and predictable system environment that you require. As a further result, you will not be able to release the 'old iron' and old software that the heritage applications use; you will still have to live with the costs and inconvenience of your old system. A less obvious implication is increasingly serious as you try to design new systems where multiple programs can access corporate data regardless of location, and where business reengineering changes the boundaries and relationships of applications and data. It is very difficult to achieve these new capabilities in cooperation with your old, disparate, unstructured technical base. Thus, important new business initiatives can be delayed or inadequately supported.

2 You could theoretically opt to satisfy that all existing applications should be migrated onto the new platform immediately. The advantage of this approach is that they then have freedom to use the portability , interoperability, location independence and system-wide access made possible by the new platform. This avoids the major problems of the previous solution. In addition, even the old programs that gain little or nothing from working with external data or applications can be expected to run more reliably and smoothly on the new platform. The one disadvantage of this solution is that it is normally totally impracticable. Most major organizations have hundreds (more often, thousands) of person-years of code invested in current systems. However keen they may be to change, the resources and time needed are simply not available. An organization that can stop new development for two to five years while it migrates old

programs is probably not dynamic enough (particularly by the end of the process!) to make good use of the result.

3   Not surprisingly, a third option is the most popular with the majority of organizations. This is to install all new applications on the new platform and to convert or replace others as fast as seems practical. There is a sense of urgency to gain the benefits of using the new architecture, but there is a healthy determination to keep costs within bounds and to have resources available for new initiatives. In this approach, a program may be converted when it needs changes of a certain magnitude, which means that a significant amount of code needs to be rewritten, or a major conversion of data is required. It may also be replaced when a new system takes over most of its function and it is practical to rewrite the small amount of code that is still needed. From a purely budgetary point of view this approach is convenient, because the business owner can participate in the decision process and agreement about funding the changes can be reached. From a technical point of view this approach phases the growth of the load on the new architectural platform and those operating it, avoiding the risk that a sudden massive conversion will cause temporary disruption.

Once again, on the principle of 'Happy the country that has no history', we prefer the third option (the boring but safe solution) for the general case. We would stress, though, that you need to take the decision yourself, based on the conflicting pressures and resource constraints you face. There may be no 'right' answer, but common sense and careful planning can avoid one that is obviously wrong.

Persuading people to use the architecture

Resistance to an architected approach

Conformance is not a trivial problem. Many technical people resent curbs on their technical imagination and freedom to use the newest, glossiest products available at a given time. It can even enhance their job prospects (with other employers!) to be expert in the most fashionable new technology regardless of whether it is what your organization needs. Many more people, in most organizations, are reluctant to organize themselves well enough to ensure that they use the right products and tools in the right way all the time. Many just do not understand the importance to the business of a sound IT architecture, and will ignore it if that seems the easiest way to go. In many organizations the technical leaders retain the 'pioneering' culture that flourished in the early days of IT, and consider a few arrows in the back a small price to pay for exploring the frontiers of technology.

There are also more justifiable reservations, often to be heard from business people rather then technologists. They may say, in effect, 'This product or package is a perfect fit for my business needs; how can IT say it does not wish to install or support it because of some commitment to an abstract idea like an architecture?'.

They have a valid point. IT exists only to serve and support the business. Since we have argued that one of the advantages of the architecture is that it allows more rapid and flexible response to business needs, we can hardly reject such a question out of hand. It is worth saying at once that there may be genuine conflicts of interest, attitude and priority surrounding so major a topic as an IT architecture, especially if it is the first. We cannot guarantee that management will never have to make compromises, or decisions that are unpopular with individuals and groups. What we are sure of, and hope you will agree after reading this book, is that the potential benefits of an IT architecture far outweigh its costs for the organization as a whole, so that every department and division should be ready to support it. Possible answers to the business people's question that started this paragraph are given below.

Methods of achieving conformance

There are various ways of trying to ensure conformance. Traditionally, IT management has believed that the drawing up of rules and stern 'policing' could bring dissidents into line. This authoritarian approach does not typically succeed for long—hence the yards of 'shelfware'. A later, and more appealing, approach has been 'quality assurance', where a very valuable group formed to define and control the quality of the IT operation is given the additional task of controlling the architecture by reviewing both it and the projects using it, to ensure that quality standards have been maintained. The problem here is obvious in the light of work over the past few years: quality needs to be built in at the start as a positive attribute. A quality assurance review can prevent a flawed product, package or application from being used before it has been put right, but will be too late to save a lot of wasted effort and money. So an architecture group must not only seek to achieve conformance through a positive approach, it must also be ubiquitous and proactive enough to ensure quality is built in at an early stage of the development process.

In the light of these considerations, three major techniques are in use by different organizations at present, and we believe the third is by far the most promising:

1   IT can make clear to the business units that the resources required to support hardware, software and packages that are not compatible with the architecture are so significant that full support is not possible outside the architecture. Thus, 'difficult' products or systems may receive limited maintenance, may be possible to run only during certain hours or at certain locations, may receive no 'help desk' support, etc. Also, there may be no guarantee that they will be able to take advantage of new and more cost-effective hardware and software as it becomes available.

2   IT may agree to support 'problem' products or projects at a price. Most organizations now have some method of assigning IT costs across business units and projects. It is not in general difficult to calculate the extra cost of supporting

something non-standard and to calculate an appropriate additional charge—although it may be harder to gain the agreement of the business unit concerned!

3   Although they can be applied in the early stages of new projects and can take advantage of quality techniques, both of the above approaches suffer from the potential problem that they can lead to conflict and escalation of differences up the management line. A positive service-oriented approach is almost certain to work better, but needs imagination, effort and resource to set up and maintain.

The recommended approach

The approach relies on providing added value to business users and development project managers who conform to the architecture. One excellent way to do this is to offer an 'architectural service' at three levels.

1   *Level 1* At the strategic level, the organization's chief architect answers questions from senior business and IT management and offers advice on the opportunities offered by technological advances in the strategic time frame to improve business performance, to reduce IT costs and perhaps to reengineer some aspects of the business. This advice is fed into the IT strategy and, where appropriate, into the business strategy.

2   *Level 2* At the feasibility stage of a proposed development project, a second level of service is offered. This helps the project to evaluate technical options for effort, cost, time-scale and risk, with an emphasis on solutions within the architecture. The architecture team can help to calculate lifetime system costs of architectural or alternative solutions—a positive rather than negative method of bringing home the cost of unarchitected approaches.

3   *Level 3* When the project starts, the architecture team assigns design effort (anything from a part-timer to several people, depending on the size of the project) to help ensure that the project team makes optimum use of the architecture. This implies of course that the architecture team must contain a pool of the organization's best designers who can be assigned to projects as required. Experience in various areas of IT shows that this sort of approach breaks down the 'them and us' attitude that closely-knit project teams tend to develop.

Of course, this approach should be combined with independent quality assurance, one of whose review criteria will be whether the architecture is being implemented fully.

Of equal significance is that if the project has an apparent need for a feature not included in the architecture, the architecture team can see this either at the feasibility or at the design stage and decide whether the need is valid and, if it is, how the architecture can be amended to accommodate it. Confidence that the architecture provides a stable base, but can be improved as necessary, will be a crucial element in acceptance by technical staff and development projects.

Management structure

An IT architecture can hope to be successful only if it is managed tightly. Unfortunately, few organizations have the structures in place today to ensure that this happens. The essential feature of the structure is that the IT architecture must have a sponsor, an owning manager and an architecture review board. The sponsor provides executive management commitment to the architecture. The day-to-day manager, reporting to the sponsor, is the owning manager. Of course he or she is not responsible for managing all activity directly, but he or she is where the buck stops. The essential long-term tool needed to support the manager is an architecture review board (ARB). Of course, this name is not sacrosanct and can be replaced by technical assurance board, joint architecture board or any approximate synonym. The board's main function is to review the IT architecture and recommend appropriate changes to it. It can be thought of as the 'guardian' of the IT architecture. It will normally be chaired by the owning manager.

Note: It will almost always be best to build on your current organization and skills if possible. You can examine your current IT structure for suitable roles and groups, and either add to the responsibilities of a group (giving it any required extra resource) or fit a new group into the structure.

The sponsor

We have discussed this role earlier and have indicated that the sponsor is a representative of executive management. Suitable candidates may be the senior IT executive, the chief information officer, or just possibly a director of a major division or department that is highly dependent on IT. The sponsor will agree with the owning manager on what needs to be done, will hold reviews of the success and the continuing relevance of the architecture, and will clear road-blocks for the owning manager when necessary. This is vital, but is very much a part-time role.

The owning manager

This individual should in our view be responsible for the following:

- initial implementation of the architecture
- conformance of applications and services to the architecture
- understanding and acceptance of the architecture by all affected groups
- currency of the architecture
- quality of the architecture
- continuing business value, i.e. that benefit is greater than cost
- a consistent policy for migrating existing applications and services to the new technical platform

- approval of deviation requests—any deviations should be minor and limited to practical (preferably short-term) considerations that are justified and documented.

We would stress once again that the owning manager does not *do* all these things: he or she is responsible for ensuring that they are done. Thus, his or her major activities will normally be to:

- ensure that the initial implementation is successful (most of the actual work will be delegated to line departments)
- establish and personally manage a conformance process
- establish requirements for change to the architecture (using the architectural review board)
- manage the change process
- continuously evaluate the cost/benefit balance of the architecture
- establish and run (periodically) the review processes
- plan and ensure the running of education of IT staff and concerned user/business groups about the architecture—within IT, those educated should include functional managers, project managers and professionals (system architects, designers, programmers, system programmers and operators)—understanding and acceptance of the IT architecture is critical to ensuring conformance
- approve and document any justified deviations from the architecture.

Given this set of responsibilities and activities in support of them, you should consider making the owning manager full-time for the first 6–12 months, since this period will be critical in gaining general acceptance of the architecture, organizing to manage it and ensuring a successful implementation that begins to yield business benefits. The amount of full-time management thereafter will depend on factors such as:

- the size of your organization
- the scope and complexity of the IT systems the architecture is supporting
- enthusiasm for the IT architecture on the part of the executive management—it may be necessary to ensure continuing and active focus
- the degree to which early acceptance is achieved within the development, support and operations groups—again, it may be necessary to maintain a strong focus for some time.

Once the architecture becomes a way of life, only the largest organizations are likely to need a full-time owning manager, but the role will be a natural part of what many people are coming to call the 'technical authority' for information technology.

The architecture review board

This is envisaged as a permanent group of senior and respected managers and professionals who work on it part-time. The full-time exception might be the organization's 'technical architect', if such a role exists. Such a person is typically a personification of the 'technical authority'. The role is technical rather than managerial, but where it exists it is very senior. Today only a few large IT departments have such a role: we believe it will become more common because it will be more essential as the trends towards a wider scope and greater business criticality of the IT function develop in the ways described earlier in this book. We would expect the owning manager to 'matrix-manage' the board while they are performing architectural functions, since many of them will not report to him or her directly. Typical functions of the board will be to:

- Review all changes to the architecture whether triggered by changes in the business, advances in the available technology or IT strategy decisions.
- Consider the impact of these changes on

  - the technical architecture definition itself
  - physical implementation decisions (particularly timing)
  - installed applications
  - existing installation standards

- estimate the costs of change
- prioritize and approve changes
- take a proactive role in defining improvements to the IT architecture.

To perform these functions properly, the board needs a range of skills. Members of the team that originally defined the architecture will be strong candidates, as will those responsible for developing and running current systems. Candidates may include (remembering that membership of the board is a part-time role):

- the architecture's owning manager (in the chair)
- the IT strategy manager (or equivalent role)
- the technical architect/authority (if the role exists)
- business analysts or managers from the major application areas
- various technical specialists in disciplines such as

  - major hardware and software platforms
  - database
  - application development
  - networking
  - operations
  - system management
  - technical support.

The size of the board should be limited to six to eight people for effectiveness. It is not a 'steering group': it makes decisions and produces deliverables, so it must be small enough to be effective in this role. Its major deliverables will be:

- a revised architecture definition
- a prioritized and costed change plan
- deviation approvals.

17.3   Other management functions

We have made it clear that many of the members of the management structure who contribute to the IT architecture will do so as part of their normal job and will not normally report in line to the owning manager of the architecture, although they will be functionally responsible to him or her for deliverables and/or architectural conformance. Managers who may be involved in architectural activities include:

- implementation project managers
- application conversion project managers
- the technical support manager
- the IT strategy manager
- the manager of the architectural service we have recommended (this person could well report in line to the owning manager)
- operations or computer services managers.

Because of the variety of approaches to structuring an IT department or division, we cannot recommend a single structure to coordinate such a diverse group. We would point out that the structure will be very dynamic across different stages of architecture development and maintenance, and we can see no alternative to some form of matrix management structure. The elements we consider crucial are the sponsor, the owning manager and the architecture review board.

17.4   Summary

The perceived problem with many consultants, strategists and planners is that they generate innovative ideas which appear superb on paper or when presented to a meeting but do not survive translation to the real world. Although we would not wholly acquit the pragmatic 'practical' critics of some responsibility for failing to implement with determination the new and often uncomfortable ideas of the 'theorists', we have tried in this chapter to show what can be done.

In looking at implementation, we have discussed both *transition* to the new technical platform and *migration* of applications to it. We have considered good and bad approaches to persuading people to conform to the IT architecture. We have provided guidance on the type of management structure required to implement, control, maintain and improve the IT architecture.

We have seen every element described here working successfully, although not yet all in one place. We have been able to give only generic guidance, and would stress that *your* solution will be unique to your environment, your skills, your management methods and your strategic aims. It is possible to have an IT architecture that works and delivers substantial benefits, but you must want it enough to put into it management attention, some structural change and significant skilled resource.

18
Right first time

Avoiding common problems

The inappropriate cannot be beautiful

(Frank Lloyd Wright)

18.1   Purpose

The purpose of this chapter is to look carefully at the essential differences between a successful IT architecture and an unsuccessful IT architecture. As with many such complex projects, the differences are often very subtle and having a view of them before embarking on such a project can be extremely beneficial. Some of the points made here have already been covered: the purpose here is to bring them all together so we can focus on them more clearly.

18.2   Success criteria

An IT architecture, just like a conventional architecture, has certain qualities. It is in terms of these qualities that we define whether or not it is a *good* IT architecture, whether it was worth producing, whether it will enable the overall effectiveness and efficiency of IT to be improved, whether it will be forgotten in 12 months' time or whether it will be remembered as the most important stimulus for change and response to change that the organization ever undertook.

There is no perfect list of these qualities, and there is certainly no unambiguous definition of them, but our experience across many organizations suggests that the qualities come under certain general headings. Why these characteristics and not others? Simply because IT architectures that we have seen in the past and class as successful *have* these characteristics, and those that we class as unsuccessful *do not*.

1 Planning

    (a) commitment
    (b) clarity of purpose
    (c) quality of sponsorship

2 Performance

   (a) evidence of method
   (b) reasonableness

3 Business

   (a) relationship to the business
   (b) right balance between standards and freedom
   (c) costs and benefits

4 Technology

   (a) taking advantage of technical opportunities
   (b) technical soundness
   (c) technical longevity
   (d) technical completeness

5 Transition

   (a) transition strategy
   (b) implementation organization
   (c) applications

6 Communication

   (a) nature of communication
   (b) quality of documentation

7 Enforcement

   (a) buy-in
   (b) management processes

The remainder of this chapter gives a brief description of each of these characteristics.

18.3 Planning

Commitment

> *The IT architecture needs commitment from all senior business and IT managers within the organization.*

Anything of fundamental importance to an organization, and information technology is almost the definitive example, needs commitment right from the top. Without the commitment it is unlikely that any relevant or lasting impression will be made. We need the commitment for the following reasons.

1   The process will almost certainly require a number of difficult decisions to be made about the business strategy and business plans—decisions that the organization may be unwilling or unable to make.[1]
2   The process will need the support, and therefore the time, of a number of senior people. Senior people are always in demand; their time is very valuable.
3   It lays down the foundation for the acquisition, implementation, use and exploitation of IT for a significant time.

The commitment for the definition of the IT architecture must be made at the very highest level. Without the commitment from senior management to the process and the result of the process, it is unlikely that the IT architecture will have the impact that it should have. The commitment must come from:

• the most senior managers in the organization
• the business managers, especially those who rely heavily on IT
• all the IT managers.

To gain the commitment, IT management must clearly demonstrate the benefit[2] of having an IT architecture, not only in IT terms but in terms that have clear relevance to the whole of the organization.

Clarity of purpose

> The reasons for producing the IT architecture must be stated clearly and understood by all parties involved.

Everyone concerned must be absolutely clear about why the IT architecture is being produced. An unwritten agreement is not worth the paper it is written on! With this in mind, it is easy to see that the reasons for producing the IT architecture need to be stated clearly.

When a large life insurance company embarked on the production of its IT architecture in 1991, the study team consisted of six people—some managers and some senior professionals. Every one of these six had a different understanding of what the IT architecture should cover, how it should be produced, how it should be used and how successful it was likely to be.

---

[1] It is increasingly common for the senior managers within an organization to back away from some of the fundamental decisions that need to be taken. This is understandable to a degree: the commercial world is a very complex place at the moment, and the rate of change is as high as we have ever seen. Where decisions are lacking, assumptions have to be made. Sometimes the assumptions that we make in building the IT architecture are a more acceptable framework within which management can make these decisions.

[2] There are two key areas of benefit. Firstly there is the benefit of *having* an IT architecture; secondly there is the benefit of *implementing* the IT architecture (see 'Costs and benefits' later in this chapter).

These differences in understanding came to light during the first two months of a three-month study, and caused quite severe problems in keeping the work on track and the team in harmony. Had these misunderstandings been exposed, analysed and resolved at the outset, a lot of problems would have been avoided.

It is never easy to write down the purpose in a form of words that is acceptable to everyone, but it is vital that it gets done. A vague objective creates a blur throughout the whole project and almost always leads to the creation of a blurred result. An oft-used argument as to why the purpose does not need committing to paper is that it is obvious. Well, if the purpose is obvious then writing it down will only take a few moments; if it is not obvious, then spending the time now to determine exactly what it is is *always* worth the effort.

Once we have the clarity of purpose, it needs to be communicated. The communication needs to cover both the purpose and the degree of commitment that is behind it.

Quality of sponsorship

The creation and acceptance of an IT architecture are not easy tasks; the support of a project sponsor is of crucial importance.

Once we have the commitment of senior managers and we have a clear statement of what we are going to do and why, we need someone to drive the process forward. This person is the project sponsor. The role of the sponsor in any project is to assume responsibility for the completion of that project.

- A good sponsor is one who gets deeply involved in the mechanics of the production of the IT architecture, who ensures that the resources that are required are made available, who ensures that those affected by the IT architecture are kept aware of what is happening and why. The best project sponsor is one who has a lot to lose if the IT architecture is not created.
- A poor project sponsor signs the project authorization forms, approves the bill for the consultancy involved and then steps back, getting status reports at regular intervals so that he or she can show up-to-date knowledge.

The process for producing an IT architecture is complex and is likely to ruffle a few feathers on the way. It needs a good project sponsor (see above) who really does understand the importance of the work and has the respect of his or her colleagues; they need to know that the project sponsor will do a good job.

18.4   Performance

Evidence of method

> *A well-thought-out IT architecture is unlikely to be produced other than by the use of a tried and tested method.*

Anyone can design a house: after all, we start drawing the things when we are about three years old. But there is a wealth of difference between a child's attempt to draw a house and the result of a professional architect. The difference is one of process—of a repeatable process. The architect learns from the experiences of others, building on and improving a process that works and in which he or she has been trained.

The IT architect charged with building an IT architecture has to have the same preparation and therefore the same advantage. It is very unlikely that anyone can produce a *good* IT architecture without a *proven* method. There is no single method that is guaranteed to work, but any method that is used repeatedly gains from the experience of past attempts, successful or otherwise.

In the many situations where we have been involved in reviewing different forms of IT architecture, we have always concentrated on reviewing what was *done*, rather than what was produced. It is the process used that is important: if it is a reasonable process then it will create a reasonable result. What is very clear is that something as complex as an IT architecture *cannot* be produced without a process that has as its objective the creation of something which meets all the characteristics of a *good* IT architecture, as shown in this chapter.

One question worth asking very early on when considering the process is whether or not there is ever a *single right answer*, a *single correct design*. If there is a single correct design, then there has to be a process for defining it; if there is not, if many designs can be considered as 'correct', then any process we do define must be capable of handling these different designs.

Back to the example of the house. At the initial stages the architect tries to gain agreement with the client as to the general shape and form of the house to be built. It is extremely likely that the architect will propose several different designs, all probably following a single theme, but all very different. The client must choose which design he or she prefers, and this selection process can only ever be a subjective one. Should the garage be on the right-hand side of the house or the left, or perhaps completely separate from the house? As far as the architect is concerned, any of these potential designs will meet the basic requirement to have a garage, but the client may simply prefer one side to the other.

In IT we have the same concept. Take a large organization trying to define a common set of software to be used on all its personal computers. Does it really matter whether the word processor chosen is product A or product B? Obviously some people will prefer one, some will prefer the other and some have no preference either way. Some obvious objective assessments can be made in terms of functionality, ease of use, cost or level of current investment, but where both products are already in use, ease of use is subjective anyway, cost is pretty much the same and functionality varies from one release to another. At the end of the day, the decision will be largely subjective. It has to be.

There cannot therefore be a process we can follow that will turn out an architecture like a car off an assembly line. Perhaps one day there will be: perhaps one day all the requirements of an organization will be able to be expressed in a measurable way, sufficient for some large and complex algorithm to produce an architecture that lays out the location of all the physical devices, defines the network connections, specifies the application programs and structures the data, but we certainly are nowhere near that today.

Reasonableness

No IT architecture is ever perfect; we should aim for something that is reasonable.

Reasonableness is another way of looking at the method and the concept of the *single correct design*. Because we know there is not a right answer, what we are looking for in an IT architecture is a reasonable answer to some very difficult questions. Although 'reasonableness' is undefinable in this context, we can immediately think of a number of characteristics that would certainly make the IT architecture an *un*reasonable one.

1 It would be unreasonable to spend too long creating the IT architecture. We cannot spend years assessing different options or different solutions; we do not have the luxury of an open-ended study. In our experience, most business managers and an increasing number of IT managers are simply not prepared to invest in projects that do not deliver real benefit in the short to medium term (this year!). What is important here is that we spend the minimum amount of time necessary to define an IT architecture that takes us sufficiently far forward so that we can start planning for and realizing implementation benefits.

2 It would be unreasonable to develop an IT architecture that required the investment of an unreasonable amount of cash. It is rare now for organizations to make really large capital investments in IT: it is much more acceptable to be able to make a predictable amount of investment over a reasonable period of time, ending up at the same point, but without breaking the bank on the way.

3 It would be unreasonable to develop an IT architecture that was so very different from today's *de facto* IT architecture that the time needed to make the required transitional changes was excessive. The reason for this is obvious: if it takes 10 years to make the transition, with the current rate of change taking place in technology and in business, the target will never be achieved. In today's environment a shorter transitional period is mandatory.

4   It would be unreasonable to develop an IT architecture which used components that no-one else had ever used or which used components from companies that are unlikely to exist in a short period of time. Risk has to be avoided where possible, and highlighted when it is unavoidable.

Asking questions about the reasonableness of the IT architecture is another way of asking the very basic question, the question that, although it is always at the back of our minds, we often tend to forget:

Will it work?

The IT architecture needs to be looked at from many angles: we have suggested time to produce, affordability, transition and components. Other angles may need to be considered, depending on each unique situation.

18.5   Business

Relationship to the business

Not only must the IT architecture be related to the needs of the organization, but the relationship must be clearly demonstrable.

This is what this entire book is about. If the IT architecture is to be successful then it *has* to have a clear relationship to the business.

A utility company decided to improve its overall customer service rating by providing a single telephone number that customers could call regardless of the reason for the call. The IT architecture that was being defined at the time defined a powerful workstation platform for all customer service personnel which integrated almost all the utility's applications. The IT architecture in this case supported the business direction and enabled the business strategy to be achieved.

An insurance company also had a business strategy for improved customer service. In this case the improved service would come in part from being able to offer the customer a wide range of insurance and general financial products, with a high degree of integration of information, support and service. The IT function had a strategy which was to support each product with the best-of-breed solution that could be purchased from external software vendors.

In this particular case, the jury is still out on how well the strategy will work out. If the business wants to integrate products and information, and the IT function wants to separate the products into different applications and onto potentially different technical platforms, then there is the potential for a gulf between these approaches which will need to be carefully monitored and managed.

Table 18.1 The relationship between business policies and business requirements

Business policy	Business requirements						
	R1	R2	R3	R4	R5	...	R*n*
Grow ahead of the market-place in all business areas			✓	✓		✓	
Provide the best service in the industry	✓		✓				
etc.		✓	✓	✓			✓

The tick marks indicate the business requirements which address a given business policy.

The business has certain requirements for IT, and one obvious measure of the success of the IT architecture is the degree to which such requirements are or are not met. In a significant number of situations where we have been involved, not only do the requirements have to be met, but we have to find some way of illustrating how they are being met. Organizations are looking for the relationship between IT and the business to be clearly documented for a variety of reasons.

The most common reason is to do with the simple need to be able to understand the things that IT is doing and which areas of the business are likely to be improved as a result. The rationale behind such a linkage may be forced so as to better understand the planned and actual benefits of IT investment. It has often been the case that the benefits promised by IT have not been realized or have been far smaller than anticipated.

Another reason, and a more positive one, is the need to support the priorities for the business imperatives by ensuring that the corresponding IT investment is set correctly. This can be a difficult one to deal with, because prioritization is never as straightforward as we would like.

Another reason, and perhaps the most important of all, is that establishment of the relationship between what the organization is trying to do and what IT is trying to do to support the organization enables a dialogue to take place. The IT architecture can provide a key contribution to this dialogue.

In its simplest form, the relationship is illustrated by Tables 18.1 and 18.2.[3] Table 18.1 shows the relationship between the driving forces behind an organization and the business requirements derived from them.

In real situations, the construction of such a table can be quite difficult. One organization that we worked with had a set of policy statements and a set of business requirements. There was little harmony between them. The policy statements

---

[3] In Chapter 13 we used a technique for relating business requirements and the technologies needed to support them. The technique here is similar, but has as its objective the laying down of a clear relationship between the key business drivers and a set of requirements to be placed on IT. The role of the tables here is to enable that relationship to be derived, communicated and tested, by both business people and IT people. The two objectives—prioritization and derivation—can very easily be satisfied by an amalgamation of these two processes.

Table 18.2　The relationship between business policies and IT requirements

Business requirement	IT requirements						
	R1	R2	R3	R4	R5	. . .	R*n*
Enable effective and efficient internal and external communication		✓	✓		✓		
Provide all customers with a single telephone contact point	✓	✓		✓			
etc.							

The tick marks indicate the IT requirements which address a given business requirement.

had been taken from an executive group who were working on overall business strategy. The business requirements were taken from a questionnaire completed by all the senior business line managers. Even a simple technique such as this can highlight such discrepancies and allow a dialogue to take place. In Table 18.1 there are two points of note:

- business requirement R3 looks like it is more important, more fundamental than any other
- business requirements R5 looks like it may be unnecessary.

Table 18.2 illustrates the relationship between the set of business requirements from the previous table and a set of IT requirements. In some situations the IT requirements would have been produced from an analysis of the business requirements, in other situations they would exist independently.

Again, the simple form of such diagrams belies their importance. When an IT architecture is produced it must be based on information provided by the business, and any way we can find to ensure that information is better understood should be encouraged.

The right balance between standards and freedom

> *Flexibility comes from having rules and standards, but no more than the bare minimum.*

The IT architecture represents a constraint on the organization. It constrains hardware, software, communications, applications and data to what is defined within the architecture. Having too many rules and regulations is bad; having too few is equally bad. Let us consider both extremes.

Information technology is exciting and innovative: organizations have to have the ability to look at new technologies, to assess their potential in terms of their own directions and policies and to make quick decisions where necessary. If the IT architecture has so many rules and regulations that its mere existence prevents such technologies being assessed and incorporated, then it is too prescriptive and must be relaxed.

One large organization that we worked with during the 1980s had a *de facto* IT architecture which was followed very closely. Applications were written either for the mainframe environment or for the personal computer environment. When a major new product was to be launched that required complete systems support from order entry through to manufacturing scheduling, a brand new suite of applications was written for the mainframe environment, even though a package solution that satisfied almost all the requirements was available off the shelf for a minicomputer.

The *de facto* IT architecture had created an environment within which people approached all problems with a somewhat blinkered view as to possible solutions.

At the opposite extreme, some organizations have a somewhat easygoing approach to the technology that can and should be employed. Reducing the rules and regulations to this level allows a much broader range of technologies to be employed, each technology being selected on the basis of its ability to support a specific requirement or set of requirements.

Another organization in the late 1980s was faced with a dilemma about its database strategy. The organization had a strategy of supporting each of its divisions in an isolated fashion, each divisional computing environment being kept fairly separate from all others. It began to look closely at what it had created, and realized that it now had critical operational data held on four completely different database management systems.

The data could not be easily accessed across the multiplicity of sources, management information systems were almost impossible to design or implement, and the range of skills that the organization was supporting was far higher than it wanted or could afford.

Such extreme examples are far more common than some would expect, but we should not really be surprised, because achieving a mid-point (see Fig. 18.1) between these extremes is extremely difficult.

What is needed is a balance, the balance being defined by an IT architecture that imposes the *minimum* set of *necessary* standards. The standards should cover a wide range of IT decision-making and should be capable of being explained, defended and modified if and when necessary. The IT architecture must allow all levels of the company the maximum freedom to act and react in the way they feel is warranted.

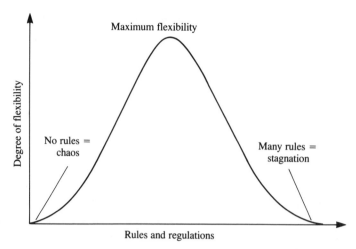

Having too many rules and regulations leads to bureaucracy and stagnation. Having no rules leads to chaos: from an individual point of view this is seen as having a lot of freedom, but from the organization's point of view there is little flexibility, little opportunity for change, because the chaos actually prevents change. A little discipline never did anyone any harm.

Figure 18.1.   Balance between chaos and stagnation.

Remember, it is far easier for the captain of a large ocean liner to change course than it is for a yacht club commodore to coordinate the changes in direction of 2000 separate yachts, each being steered by someone totally convinced that he or she is already going in the right direction.

Costs and benefits

There are costs and benefits associated with having the IT architecture as well as implementing the IT architecture.

There are three cost areas fundamental to an IT architecture that need to be understood in advance.

1 The cost of creating the IT architecture in the first place. This relates directly to the time that has to be put into the study by members of the organization and people from outside the organization who are brought in to help (consultants skilled in definition of IT architectures and technicians skilled in certain areas of information technology).

2 The cost of the transition[4] from the current state to that defined by the IT architecture; the migration costs. This is almost certainly the largest of the three cost areas, and any good IT architecture must include a transition plan that minimizes such costs and ensures that they are spread carefully.

---

[4] The word 'transition' is preferable to 'migration', the latter being unfortunately associated with birds flying in one direction in the summer and another in the winter. We should try to avoid such frequent and drastic changes in direction. Transition at least suggests a one-way process.

3 The cost of maintaining and enforcing the IT architecture. This includes the time taken to keep the IT architecture relevant and current, the time to ensure that people are aware of what the IT architecture means, and the time taken to maintain a check on development and purchasing decisions such that the IT architecture is supported and enforced.

Against these costs, there are a number of benefits. The most important concept to understand regarding such benefits is that they fall into two areas: benefits of *having* the IT architecture and benefits of *implementing* it.

The specific benefits of implementation have to be defined by the study that defines the IT architecture in the first place. The benefits of having the IT architecture can be considered generic to most organizations, and would include the following.

1 Less effort expended on architectural issues in each developmental project. The IT architecture provides a common base for all development projects and as such, represents a significant saving, allowing the development projects to concentrate on delivering business function and business benefit.
2 Increased confidence across both the business and the IT areas that decisions are being made on a well-thought-out basis.
3 Faster decision-making, because most of the complex architectural decisions have already been made, and made in a common manner across the whole organization.
4 Better support from vendors and other 'supplier' organizations, because the IT architecture is an effective means of communicating the directions and requirements of the organization.
5 Increased ability to maximize the efficiency of the various IT functions as a result of the fact that the IT architecture clearly lays down the technologies that are to be used and the way in which they are to be used. This allows precious skilled resource to be developed and concentrated on the issues at hand.

In every situation that we have worked on, the cost and benefit areas varied, but have not varied significantly from those shown above. However, in every situation there are many unique costs and benefits that need to be drawn out.

18.6 Technology

Taking advantage of technical opportunities

> *Technology is varied and complex: to take advantage of it we need to understand it, and to understand it properly we may need help.*

Firstly, a little apocryphal story.

A large company performed a survey of the skills of a selection of its employees. In one regional centre there were around 20 professionals, some of whom had been in the business for around 20 years, some for less than two.

The skill survey asked about 100 questions, to be answered on a scale of one to five, 'one' meaning that the person had a poor knowledge of the subject area, 'five' meaning that the person had an excellent knowledge of the subject area.

The result clearly showed that the people who had worked on IT for many years assessed their skill level as far lower than those who were relative newcomers.

This illustrates a problem that is rife within our industry, typified by the expression '*a little knowledge is a dangerous thing*'. The complexity that we have to deal with in IT today is far greater than it has ever been in the past, and it is never going to be simple again. Figure 18.2 shows some of the results of the *acronym extrapolation* that is taking place: it seems that a new acronym is created each and every day, at least. A significant proportion of the complexity in terminology comes from the manufacturers who believe that we are impressed by this. Another significant proportion comes from the various regulatory bodies and standards organizations, and what they lack in quantity, they certainly make up for in quality!

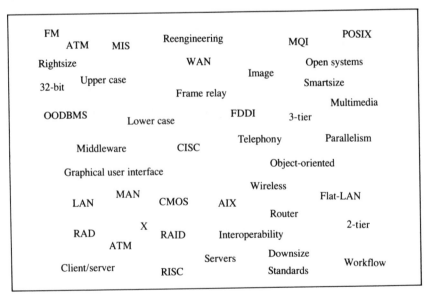

Figure 18.2.   Jargon.

The IT industry is getting excited about a number of fundamental 'technologies', such as:

- open systems
- document image processing
- multimedia
- client/server
- workgroup computing
- wireless communication.

If the IT architecture does not take a position on such technologies, if it does not get beyond the vendor hype and the glitzy journalism, then it will have failed. These (and others) are such fundamental technologies that they *must be* assessed as to their potential within the IT architecture. Failure to do this leaves the organization potentially exposed due to the vast amount of resource being applied to these areas by vendors, standards bodies and the competition alike.

Technical soundness

The building of an IT architecture requires hard work, clear thinking and a fair degree of good old-fashioned pragmatism.

Pragmatic means *having no illusions and facing reality squarely*. What is *reality*? It is a whole bunch of things, we all know them; there is no magic list. Let us go through some examples.

Components

The IT architecture starts out as a logical construct and ends up as a collection of components, technologies and processes. The components that we select should be capable of fulfilling a number of requirements. Prime among these requirements is the ability of the components to meet the requirements of the organization that the IT architecture has identified, analysed and documented.

But if we take a product such as a database management system, for most organizations we could select from a list of about six or seven database management systems that meet the functional requirements. However, only some of these components have the industrial strength, the vendor support and the backing of hundreds of thousands of other similar organizations that are needed in order to be deemed a *reliable* choice. Meeting the functional requirements is only part of the problem: we have to plan to do it with products that are going to stand the test of time.

Interfaces

When populating the IT architecture with components, we build a series of interfaces between the components that have to be considered in some detail. For example, the database management system we mentioned above has to have interfaces to:

- the operating system
- the media manager
- the security system
- programming languages
- operational products and procedures
- end-user access tools
- communications products.

Each of these interfaces must be considered carefully. Supporting products is one thing; supporting the interfaces between dissimilar products is something far more complex.

Vendors

Love 'em or hate 'em, we cannot do without the vendors of IT equipment. In the past, some organizations stuck with a single vendor, basing this decision in part on the belief that if all components were selected from a single vendor they stood a good chance of working reasonably well.

Some organizations chose to go with two vendors, trading one against the other in an annual battle of credibility and pricing. A *dual-supplier* policy gave benefits in the area of pricing, but forced organizations to devote key staff to managing the interface to the two vendors.

The rest of the world adopted a 'best-of-breed' policy, choosing products that seemed to be the best at doing some specific task. The cost of the integration of the various products was accepted as a cost worth paying.

There is no right answer here; there is no *best* approach to the subject of the vendors. What is important, however, is that as the number of components in the IT architecture increases (almost exponentially!), organizations think about what specific policy they are going to adopt, and understand the implications of the policy.

Skills

If the IT architecture being developed is different from the *de facto* IT architecture that already exists (and it may be very different), then it will require different skills. Some skills will come from the organization itself; some will have to be developed or imported. This all seems quite straightforward and easily acceptable to most organizations. What is perhaps more difficult to accept sometimes is the inability to grow or import the correct level of skills in the correct quantity.

Ten years ago everyone wanted COBOL programmers; now everyone wants C programmers. They are around: not in high volume, but they are around. But the ones that exist may know little if anything about the organization itself. The skills in existence in most organizations are a carefully crafted blend of relevant skills and experience, both business and technical. Making a major shift is fine, but we have to remember that it may take some time for the rest of the organization to catch up with us. This needs to be borne in mind not when we consider which direction to move in, but when we consider how fast we should make the move.

Technical longevity

A large number of products around today will be gone tomorrow: the IT architecture should not be unwittingly dependent on them.

It is a simple fact that every organization has available to it exactly the same technology as every other organization. What differentiates these organizations in IT terms is their ability to select the right technology and utilize it in the most effective and efficient manner.

Investing in technology has some similarities with investing in the stock market: there are winners and losers. Some investments will deliver great benefits in the short term but with an associated level of risk. Others will deliver lesser benefits, but over a far longer period.

It is important that the components of the IT architecture that are of crucial importance, the parts that are fundamental to the IT architecture, should be carefully selected. In most organizations there are four key product areas.

1 *Operating systems* So much depends on the operating system chosen that their selection is critical. The operating system dictates, for example, which application programs can be run, how well they can be run, how secure the data will be and how reliable the overall environment will be.
2 *Database management systems* Getting data into a database management system is expensive. Once the data is captured, the development of access routines, back-up routines and application programs adds to the cost. The database management system must be carefully selected to ensure that it will provide what the organization requires for some time to come.
3 *Communications protocols* As more and more hardware, software and data gets distributed across more and more geographic parts of the organization, the dependency on the communications protocols becomes vital.
4 *Programming languages* Certain programming languages work in some environments and not others. Although this is becoming less of a problem, with organizations focusing on a small number of languages that are available across many environments, the skills required to support multiple languages

and the problems caused by having some applications written in one language and some in another make this an important issue for some time to come.

Technical completeness

Everything covered by the IT architecture should be understood; the interfaces to everything not covered by it should also be understood.

Figure 18.3 shows a simple schematic which illustrates three different manifestations of the problem of completeness.

1   All the component parts of the IT architecture must fit together, representing as they do the IT architecture for the part of the organization that is within its scope.
2   The IT architecture usually does not cover the entire organization: some parts may be specifically excluded for a variety of reasons.
3   The IT architecture does not cover external organizations such as those of customers or suppliers, but the IT architecture must understand the interfaces to such organizations that may be required.

No IT architecture can cover everything. In most organizations there will be sections that for one reason or another are deemed 'outside'. For example, a small internal publishing centre within a large organization may use equipment that is seen as being outside the control of the IT architecture. Nevertheless, the interfaces to these excluded sections are clearly part of the IT architecture.

The part of the organization that is within the scope of the IT architecture must be defined clearly within the IT architecture. The components that are identified to

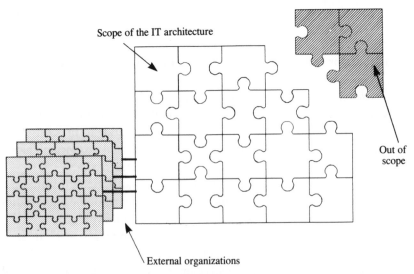

Figure 18.3.   Interfaces inside and outside the organization.

support this part of the organization must be defined, and the interfaces between them defined also.

In addition, the interfaces between the components needed to support the IT architecture and the components that are outside the scope of the IT architecture must be defined clearly. It is possible to impose an IT architecture on some external organizations, for example agents or suppliers. For other organizations we must simply accept that we have to work with something that is imposed. Often, this can lead to changes in the IT architecture that is defined in order to ensure that the interfaces that are beyond our control can be supported effectively.

18.7   Transition

Transition strategy

> *The process by which the IT architecture will be implemented must be well understood by everyone involved.*

A new organization on its first day of operation is as close to a green field opportunity as IT will ever find. In all existing organizations there is the existing IT infrastructure to worry about; our starting point may not be a desirable one, but it is the only one we have got. Imagine how much more difficult the traditional architect's task would be if our requirement were for a six-bedroom house and the starting point were an apartment on the twentieth floor. The obvious solution may be to sell the apartment and invest the money in a new six-bedroom house. If only we could do something similar with our IT investments.

In order to build on the *heritage*,[5] the IT architecture must consider the strengths and weaknesses of the current environment and try to exploit the former and eradicate the latter. An objective assessment of the strengths and weaknesses of the current *de facto* IT architecture is an excellent place to start.

The specific transition issues that need to be considered very carefully include the following.

1   The overall cost of the transition and how that cost is phased over time. Any period where the transition cost is excessively high must be well thought through and well justified. Unfortunately, one of the rules in this game is that the things that are relatively inexpensive to change usually have the least benefit, the major benefit coming from a small number of fundamental and costly changes.
2   The ability to make changes should not be underestimated. Most organizations have accepted that change is a fact of life and some organizations seem to live

---

[5] The existing IT infrastructure is often described as *legacy* or *heritage*. Which word you use can give some indication of how you view this infrastructure. A legacy is something that gets passed down through the generations when someone dies. It may or may not be welcome. Heritage has a much more attractive feel, usually being applied to something that we own collectively and feel proud of.

reasonably comfortably amid continual change, but for all other organizations change takes time, it must be well planned and sufficient time must be taken for people to accept and absorb the changes.

3 The overall sequence in which the transition should take place is hardly ever obvious. Cost avoidance is an important contributor to the planning process, but it is not the only one. In a large number of the situations that we have been involved with, specific actions that had to take place at specific times have tended to drive the migration strategy.

Implementation organization

The organization must have in place a means of implementing the IT architecture.

It may well be the case that the implementation of the IT architecture is such a significant piece of work that it has to be broken down into a series of projects and managed as such over a fairly long period of time. A steering group to oversee these projects will be necessary, and a number of management processes (see 'Management process' later in this chapter) will be required. Within IT, we are used to such an approach; we are used to the use of projects in this way.

However, not everything in life can be achieved through the use of a finite series of projects. For some things, an approach that sees a number of changes in the way things are done on a day-to-day basis is more suitable. Such an incremental approach may well be the best option for implementing parts of the IT architecture; specific projects may well be the best option for the other parts.

All we are really saying is that care needs to be taken over the approach to implementation. Do not simply assume that a series of projects is necessary: look what can be achieved by making relatively minor changes to the way in which everyday tasks are performed.

Applications

The IT architecture must be consistent with the applications that exist, the applications that will exist and the way in which they are being developed.

Organizations get their application programs from a variety of sources:

- some they build in-house using their own development staff
- some they buy from other organizations with similar requirements
- some are specifically built for the organization by third parties
- some are bought 'off the shelf' as packages.

The IT architecture should address which options will be used in the future and how those options will be managed. Without a clear understanding of where tomorrow's applications are going to come from, a number of parts of the IT architecture will be correspondingly vague.

Having sorted out the preference for the acquisition of application programs, the IT architecture has to support the applications in an effective way. An IT architecture *cannot* be defined without knowledge of what applications will exist and where the applications will run, or what data will exist and where that data will be placed. This is illustrated in Fig. 18.4.

This figure is a very simplified view of a very complex subject. It shows on the left-hand side the real-world objects on which an IT architecture has to be based, and on the right-hand side the IT architecture that must be defined. The IT architecture shown here has three major components: the data architecture, the application architecture and the technology or technical architecture (see Chapter 14).

A structured understanding of the places, people, processes and data, as indicated by the real-world objects in Fig. 18.4, is often called a *business model*. Unfortunately, the phrase is often associated with long drawn-out projects to 'define the organization', which seem to absorb vast amounts of time, produce enormous reports and add no value whatsoever. This is the cynical view. The realistic view is that an understanding of these objects is of paramount importance and that the understanding does not necessarily have to be very detailed. The usefulness of such a model as a precursor to producing an IT architecture is illustrated in Table 18.3.

An IT architecture produced without the information given in Table 18.3 would probably be a very subjective one, and its value to the organization would be low. The information is essential at some level, the table just shows how much vital data is dependent on a basic understanding of four simple areas.

Having a list of locations or users is itself important, but being able to relate such information to the other key information as shown in Table 18.3 provides a great

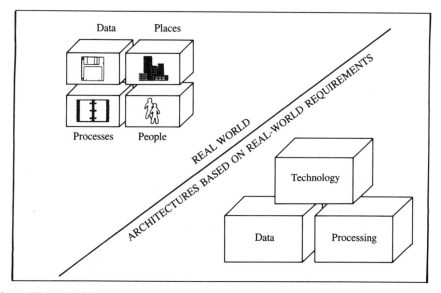

Figure 18.4.   Architectures and models.

Table 18.3   Relationship between real-world objects

	Locations	Users	Processes	Data
Locations	Hierarchy and geography	Who works at the location	What processes are performed at the location	What data is needed at the location
Users	Where specific users actually work	Organization and responsibilities	What processes specific users perform	What data is needed by specific users
Processes	Where a given process is performed	Who performs a given process	Process flows and workflow	What data is needed by a given process
Data	Which locations data needs to be accessible to	Which users need access to the data	Which processes need access to the data	Data model and data structure

deal more useful information. Some still believe that gathering and analysing such information is a bureaucratic exercise only—ask them which of the above pieces of information they can build an IT architecture without.

18.8   Communication

Nature of communication

>   *The IT architecture must be documented in a way that is clear, relevant and accessible.*

If we produce an IT architecture, what do we get at the end? What are the tangible results of going through the process? Well, the IT architecture has to be documented, so there must be at the very least a document that contains all the details. But is that enough? No, it is not.

   The IT architecture is the common map of IT for the organization: it represents a target, some desirable state. To be *common* it has to be *known*, and there are few ways of communicating knowledge that are worse than a thick and detailed document.

Several years ago in a meeting with representatives of a data architecture department of a large organization, the following conversation took place.

Q: Do you have a data architecture for the whole organization?
A: Yes.
Q: Do all the relevant groups across IT and the business agree with the data architecture?
A: Yes.

Q: How did you obtain this agreement?

A: We printed 35 copies, sent one to each department and gave them a month in which to point out errors or omissions.

Q: Did you get any feedback?

A: No.

Q: How big was the document?

A: 850 pages.

There are probably an infinite number of levels of IT architecture, each varying from the others in terms of the detail that it contains, but in practice we can group them into three levels. These levels are illustrated in Fig. 18.5.

The visionary level

This is a high-level view of the IT architecture and is very concise. The purpose of this level is to enable senior executives and senior management, whether from IT or not, to gain a perception of the IT architecture and what it may mean for themselves and for the parts of the organization that they represent.

The management level

This contains more detail and is consistent with the visionary level. The purpose of this level is to identify the major parts of the IT architecture so that decisions can be made about things such as relative priority or responsibilities.

This is the correct level at which an IT architecture should be aimed. The visionary level can and should be created as a summarization of this level, and the

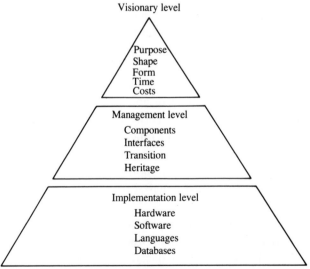

Figure 18.5.   The three levels of an IT architecture.

following level—the implementation level—is the result of further definition work on the IT architecture as implementation takes place.

The implementation level

This final level is aimed at implementation. It is detailed because it has to specify exactly what will be implemented and how. There is normally no single copy of the implementation level of the IT architecture; it will exist as detailed documentation associated with a particular implementation project.

An analogy

To gain a better understanding, we can relate these different levels to the architecture for a house. The visionary level is a schematic showing the external views of the house plus a layout for each floor that shows what rooms exist and how they are arranged. The management level is a more detailed definition of each of the floor plans, showing external and internal construction, sizes, standards that will need to be followed and so on. The implementation level is a detailed blueprint for the house, showing all the measurements, the specification of the materials to be used, the ways in which the various parts of the building will be connected and the standards and regulations that must be followed.

The IT management of a large manufacturing and marketing organization wanted to build a system for handling spare parts. For this they needed (a lot of) funding. At one of the initial meetings, the head office personnel responsible for granting the funding asked to see 'the architecture for the system'. The IT management team huddled and debated this for a while, and promised to produce one in two weeks' time.

Back at the office they commissioned a senior analyst to produce a 'system architecture'. The analyst understood how to produce a system architecture: it had to consist of applications and data and the relationships between the applications, between the data and between the applications and data. This would take time, but only two weeks were available, less the time to review the work (say two days), the time to produce the overhead foils to present it (say another day) and the three days that had already expired. This left the analyst with four working days to 'architect the system'.

The analyst refused and was replaced by someone who promised to deliver, and deliver she did. On the due date, three overhead foils were produced like rabbits out of a magician's hat. The head office people were impressed and, after a reasonable period of time, funding was granted.

> The overhead foils were never looked at again: they bore no relationship to the way the system was eventually designed. They were useless. But were they? The people who understood money but did not understand IT wanted to see what they were being asked to pay for, and that is exactly what they were shown. The fact that it bore no relationship to the final product is totally irrelevant.

The point here is that we have to document the IT architecture, but we have to be sure that we document it at the right level for the audience. For an IT architecture, more than one level will certainly be needed (see the next section).

Quality of documentation

We have already said that the IT architecture has to be documented, but we have hinted at the fact that the success of an IT architecture should not be assessed on the basis of the size of the document that is produced. More important than the document is the set of changes that the IT architecture brings about. Nevertheless, we have to produce a document that defines the IT architecture at any given point in time. Likely contents for this documentation include the following.

- Management overview

  - purpose
  - the vision
  - costs and benefits
  - management processes
  - outline implementation plan

- Background information

  - business plans, policies and requirements
  - current IT infrastructure
  - givens, standards and practices
  - assumptions
  - principles

- Requirements

  - critical business requirements
  - critical IT requirements

- IT architecture

  - building blocks
  - functional capabilities and characteristics
  - components

- Transition
    - transition principles
    - transition plan
    - sub-projects

This does not necessarily make the IT architecture definition report a large document, but it does make it a very vital one. Captured within this document are four key pieces of information:

- where the organization is starting from in terms of business and technology
- where the organization wants to get to in terms of plans, policies and basic business requirements
- what IT architecture the organization needs to implement in order to achieve the above
- how this IT architecture is implemented.

None of these are static; they will change very quickly (see 'Management process' later in this chapter). In order for the document not to become out-of-date, there must be easy ways in which it can be communicated and changed as necessary.

As we mentioned earlier in 'Communication', there are possibly three levels of detail to an IT architecture. The above document is aimed very firmly at the *management level*. The higher level view, which we called the *visionary level*, is a summarization of the major parts of the IT architecture and, logically, should be included within the management overview as indicated.

The more detailed level of the IT architecture, the *implementation level*, exists to support implementation projects and is not required to back up the IT architecture. As such, this detailed level should become part of the documentation associated with the various implementation projects, with simple references to it from the IT architecture document itself.

18.9   Enforcement

Buy-in

> *The IT architecture cannot be ignored by anyone.*

This was covered in some depth in Chapter 17, which concentrated on the people and the processes that are required to ensure that the IT architecture is followed, and therefore the benefits are achieved.

The IT architecture represents a set of rules for IT to follow to enable the creation of an integrated and efficient technical infrastructure, on which the organization can succeed. Nevertheless, there will always be people who read as far as '. . . *a set of rules* . . .' and then concentrate on working out how the rules can be circumvented. To a large degree this can be avoided by good management processes and good communication, but not always.

Because the IT architecture must have a process that allows certain parts of the organization to 'opt-out' for a variety of reasons, this is often exploited as a means of avoiding the rules. As more and more of the IT infrastructure is subject to this clause, fewer and fewer of the benefits of having it are actually realized.

The commonest way of avoiding the IT architecture is to exploit the difference between tactical and strategic solutions. The IT architecture is a strategic statement of what needs to be built. A tactical solution is often seen as justifiable when the solution that is seen as strategic is too expensive, will take too long or perhaps is too high-risk at this point in time.

This all assumes that there is a clear definition of *tactical* and *strategic*, but this is not in fact the case. If a particular solution meets today's requirements and is thought likely to be able to meet future requirements, or at least those that we can envisage at the moment, then that is fine; that is what we want. If a solution is unlikely to meet future requirements, or meets only some of today's requirements, then that is a problem. It does not mean that we cannot implement it; it just means that we implement it in the knowledge that it may cause us problems some way down the road. 'Tactical' and 'strategic' do not really come into it. The real question is whether the solution is a valid and viable solution, now and for some time to come. If it is, then we proceed; if it is not then we raise the issue and get a decision made.

Management process

> *The IT architecture is subject to continual change: there must be a process whereby this change can take place.*

When we talk about an IT architecture, remember that although it has many purposes, it is above all a *plan*. We must get away from a common perception of an IT architecture as being a static view; it is dynamic and must continually change to reflect the changes in the environment. As a plan it will always be with us, forever being corrected and extended, always representing what we are trying to achieve.

A reasonably large banking organization commissioned the production of an IT architecture in response to a perceived need to understand how the proliferation of personal computers should best be controlled. The IT architecture should cover all aspects of IT in all areas of the business, but notably the branch environment where the existing equipment was reaching the end of its life and would therefore have to be replaced, hopefully with technology in line with the overall IT architecture.

However, this same organization had already produced three IT architectures, two of which covered exactly the required area. Unfortunately they were all at least 12 months out of date.

IT management were right to believe that things had changed significantly in the past 12 months, but were wrong not to have anticipated this a lot earlier and understood that they needed a process for keeping their work up to date.

An IT architecture has to be more than a contemporary record or assessment; it has to be the initiator and subject of a process that is deeply concerned with maintaining its applicability and relevance to the needs of the organization and the current state of available technology.

Tables 18.4 and 18.5 show the sorts of changes, originating in the business and in IT respectively, that organizations must continually, or at least periodically, feed into the IT architecture.

Managing these changes is not an overhead. We cope with them as best we can every working day; the IT architecture simply gives them a basis for assessment. When we identify some problem or opportunity it can be measured up against the IT architecture:

- does it fit?
- do we have to do anything different?
- are we on the right track?

Table 18.4   Possible business initiators

Business
Organizational changes and restructuring activities
Announcement of new products or services that have to be administered
Geographic changes, new premises opened, old ones closed down
Policy changes in terms of offloading or outsourcing facilities
Profitability concerns, cost reduction exercises
Mergers, acquisitions and disposals
Major checkpoints in financial arrangements such as leasing arrangements for significant IT investments

Table 18.5   Possible IT initiators

IT
Building of a major new application where the technology decisions are not obvious
Incorporation of new development tools or techniques that may affect the technology platforms
Building of major databases or the rationalization of duplicate or fragmented data
Recognized need to standardize on specific hardware or software platforms
Implementation of new network components such as EDI or local area networks
Incorporation of newer technologies into the existing infrastructure, such as image, voice, client/server or multimedia.
Perceived problems with hardware or software elements of the current infrastructure

We have a focus for handling change in a much more objective fashion.

One client that we worked with used to be a navigator in a navy fighter plane. He quoted an interesting analogy. Imagine a flight from Paris to London in a fast military jet aircraft. When the flight plan is filed, it consists of a number of stages, each representing a certain distance travelled in a certain direction.

All is well, the course is worked out, the navigator is relaxed and the plane takes off. But the plane does not arrive at the prearranged checkpoints: it is usually some distance off. The navigator needs to calculate a new direction to get the plane back on course for the next checkpoint. There is no point in the navigator complaining to the pilot; any delay simply makes the problem even worse.

When you are travelling at supersonic speeds there is no time to sit back and hold a meeting; you simply need to accept that there is an agreed destination, the objective is to get there and any problems encountered *en route* are unfortunate and unavoidable and simply need to be taken into account as quickly and efficiently as possible, to get the plane back on course.

The process for keeping the IT architecture current and relevant requires a number of processes to be put in place. These are illustrated in Fig. 18.6 and are covered in more detail in Chapter 17.

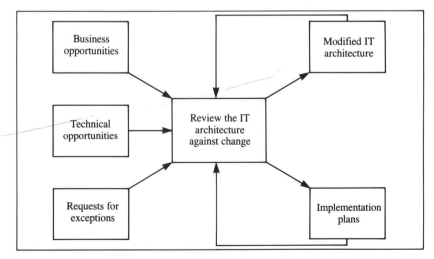

Figure 18.6.   Management processes.

18.10   Summary

This whole chapter is a catalogue of experience. The exact nature of an IT architecture differs so much from organization to organization and from industry to industry that it is almost impossible to lay down rigid rules that should be followed. All we can do, and all we have tried to do in this chapter, is to provide some food for thought: some ideas, based on the experiences we have had in trying to improve the process for defining and managing the IT architecture.

19
So, where do we go from here?

Lord Ronald . . . flung himself upon his horse and rode madly off in all directions.

(Stephen Leacock, 1869–1944)

We said at the beginning that this was a book about both business and technology, and we set out in the first two parts to provide an overview of these two wide-ranging subjects. It is certain that we missed things out, some intentionally and some unintentionally. What was covered was included with the intention of showing the nature, degree, speed and importance of *change*, in both the business world and the information technology world.

Although the changes in business and technology have been covered separately, the vital point is the degree to which the changes are related. Technology provides opportunities for some organizations to do things more efficiently than others, and sometimes it enables them to do things that others simply cannot attempt. It is certain that the successful application of well chosen and cooperating technologies is becoming a key differentiator between the organizations that succeed and those that do not.[1]

Although much of the technology exists as commodity items that are available to all, some organizations will be better placed than others to exploit it. Successful organizations will be those that solve the problem of communication between people who understand the business, its challenges and opportunities and people who understand the same aspects of information technology. Architectures are an essential component of that language. This is as true for information technology as it is for any other important part of infrastructure (e.g. buildings or transportation systems).

Many organizations today are making heavy investments in people, time and money that we believe are destined to a degree of success far below initial

---

[1] We leave the following questions as exercises for the reader. *If IT is a key differentiator of the relative performance of organizations in an increasingly competitive world, is it possible that most enterprises can outsource the whole of their information technology operations? Is it not more likely that the successful companies will keep the parts of IT that are key to their success to themselves, and have these built on an architectural foundation?*

expectations. Every month in the computer press there are examples of projects that have failed, schedules that have been missed, users who are left dissatisfied or budgets that have been grossly surpassed. We are not suggesting for one minute that IT architectures would avoid all of these problems: that simply is not true. What we are saying, however, it that IT architectures provide a common language for dealing with change, and that trying to embark on major changes in IT without them greatly reduces the chance of success.

Producing IT architectures is not easy. It requires good people, experience and a methodical approach. We have outlined some of the features of the last, but no book can provide you with the people or the experience. They can come from only two places–within your organization and outside. Ultimately, any architecture you produce has to be *yours* in style, content and implementation. You cannot totally outsource its production. So we urge you to take some of your best people from the business side and from IT and set them on the path described in Part 3 of this book. They will find it hard, and you will probably also need some outside help, but there is no substitute for the experience of trying. In fact, we have noted in one organization after another the benefits that come from the exercise itself, whatever its end point. Putting a team together with the remit to discuss business and IT issues at such a fundamental level is almost always of great benefit in its own right. It builds a level of understanding and a communication channel that will be of great use in the future.

As we said, you may also want some outside help. A word of caution is appropriate here. The IT industry is full of people with the title 'consultant'. It is a fine title—the authors use it themselves—but it is used very freely and widely. In an area as important as IT architectures you owe it to yourselves to use the best. Do not be tempted to get cheap labour, and do make sure that the individuals you are offered have experience and a track record in this field. Try to make sure that they will work methodically with your people, and that they will be comfortable with both the business and the IT aspects of the work.

If at first you do not succeed, try and try again. Each time you will be surprised at the spin-off benefits of the exercise itself, and eventually you will arrive at a robust architecture on which your organization can base its future. Perhaps the most important point of all is that through this work you will be ahead of your competition, and well placed to make better and better use of information technology as it continues its rapid evolution.

Bibliography and References

She or he should (a) be multiskilled; (b) choose and master an area of special competence; and (c) transmit that special knowledge to others. . . .

(Tom Peters, *Liberation Management*)

The preceding pages have covered a wide range of topics. We should be delighted if readers now wanted to explore in greater depth some of the ideas presented. There are many books that will help them to do that. Here is a short selection of some that we believe readers will find useful and stimulating.

Business trends and ideas

Drucker, P., *For the Future: the 1990s and Beyond*, Dutton, New York, 1992.

Hammer, M., Reengineering work: don't automate, obliterate, *Harvard Business Review*, July 1990.

Hammer, M. and Champy, J., *Reengineering the corporation: a manifesto for Business Revolution*, Nicholas Brealey, London, 1993.

Handy, C., *The Age of Unreason*, Business Books, London, 1989.

Harvey-Jones, J., *Managing to Survive: a Guide to Managing through the Nineties*, Heinemann, London, 1993.

Kennedy, C., *Guide to the Management Gurus*, Century Business, London, 1993.

Mills, D. O., *Rebirth of the Corporation*, John Wiley and Sons, New York, 1991.

Peters, T., *Liberation Management: Necessary Disorganisation for the Nanosecond Nineties*, Macmillan, London, 1992.

Taylor, F., *Scientific Management*, Harper, New York, 1911.

Thompson, J., *Organizations in Action*, McGraw-Hill, New York, 1967.

Wiggenhorn, W., The language of quality, *Harvard Business Review*, July 1990.

Information Technology

Bearpark, K. and Beevor, P., *Computer Communications: A Business Perspective*, McGraw-Hill, London, 1993.

Clarke, A. C., *Profiles of the future: An Inquiry into the Limits of the Possible*, Gollancz, London, 1982.

Gray, P., *Open Systems: A Business Strategy for the 1990s*, McGraw-Hill, London, 1991.

IBM Dictionary of Computing, McGraw-Hill, New York, 1993.

Kerridge, C., *Microchip Technology—the Past and the Future*, John Wiley and Sons, Chichester, 1984.

Larijani, L., *The Virtual Reality Primer*, McGraw-Hill, New York, 1993.

The relationship of technology, business and society

Business transformation through information technology, *IBM Systems Journal*, Vol. 32, No.1, 1993.

Keen, P., *Shaping the Future: Business Design through Information Technology*, Harvard Business School Press, Cambridge, MA, 1991.

Morton, M., *The Corporation of the 1990s, Information Technology and organisational transformation*, Oxford University Press, Oxford, 1991.

Porter, M. and Millar, V., How information technology gives you competitive advantage, *Harvard Business Review*, July, 1985.

Zuboff, S., *In the Age of the Smart Machine: The Future of Work and Power*, Basic Books, New York, 1988.

Architecture and design

Athey, T., *Systematic Systems Approach: An Integrated Method for Solving Systems Problems*, Prentice-Hall, Englewood Cliffs, NJ, 1982.

Beam, W., *Systems Engineering: Architecture and Design*, McGraw-Hill, New York, 1990.

Boardman, J., *Systems Engineering: An Introduction*, Prentice-Hall, Cambridge, 1990.

Index

Further Titles in the IBM McGraw-Hill Series